VOICES OF AMERICAN H[OMEMAKERS]

VOICES OF
AMERICAN
HOMEMAKERS

Eleanor Arnold
Editor and Project Director

Indiana University Press
Bloomington & Indianapolis

The paper used in this publication meets the minimum requirements of American National Standard for Information Sciences—Permanence of Paper for Printed Library Materials, ANSI Z39.48-1984.

∞ ™

Manufactured in the United States of America

Library of Congress Cataloging-in-Publication Data

Voices of American homemakers / Eleanor Arnold, editor and project director.
    p. cm.
  "From an oral history project of the National Extension Homemakers Council, on the occasion of their fiftieth anniversary."
  Originally published: Hollis, N. H. : National Extension Homemakers Council, c1985.
  ISBN 0-253-12986-9. —ISBN 0-253-20799-1 (pbk.)
  1. Home economics—United States—History. 2. Housewives—United States—Interviews. I. Arnold, Eleanor. II. National Extension Homemakers Council (U.S.)
TX23.V65 1993
640'.973—dc20
                                 92-2150

1 2 3 4 5 97 96 95 94 93

*There isn't anything
more honorable, or that
takes more ability than
being a homemaker. It takes patience,
it takes knowledge, and it takes endurance
for a woman to really be a homemaker.*

*There is a difference between a homemaker and
a housekeeper. A housekeeper keeps a house clean,
keeps it picked up, cooks meals. But a
homemaker does it with love. Love for
her family, love for her mate.*

*There is a lot of difference, and I
am proud to be a homemaker.*

Jalie Martin, New Mexico

grandma,

This book made
me think of you and
your life. I hope
you find these stories
interesting and that they
remind you of some
of the good times in
your life.

Love,

Mary K.

July 1994

TABLE OF CONTENTS

FOREWORD

With the publication of this book, a remarkable citizens' history venture reaches not a culmination but another milestone in its five-year effort to document the domestic lives of American women. Like the project's other activities, *Voices of American Homemakers* merges serious and popular history, anecdote and reflection, professional and lay contributions, and concerted as well as individual effort.

Inspired by a successful Indiana oral history program, project planners developed an ambitious and comprehensive national proposal that won support in 1981 from the National Endowment for the Humanities. Vital to the project's scope and success were its sponsoring organization, the National Extension Homemakers Council, and its director, Eleanor Arnold. The Council offered a nationwide coordinating network, the focal point of its 50th anniversary, and a large membership pool of volunteer workers and informants. Eleanor Arnold brought talent, diplomacy, tenacity and inexhaustible energy to every facet of the work, including authorship of this book. Assisting her was a cadre of enthusiastic professional historians.

The results of such unusual collaboration have been impressive. Dozens of volunteer interviewers in 37 states collected and processed over 200 oral histories of women who devoted their lives to the unglamourous but elemental task of raising families and managing households. Guiding and evaluating their work were professionals in the field of oral history. Complete sets of these voluminous testimonies will be deposited in major libraries in every state, providing future historians and students with a rich collection of first-hand accounts.

This book offers readers a sampling of the collection, organized around key themes and findings from the interviews. The textual and visual memories preserve both the details and the attitudes associated with an occupation that has dominated the life experiences of American women. The dignity and importance of homemaking in American social history has been largely neglected by scholars. *Voices of American Homemakers* joins several recent studies in filling this void. It deserves the attention of historians as well as the millions of homemakers whose experience it illuminates.

Cullom Davis
Sangamon State University

EDITOR'S NOTES

A few notes may aid the reader's understanding of how this book has been edited. The book is composed entirely of words from the taped interviews of the homemakers. My task, as editor, was to select these words and place them in a coherent order, so that these women could share their lives and experiences with you.

In order to make their words clear, I have had to omit false starts, repetitions, and extraneous material for the sake of brevity and coherence. The words, however, are the words they spoke; and the meaning is not changed.

Occasionally words or phrases will be found in brackets [ ]. Here I have added something to make the sense of an excerpt clear, or to explain the meaning of a word. Example: pie plant [rhubarb]. An immediate explanation seemed less distracting than a glossary or footnotes.

Words set in bold type are the words of the person conducting the interview. In the back of the book is a list of interviewers and narrators, so that the interested reader may find who has conducted any interview.

The name following the excerpt is the name of the person who was interviewed. Her age (where known) and her state are included to help the reader place the era and the locale from which these memories came.

Visual material included in this book came from the material collected by the homemakers, unless otherwise noted.

There is no way to put into print the different voice qualities and pronunciations. One must supply from the imagination the clipped Eastern voice, the comfortable Midwest speech, the southern drawl and the Scandinavian accents of a North Dakota immigrant, which serve to emphasize the diversity and yet the sameness of this fine nation of ours.

INTRODUCTION

This book is one of the products of an oral history project of the National Extension Homemakers Council, and it can be better understood if we understand the organization, the project, and the women whose lives it records.

The Organization

The National Extension Homemakers Council, Inc., is a nonprofit educational organization made up of 30,000 organized groups, or clubs, in 44 states and two territories, with a membership of approximately 500,000. It is one of the largest organizations of women in the United States. Although membership is open to everyone, because of its rural heritage, a large percentage of its members are rural and small-town residents.

The clubs which comprise the NEHC are the audience groups of the home economists working with the Cooperative Extension Service, just as 4-H clubs are the audience group for Cooperative Extension youth education agents.

Throughout their history, Extension Homemaker clubs have been known by several names in different states. These include Home Economics clubs, Home Bureaus, Home Units, and Home Demonstration clubs. Most are now called Extension Homemaker clubs.

The background of Cooperative Extension work dates back to 1862, when President Abraham Lincoln signed the bill which created land-grant colleges in every state. These colleges were charged with teaching agriculture and mechanic arts, without excluding other branches of learning, and they were provided land grants from the government. This land was sold to purchase a college site and set up an experimental farm.

In 1914, the Smith-Lever Act provided for mutual cooperation of the United States Department of Agriculture and the land-grant colleges in conducting "practical demonstrations" in agriculture and home economics to persons not attending these colleges.

The result of this and other related legislation has been the familiar county Extension office, working with agriculture, home economics, and youth education programs and bringing the resources of the colleges to the people.

In the home economics area, specialists from the universities began bringing educational material to women in various ways, including organized classes. These classes were soon formally organized into clubs which met regularly for educational lessons. Typically, these clubs met in the member's homes, either semi-monthly or monthly.

In the beginning, home economics specialists attended the clubs and gave demonstration-type lessons on some aspects of homemaking. Later, as clubs multiplied rapidly, the concept of leader training was used, whereby one or two members from each club in the county came to a single meeting where they were trained by specialists on a subject. These members, in turn, gave the training to the members of their own individual clubs.

At the time the first clubs were being organized, there was a great lack of information on home economics-related subjects. Women learned from their mothers, and new methods in homemaking spread very slowly. The women were anxious to learn and to improve their skills; therefore, the new clubs were very popular. In a time when rural social life was very limited, the social aspects of the club meetings meant a great deal to these isolated women, also.

As more clubs organized, a network of county, district and state affiliations was formed, with extension agents servings as advisors, but not members, of the clubs.

In the early 1930s, the need for a national organization began to be felt all over the United States. Miss Grace Frysinger, a senior home economics program leader in the Federal Extension Service, was particularly interested in furthering this kind of an organization, as were several state Home Economics leaders. In 1934, several representatives of state home economics Extension groups were invited to participate in a Rural Homemakers Conference in Washington, D.C. These delegates expressed the need for a national organization that would provide an opportunity for homemakers to share ideas and experiences for the improvement of home and community life. They felt that such an organization could represent the interests of homemakers in matters of regional and national concern.

In September, 1935, presidents of twelve state Extension Homemaker organizations met in Columbus, Ohio, and definite steps were unanimously agreed upon. A committee was to draft a constitution for the proposed new organization. This constitution was to be submitted to the states prior to the adoption at a national meeting.

An executive committee was elected to serve until the next meeting. These officers were charged with planning the next meeting and with inviting other states to join in the establishment of the national organization.

The next national meeting was set for June 8-10, 1936, in Washington, D.C., just prior to the Triennial Conference of the Associated Country Women of the World.

And so, in June, 1936, an organizational meeting was held in the auditorium of the U.S. Department of Agriculture in Washington. Representatives from the states joined in adopting a constitution, selecting a name, and electing officers for the new national organization.

The name chosen was the National Home Demonstration Council, as most clubs were then known as Home Demonstration clubs. In 1963, the name was changed to the present National Extension Homemakers Council. Officers elected in 1936 were: Mrs. Guy Roop, Virginia, president; Mrs. Ernest Overton, Nebraska, vice-president; Mrs. R.T. Douglass, Louisiana, secretary; and Mrs. Walter Hill, Michigan, treasurer.

From this first beginning, the NEHC has grown to its present size and influential position. It serves as the coordinating organization for its nationwide membership and represents the interests of homemakers in many different ways.

Through membership in the Associated Country Women of the World organization, the NEHC and the member states work all over the world for the betterment of country women and children. The NEHC is represented at United Nations headquarters in the nongovernmental organizations sector.

Truly, the isolated countrywoman of 50 years ago has extended her influence around the world.

The Project

In 1981, the NEHC Board of Directors began to plan for the celebration of the fiftieth anniversary of the founding of their organization, which would occur in 1986.

Noting that there was a successful oral history project in progress in Indiana, the board asked Eleanor Arnold, director of the Hoosier effort, to direct a similar program at the national level, with the Indiana effort serving as the pilot project.

Two grant proposals, the first a planning grant and the second an implementation grant, were funded fully by the National Endowment for the Humanities, and this funding made the extensive project possible.

The aims of the project, as stated in the grant proposal, were as follows:

1. To understand and document the richness and worth of home-

makers' lives and how these lives have affected the fabric of American life.

2. To make a significant contribution to the scholarly world by generating valuable primary resource material about an almost completely undocumented segment of society, the homemakers.

3. To make the average homemaker aware of the value and dignity of her life.

4. To provide disseminations to both the homemakers and to scholars, so that the work of the project will have lasting and widespread value at national, state, and local levels.

Working with well-known names in the fields of oral history and women's history, the plans for the project were laid. The aim of the project went beyond organizational history and became an attempt to document women in their role as a homemaker, using the interview process.

Two interviewers from each state were trained at a two-day workshop and then asked to make one interview and send it in to their instructors for critiquing. After that, they were asked to make five interviews per state within the confines of a prepared list of topics having to do with women's lives and their homemaking role.

Visual materials were gathered at a workshop a year later, as the membership of the organization was urged to share photographs and other such material for inclusion in the project.

In 1983, a seminar on the role of women as homemakers was held. Using material excerpted from the completed interviews, a panel of six humanists researched, wrote and delivered papers on various aspects of the homemaking experience. Topics included Rural Women's History; Technology and the Homemaker; Changing Patterns of Child-rearing; Homemakers, A Changing Statistical Profile; How Homemakers and the Extension Homemaker Association Help Each Other; and a preview of the rest of the project.

In 1984 at the NEHC conference, a slide/tape program was introduced. Using only the voices of the women from the taped interviews and photographs which had been unearthed by the project, the producers had made a thirty-minute program emphasizing the history of homemaking and of Extension Homemakers, with the last segment focused on the values of the homemakers. With the funding from the NEH, one copy of this program was sent to each state, where it has proved very popular, with nationwide exposure.

The publication of this book in 1985 marks another milestone of the project. Once again, using the material collected from the homemakers only, a project dissemination tells the story of these fine women and what their lives, their work, their clubs and their values have been. First sales will occur at the NEHC conference in Estes Park, Colorado, in 1985.

As the project nears its end, 219 interviews have been made. The youngest interviewee was 27; the oldest was 100. One man, a member of Extension Homemakers, was interviewed. The ages of many of the narrators are in the 60 to 80 year range, with a good sprinkling on either side. The states are listed in the back of the book, but the interviews were conducted ocean to ocean east and west, and Alaska to Florida north and south.

At the close of the project, copies of all the tapes and of the bound transcriptions will be donated, one per state, together with a copy of the book and the seminar proceedings. This will make a valuable archive for future researchers in this sparsely documented field.

Perhaps the most outstanding finding of the research has been the simple fact that homemaking experiences are so universal. Butchering in Hawaii and Alabama is so much the same; washing by hand on a washboard knows no state limits. Love and concern for one's family is the paramount experience of all women interviewed. Backgrounds vary from ranches to farms; from treeless prairies to sandy swamps; from old established communities to new settlements; but the homemaker still fulfills the basic function of keeping the family intact.

A consultant of the project, D'Ann Campbell, Dean of Women's Affairs at Indiana University, summed it up nicely when she wrote, "This project makes a long-overdue inquiry into the lives of a major group in our nation's population. It is women's history in a distinctive form, in no way ideological, but rather the discovery of a nearly invisible and inarticulate, and surely undocumented, segment of women who are yet one of the main forces in our nation's history."

The Women and their World

In order to understand the women, we have to first understand the conditions of their lives and the world they lived in.

Our narrators tell of their lives as children and women, mainly in the era from about 1890 to 1940, a time of busy, industrious, small communities and rural areas. During those times, each extended household was almost self-sufficient in producing the basic requirements of food and shelter. However, much interdependence existed among neighbors, both for help in work too large for one family to perform and in their social life.

Farms, ranches and small towns were isolated and self-contained. Miles were long when only buggies and early automobiles were available, so most shopping, social events, schools and churches were within a few miles of home.

Yet life was far from dull. Without modern aids to enjoyment, the people made their own entertainment. They gathered together and made fun out of work, whether butchering or raising a barn, and they met often at school and church for social events which grew out of community life.

A strong sense of remembered gaiety and joy runs through their recollections. Walking to the one-room school and playing out at recess was fun; Sunday afternoons when the young people congregated together were anticipated all week; there was excitement and anticipation on

butchering day. Over and over again words like "fun" and "had a good time" appear. Life was hardworking, but these people were not rebellious or resentful. They tempered their labor with good times and their high moral beliefs with good humor.

In the household, the province of our narrators, there was a complex interdependence in which the homemaker was essential to the whole. The household itself was generally large, consisting of the wife and the husband, many children, perhaps one or more grandparents, unmarried uncles or aunts, or orphaned cousins. To this assemblage might be added one, two or more hired men or cowboys, the occasional hired girl, and numerous guests, invited or drop-in.

Members of the family worked together as parts of a smoothly functioning unit, with each having an important role to play. Husband, wife, children and other household members had areas of responsibility.

Care of the family, plus care of the house and garden, was generally the province of the homemaker. She planted the garden, hoed it, and canned or dried the produce. She picked the fruit in the orchard and preserved it; she milked the cow and churned the butter; she raised the chickens and gathered the eggs. In addition she cooked the meals and baked the bread; she cleaned and swept; she washed and ironed; she bore and raised the children. Her home remedies kept the family healthy and she participated in community life fully.

If she were thrifty and hardworking, she could sell enough excess butter, cream, eggs and chickens to pay for shoes for the children and to buy fabric she could make into family clothing.

In addition to her household chores, many women helped routinely with farm and ranch work, particularly at planting and harvesting times.

It is not surprising that a widower married again very soon. His choice was often between remarriage and breaking up his family, since the household of that time required a functioning full-time homemaker to do the many chores which fell in her sphere.

The homemaker of that day did not have to be assured that she was needed. It was a fact of life.

It is hard to realize the amount of hard physical work which was required. There were very few labor-saving devices. Water had to be carried in from springs, or, with luck, an iron pump. Laundry was done by heating water on a wood-burning cookstove and rubbing clothes on a washboard with homemade lye soap. Milk was carried in buckets to the house for straining, skimming and separating, then skim milk carried back to the pigs. Neither electricity nor gasoline motors were generally available to substitute for woman power, and most chores involved lifting, carrying, digging, pumping or pouring—all using energy and muscle.

And, since most families were large in those days, the young homemaker of the day was much of the time either pregnant or a nursing mother.

The day began early, since most outside work must be done by daylight. Cows had to be milked regularly and chickens required daily care. In the summer the added chores—gardening and canning—effectively used the extra daylight hours. Narrators tell of carrying a kerosene lamp to the wood cookstove to see if the water was boiling around canning jars in a washboiler at ten at night.

Of course, the homemaker did have help in some instances. Children, as soon as they were old enough to understand, had their chores and were expected to do them. Any member of the extended family in the household would expect to help. A grandfather or uncle too old to work in the fields might do the gardening, and a grandmother would often do all the mending and some of the cooking. The neighbor girl who had graduated from the one-room school and was not yet married was available as a hired girl, either during the busy summer or year-round.

Still, the main responsibility for the household was with the homemaker and she responded to it nobly.

The homemakers of the time, though they were so busy and tired, were always working toward better goals for their families. They emphasized the necessity for education for their children, often making real sacrifices to accomplish this. Although most adjuncts of so-called gracious living were beyond their reach, they worked with what they had. Pretty dresses and curtains made from printed feed sacks, embroidered pillowcases from bleached flour sacks, flowers tucked into their vegetable gardens—all satisfied their need for beauty in their and their family's lives.

These women took very seriously their task of raising future generations. They strove by example and precept to teach honesty, religious beliefs, and the rewards of productive labor. Their moral values were high, and they expected the same of their children.

With the coming of gasoline engines and, more importantly, electricity, much of the hardest labor was very slowly taken over by machines in the later years of the narrators' lives. The back-breaking drudgery which had been part of every homemaker's life was virtually eliminated. The health of the women improved and photographs no longer show so many women who are old before their time.

With less time required for household tasks, the homemakers found themselves with a certain freedom to choose how they would spend some hours of their lives. This time was utilized in different ways. Undoubtedly standards of homemaking and of the family's personal cleanliness were upgraded, and more home improvements were made, when time was available.

Homemakers had more time to spend outside the physical limits of their house and environs. Many helped more in the family business, whether farm, ranch or trade. Many took outside employment to supplement the family budget, or did volunteer work in church and community activities. As these non-household activities became more numerous, many homemakers found themselves increasingly busy. Since they still generally bear the homemaking role, the homemakers of today may find that they spend more working hours than did their ancestors who were doing their household tasks manually.

The narrators of the project hold a unique place. They are able to remember a very different world, but they live in the present world. Such a great change may never again occur in a lifetime. Their memories and judgments have real worth.

These are women whose lives inspire admiration and respect. They are women of strength, resolution and common sense. They could deal with difficulties with patience and wisdom. They were innovative and creative in their use of the simple materials with which they worked. They were experts in making do and getting by—and they did it well.

Working with what they had, they were able to create loving and pleasant homes, be good neighbors and friends to those in the community, to rear fine families, and to be good helpmates and companions to their husbands. Yet they never lost their sense of personal worth and their quiet dignity.

The basic tenet of this project has been to prove, both to the world and to these women themselves, that their lives have had value, dignity and worth. Their memories are the best proof that could be offered.

Eleanor Arnold
R.R. 2, Box 48
Rushville, Indiana 46173
317/932-5204

THE HOMEMAKER
AND HER LIFE

*"We had lots of fun when we
were young. There was a lot of
fun in big families, but it
was hard work, too."*

Elizabeth Meyer, Minnesota

Little girls grew to womanhood in a world centered around home, family, church and school. Communities were small and close-knit, with a great deal of interest and concern for their inhabitants.

Hard work and chores were an understood part of the youngster's life and made her feel that she was an integral and necessary part of her family structure.

One-room schools dotted the countryside. Walking to school carrying a lunch pail brought education to everyone, but it took determination to achieve advanced schooling.

Many times girls just out of school, and with very little additional schooling, returned to teach former classmates.

Recreational activities, dating and courtship centered around the same community centers of church and school. Girls were closely chaperoned.

Marriage, usually to a local boy, generally came early, and was often accompanied by a chivaree and an infare dinner. Sometimes the newly wed couple lived for a short time with the parents before "setting up housekeeping."

Large families were usual, and children were born in the home with midwives and country doctors in attendance.

And the cycle of another child's life began again.

GROWING UP

I'm very grateful that I was brought up in the country. I think of all the happy days that I had out on the farm. One of my school pals and I saw a cat having kittens one day, and we helped her along. We could go out and milk a cow if we wanted to as we went through a field. You love the outdoors. I would help my grandfather and we would work in the orchard. Then you had your garden and your fresh vegetables. Always had fresh meat—chicken every Sunday.

I had a favorite chicken one time that I carried around, and I fed it until its breast just dragged the ground. I remember my great-uncle Pete was there, and he said, "You're gonna kill that chicken, just as sure as I'm alive. You're feeding it to death." And, by gosh, the next week it was dead.

I used to go and get turtles for pets. I used a small chicken coop that we had for setting hens. My grandfather would feed them for me once in a while, but this one day, one bit him. He opened the door, and they scattered pretty good. I never had another pet turtle (laughs).

My aunt had a cat, Boo-boo his name was. He was quite old and she just loved him. So he died, and one other girl and I buried him alongside of the barn. We got down on our knees and we said a little prayer for the cat.

So many little things come back to your mind that make you think of happy days. You know, when you are a kid, you really are happy.

Mabel Hughes, 82, Florida

I grew up on quite an isolated ranch. I didn't have any playmates. I had a brother [then two younger sisters]. The only way we had to go anywhere was horseback, and until I got old enough to open and shut gates by myself, I couldn't just hop on a horse and go somewhere to visit any neighbor girls. We didn't have any school until I was ten years old, so in those early years we were pretty much on our own.

But after I started to school, there was more socializing. I lived on a horse. I could ride horseback as far back as I can remember. I had a good life. It was lonely at times, but I loved to read, and whenever I had anything to read, everything was fine.

A lot of the time I didn't have anything to read, because we didn't even get the mail very often—just a few times a year. The post office was a long ways away. When we did go visiting, I borrowed everything that they'd let me have to read. Then I'd be all right for a while. But that was the kind of childhood it was.

Nellie Yost, 76, Nebraska

I can say something that not very many people can say. I went with
my father in the run in western Oklahoma. That was in 1892 and I was
not quite five years old when we went down there.

I started to school the fall I was five. During that time I had Carrie
Nation as a Sunday School teacher. Not very many people can say
that. They lived there; her husband David held services for us and she
was a Sunday School teacher.

In Oklahoma we lived in a dugout, several dugouts, with a tunnel
between. On the hillside there was a big sandpile and we had a playhouse on this sandy hillside. We played dolls and housekeeping.

Vivian Jefferson, 95, Arkansas

Fun on an overloaded burro.

I grew up in a home that stressed a lot of Japanese culture, because
my father and my mother both came from Hiroshima and my parents
felt that when they had enough money that we would be going back to
Japan as a family. So, being the firstborn and being a daughter, my
mother educated me and taught me in the Japanese tradition. Even
though we lived in California, she wanted me to be prepared to go to

Japan and be accepted as one of them, so I did have a very strict Japanese background.

Misaye Uno, 65, Colorado

I grew up in Kula. We had five girls in the family, and then my brother came along. We had a five-acre little farm where we raised our vegetables, and a couple of cows and pigs.

I remember my grandfather lived in a little house way down at the end of the field. When I was young, I used to go to *tutumaka*—my grandfather. He was Hawaiian. My mother was Hawaiian and this was her father. I used to spend quite a bit of time with my *tutumaka*. He spoke only Hawaiian to me, so I was the only one in the family who could understand. Today I can still understand Hawaiian.

My father was Chinese and he wanted us to be good in school. We had to read, and we had to make good grades. My parents were not as strict as some of our Portuguese neighbors were. Being Chinese, my father was a good cook. My mother would rather work out in the garden. She loved to make flowers. We played a lot. I had a very carefree childhood.

Mary Soon, 60, Hawaii

I think back on the good times we had. We had a happy childhood and a happy young life. It was altogether different from what it is today, because we didn't get very far from home. The church and the school were the social centers at the time we were growing up. We didn't go very many other places, except to neighborhood parties, and we all did our own entertaining. We weren't entertained, like the young people are today.

We'd be first at one house on Sunday—that was our special time to play together—and then somebody else's house the next Sunday. We would have neighborhood parties, and that would be from one home to another and that would be through the week. And the things that went on at the schoolhouse and the church was our social life.

On Sunday afternoon we'd meet and jump the rope and play hide-and-seek, and drop the handkerchief, and all those things until we grew older and outgrew those things. But until we got in high school, that was what we entertained ourselves doing.

Zelma Blocher, 81, Indiana

When I was growing up, every kid had a horse. Usually the horses that our parents bought for us to ride as children were horses that were Indian horses, because the Indians really tamed the horses. You could get on on either side, and any number of people could get on.

I remember one little episode when there were five of us on an

Indian pony that belonged to my cousins. We got the giggles and we fell off over the horse's tail, one by one, and that horse didn't object at all. He just stood there and let it happen.

Jennie Williams, 89, Wyoming

We hardly ever went anywhere. Our amusement was done in our own homes, among our own selves. We had neighbors two or three

Children looked forward eagerly to going barefoot, and parents appreciated the saving in shoe leather.

miles, and sometimes we would ask our mother if we could ask them to come home with us on Sunday. They stayed all day Sunday after we went to Sunday School and church.

Sounds like a happy home.

It was indeed. My mother, who was a Chickasaw Indian, spoke very little. When she did, it was very soft and if you weren't used to her voice, you couldn't hear her. My father spoke very loud. He ruled the roost, all right (laughs). He was a very strict man, but he loved each one of us and we were very well taken care of.

Elba Johnston, 79, Oklahoma

As far as clothes were concerned, the families always passed on the clothes, from their kids to the kids below. So the clothes just made the rounds.

We all had good clothes, I especially. I had one aunt who had only one child. That kid had only real silk panties, and everything of the very best, and all of her clothes were handed down to me. So I had real silk panties.

All the other kids in the truck [which took us to school]—when I used to climb the sides of the truck—they used to get so angry with me, because I had silk panties, and they had the rice bag kind (laughs).

Julia Souza, 62, Hawaii

In the wintertime, our clothing was long-handled underwear and black or brown long stockings that you pulled up over those said long johns. If you were careful, you didn't get any bulges in them. If you weren't careful, you had lumpy legs.

If you happened to tear those stockings, and you didn't get around to get them mended, once in a while we'd take the shoe polish bottle and fill in the hole with shoe polish. 'Course, it didn't help the looks of your long drawers any (laughter), but it worked (laughter).

Dorothy Personette, 77, Oregon

Especially I can remember that we had to find a dandelion in bloom before we could take those cotton-picking old long underwear off. Then we could take them off, and we could go barefooted. Then spring was here.

Estella Myers, Michigan

We would all get around the dining room table at night and my mother would do the hand sewing, because she had to sew a lot, having five daughters. We children would do our lessons, and our father would help us with our lessons if we had any problems. He was a great person to make sure you had your arithmetic. He'd pound the table, and say, "I'm going to pound this into you if I have to stay here all night!"

Then when our lessons were over, we played games like bunco and Parcheesi. We had Cootie, and anagrams and Flinch. As we got a little bit bigger, our mother and dad taught us how to play pinochle.

Dorothy Tolley, 67, Arkansas

One of my uncles and his wife—they had eleven children. Then with our family of three children, we played together and had a wonderful time. We had our games that we could all play together—nothing bought. We played black man, hopscotch, hide and go seek, marble games, spin the top, jump the rope, and just games like that.

Opal Cypert, 68, Arkansas

Homegrown inexpensive pleasures, like fishing, were well-remembered parts of growing up.

We'd have a little softball game on Sunday afternoons at somebody's house. Couldn't afford a ball bat in those days. We hunted up a board, probably a 1 by 4 inch, or something of that sort for a ball bat. The ball was made by somebody raveled up an old sawmill sock. If we were lucky, we had a sponge ball in the center, and we wrapped it with twine. That was our ball.

I remember one year my aunt sent me a paper doll—a cutout paper doll that you could cut out the clothes and hang on it. My mother would not allow me to cut out that doll. I was brokenhearted. But down at the store Dad sold crackers from a cracker barrel, and there was a big white pasteboard disc in there. I traced a pattern from that doll and made dolls on this disc. I had oodles of dolls.

I think now how wise my mother was. Look how much more fun I had creating my own dolls. If she had allowed me to cut that other doll out, they would have soon grown old to me and would have been discarded. As it was, it furnished many hours of pleasure.

Edith Gladden, 63, Missouri

I felt like a member of the [Homemaker] club, because my mother was in all the time I was a girl growing up, and I always looked forward to getting to go to club every month with her.

Back then, club was an all-day affair. They took their dinner in their baskets, and of course there was about as many children as there were women. That was a big deal to get to go play with all the children on club day. We had a big dinner and then the kids got to play and, the best I remember, the women quilted.

And in the wintertime, when school was going on, that really upset me 'cause my mom could go to club without me.

Mary Ann Hoskins, 49, Indiana

Most every summer we would have a long weekend on the Verdigris River. We camped and fished. That was a good outdoor experience with the family.

My father would pitch a tent. He usually would have some young man working in the store, and they would go out at night in the boat and set the trout lines, and then get up in the morning and take the fish off the hook.

Did you eat the fish then?

Yes, my mother would make biscuits in an iron Dutch oven on the bonfire, and we'd have fried fish and biscuits.

You have some fond memories.

Evelyn Alden, 74, Kansas

The young folks of the community—and they didn't all have to be one age, families sorta went together—we would start at the farthest out and they would begin to walk and pick us up as they went along, and came to the next house. Then we'd go to somebody's house for a party. We didn't have to have big preparations, or decisions about a party. We just went and all had fun together without any plans.

Maybe if they had some apples, they passed them around, or we'd pop corn, or have a few cookies. That was the kind of entertainment we had.

And Sunday afternoons we'd get out and walk that way, and maybe walk out wildflower hunting, or just out in the woods—sit on a log, talk, sing songs.

We went on possum hunts. Oh, that was gorgeous. Right now, when I see a big round moon in October, I think about the possum hunts. They'd build a big bonfire and the boys, most of them, would get out and take the dogs and hunt. But the rest of us sat around the fire and told tales, and sang songs. We liked to tell ghost tales sometimes—if we didn't get too scared.

Tressa Waters, 85, Tennessee

I had two brothers and one sister. My sister was the youngest and the two brothers were next to me. They were hellions.

I remember my brother was a great fisherman. He liked company sometimes, so I'd have to go fishing with him. One time he was digging angleworms and I just went to see what he was doing. So he held my dress, and poured a whole can of angleworms down my front (laughter). That's the kind of terror I went through.

Lillian Blonien, 68, Wisconsin

When we were kids, we had big zinc tubs to take a bath in. We'd heat the water in a [wash] boiler and then we'd put it in the tub. I was stomping on the water one time—must have been about four years old—and Mom, she wanted to know why I was splashing all that water. I says, "Somebody lied." I says, "You can't walk on this water." I had had the Sunday School lesson that Christ walked on the water, and I was trying to walk on that water in that tub. But I never did accomplish it (laughter).

Then I seen a hen lay an egg one time. Mother always said an egg come from under their wing. I went in and told her that I knew better than that, I'd seen where that egg came from (laughs).

The first balloon I ever seen was—oh, I was probably fourteen. I said, "Huh, anyone can do that." So I got Mother's umbrella and I climbed up on the barn and I jumped off into a pile of horse manure! My mother whipped me, because the doggone umbrella turned wrong side out.

You must have been a character.

Oh, I was a character.

Estella Myers, Michigan

We had a lot of fun as a family. My mother liked to laugh. We always had a lot of people around. I have an older sister whose husband plays the piano. He sits down and just plays, and we sing. That's one of the warmest memories of my childhood. He'd come at night and he'd sit down and start playing, and we'd just sing. That's still one of my favorite pastimes. So we had a very happy home. Nobody was ever worried about Johnny Jones next door having more, or having less. That way we were just brought up with very basic values.

Eleanor Whittemore, 55, New Hampshire

We made willow whistles in the spring. You take a twig and slit the bark on it and pound it, and you make whistles. We used to split strips off of the cedar posts and make bows and arrows, which was a lot of fun.

We swam in the ditch, and we hunted polliwogs and little minnows.
Dorothy Personette, 77, Oregon

We would save all the cans, cartons, anything we could find, and we set up our own store, and we had play money that we made ourselves, and we played store, day in and day out.

I think it probably helped us learn to add and subtract. It kept us occupied and Mother knew where we were.
Hazel Leininger, 59, Colorado

When I was growing up, for entertainment we had parties, square dances, quilting bees, bean stringings, corn husking, apple peelings, and general get-togethers. We loved to horseback ride, too.
Mary Fouts, 72, Kentucky

We had a place we could swim down in the Umpqua River, and the whole neighborhood would come down in the afternoon. It was sort of sandy out so far, and then you had a ledge of rocks. This is where the people who could not swim first practiced. Then when they were able to swim a little better, they'd go to the next ledge. Then when you finally could swim well, you could go past that one land out in the main part of the river.
Marie Brown, 64, Oregon

What do you consider to be the greatest joy in your childhood?
Ours was a simple life, but I think the most cozy thing that I think of right now was getting everything completed for the day. My father always built up a great big fire at night. He loved to sit by the firelight. Mother was an excellent reader. To hear Mother read at night was one of the highlights of the day.
Elizabeth McAdams, 69, Alabama

Chores

There was a big family of us. We had fifteen children in our family, with three sets of twins. We each one had our chores to do. First thing [after coming home from school] was to change our dresses, so we'd be nice and clean for next day.

You wore the same dress the next day?
Practically all week, because my mother washed on a board, and we had to be very careful with our dresses.

But we always knew what chores we had to do. Some got the water in for the night, some got the coal and the wood, some to the barn to milk. Everybody went right to their chores and got them all done, and then after supper of a night, we all got our lessons.

Mary Sheeks, 73, Indiana

It was my job to bring in the wood to fill the stove each night and to bring in water to go in the reservoir which we heated in the wood stove—our only source of hot water. Also, we had to carry water and fill up the iron kettle to do the laundry.

Margie Brookshire, 60, Kentucky

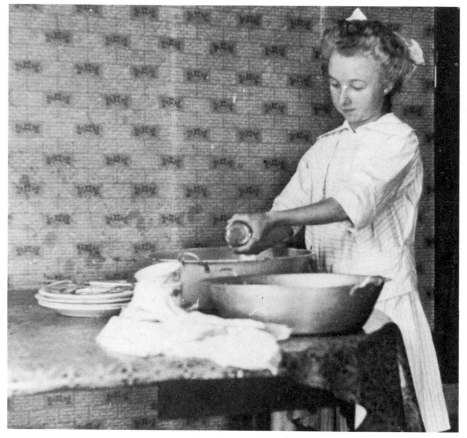

Washing dishes was generally the
young girls' chore.

I grew up on a farm in a large family of fourteen in number. My mother was a good, industrious housewife who helped on the farm at intervals, when she wasn't nursing babies. I am the seventh child, which means that I had to help with the babies as early as I was strong enough.

Sallie Bell, 74, Alabama

I learned to wash dishes with the dishpan down in the chair. My brothers did help me at night to dry the dishes.

Theo Hammond, 82, North Carolina

I learned to cook the year I was twelve years old. My father died of pneumonia and left my mother with eight of us at home. Mother had to go to the field to show the boys, 16 and 15 years old, how to farm.

That was the year I canned my first food. My mother taught me how to make biscuits, how to make light bread, and egg custard. I had three brothers and they were hard to fill up.

Essie Simmons, 81, Arkansas

Life was hard. My mother, when I was five years old, married my stepfather and they had six children, so I didied and played with them, raised them up and helped with them. And, land's sakes, I helped feed the hogs every morning, and I helped milk. I had a little three-legged stool, and he could depend on me to get my old cow milked. And then they used to cut the corn and put it in the loft, and then you'd go up and throw down jest enough to feed the cows and horses. I always liked to do that.

Mary Foltz, 89, Indiana

We had to make our beds. I used to make my brothers' beds, also. I used to do the dishes on a bench. My mother used to put a little bench in front of the sink, and I had to do the dishes and wipe the dishes.

I had chores to do after that. One of the first things was to empty all the chambers. You never threw away anything that was in a chamber. You had to mix it with water. She [mother] taught me the combination of how much water and how much urine. Then we had to mix it up, and then I used to go and put that on the vegetables and the flowers in the garden.

The second chore was—my grandfather was bedridden for many years. He couldn't eat anything that was rough. She used to make Portuguese soup and all those beans that they used to use for thickening, like peas, or white beans, or red beans—they had to be peeled. You'd bring it to a boil and you'd let it stand. Then I had to take off the skins of the beans.

Then after that, I had to go out and pick fresh flowers for the altar. Every day, their little altar had fresh flowers. Then I'd do the ironing.

There was no time for idleness. They *never* let you be idle. Their day

was bang, bang, bang (pounds). All day long you had chores to do.
    Julia Souza, 62, Hawaii

My dad believed idleness was the devil's workshop, and if we ran out of anything to do, he would send us out to dig up Johnson grass by the roots. Today, I hate Johnson grass, and when I see it, I have the urge to dig it up.
    Billie Jones, 72, Louisiana

Everyone worked together when the cotton was ready to pick, including the youngsters.

My work in growing up consisted of chores at home and working in the field, sowing seed for early planting, hoeing or chopping, carrying water to the field, picking cotton, pulling corn, and any other farm work as needed—other than plowing. My brothers, who were nine in number, did all of the plowing and other work which had to be done by machine.
    Sallie Bell, 74, Alabama

I learned to milk when I was five years old. I remember this cow named Tiny, and my dad always let us all learn to milk on her, because she was tiny and she was easy to milk.

Pearl Mehl, 67, Colorado

As a youngster, I had a dog which I made a work horse out of him. He would pull my little wagon. I'd haul apples out of the orchard into the cellar, and [he] made my life more enjoyable—more play than work lots of time. My father came home one day and he'd asked me to make some sweet potato ridges, so I harnessed up the dog and hooked him to a shovel and let him pull the shovel. I was making real play out of that.

Ansel Peterson, 76, West Virginia

We hoed corn from one end of a big long bottom to the other. Now a hillside may be rocky and rough, but I want you to know, when you bend your back in the hot sun to hoe in a good sandy bottom, you're sure working.

Corria Ratliff, 82, Virginia

I remember assuming the responsibility with my older sister—we would ride, probably two miles, and water this herd of cattle. You didn't turn the pump on and have the water come gushing. You lifted it up with a bucket and a rope and put it in the trough.

We took turns getting the horses in the morning, feeding the chickens, and household chores, like filling the lamps with kerosene, washing the separator and the dishes.

It was a team effort, we all had our work to do. More was expected of us as we grew older, but we felt part of a team.

Marjorie Pontius, 65, South Dakota

Holidays

We made quite a to-do of Christmas. At Christmas time we had our fireworks. My brothers got firecrackers. You didn't get a lot of presents, like you do now. When you was a little girl, you got a china-head doll.

We always hung our stockings by the fire, and you got an apple, and an orange and nuts, and candy, and that present. It was always at the top of the stocking.

We had a two-story house, and we'd all run downstairs to see what Santa had left us. [There] would be a long Roman candle in every stocking. We took those socks back to bed with us.

We always raised peanuts, and we'd pick out a barrel of peanuts and everybody could help themselves. We had a lot of neighbor children visiting us, because our father and mother really took care of us. One year my father went out and bought a bunch of bananas and hung them up. The neighborhood children just thought that was something—to have your own bunch of bananas.

Essie Simmons, 81, Arkansas

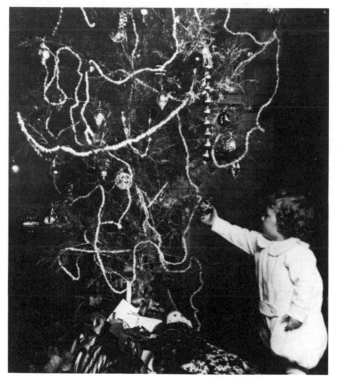

A Christmas tree hung with popcorn garlands and a few ornaments fascinates this youngster. A toy horse-drawn delivery truck and stuffed dog sit under the tree among more wrapped gifts.

I remember especially one Christmas when I was a little girl about seven years old. The day came and it was storming terribly, and my father said, "I don't think we should try to go to your mother's today. It is just so bad." And my mother said, "Oh, it's Christmas, it's just once a year. I think we should try to go."

So she got us children ready, and my dad drove up by the front door with the team hitched to a big old sled and in the sled was straw. It was really a wagon bed on a sled. There was straw and horse blankets, plenty of horse blankets. We all got in the thing and started over to her mother's, and it *was* a very, very bad day. We hovered under the blankets, and my father could hardly see to drive, the snow was blowing so badly.

But after a while we come to my grandmother's house, and they all rushed out shouting, "Christmas gift." The air was just full of love and understanding, and it was warm and cozy in the house.

A Christmas tree had been shut off from the rest of the house in the parlor, and no one was allowed in there until after dinner. We had a wonderful dinner of goose and sweet potatoes and all the fixin's; homemade bread, mince pie—everything you can imagine. And when the meal was over, my grandfather went and brought out a little box of candy—just a small, small box of chocolate, for a big family—and he passed it around. Each fellow got one piece of chocolate candy, and that was a treat of a lifetime.

After dinner we went into the parlor where the Christmas tree stood, and it was a sight for anyone to remember. It was a huge tree that reached clear to the ceiling and it was lighted with real candles. I was a little girl, and I stood back and I looked, and there was a doll dressed in pink, way up in the top. I had many little cousins, and I thought, "Oh, I wish I had that," and, lo and behold, it was my portion of the Christmas for that year. I can never forget it as long as I live.

Floy Chapman, 80, Illinois

At Christmas time at the country schools there would be the Christmas tree that the whole community participated in. This was the main activity at Christmas. It was a community thing, rather than a home-type Christmas celebration.

You'd go to these Christmas trees, and there the children would go in with the candles burning on the trees, which we know now is very dangerous. But there would be many children there, and our eyes all aglow with hope that we'd have a doll on that Christmas tree.

Then, when Santa Claus jumped in the front door, there was bedlam almost, with the screaming children. Some of the smaller ones would be afraid. Of course the older ones recognized what this was.

Jessie Halsell, 68, New Mexico

Do the Norwegians celebrate Christmas any different? Did you have ethnic things that you did at that time?

My mother was so particular on Christmas Eve. We had to all be clean. Everything had to be clean for Christmas. We all had to take a bath, and change our clothes and be nice for Christmas Eve. Then we had a lutefish supper and all the goodies that goes with it.

And my folks would invite somebody over for Christmas Day, and we had the Christmas tree in the home, and we children would join hands and go around the tree and sing those Christmas carols in Norwegian and in American.

Did you have lights on your Christmas tree?

Yes, we had candles. They had to watch that so careful. We had the real trees, and they had somebody that watched it all the time. They never had a fire. When they burnt down, they'd take them off.

Cora Lykken, 89, North Dakota

We belonged to what they called the "Tin" church north of town, and they would have a Christmas program—with singing, and the pastor would be there and do some reading. And some of the kids would speak a piece.

And then he had a custom he [pastor] got started that they all got to hold hands, the whole bunch, and go around the Christmas tree and sing "Nu har ve Jul ejen." That's Danish, you know.

What does that mean?

Now we've got Christmas again. And it goes on "Laut til Paske." That means it'll last till Easter. The kids always enjoyed that, because they could easily sing.

Anna Sorensen, 83, North Dakota

We always celebrated Christmas, and I can remember in my early married life that my husband always had to have a Christmas tree. This one year we had so much snow that we couldn't get out and get a Christmas tree, and he brought in a big tumbleweed and we decorated that tumbleweed for our Christmas tree.

Mary Moore, 73, New Mexico

The first Christmas tree I can remember was a little dead cottonwood only about two or three feet high. It had come up in the meadow and died. It was just too dry in there.

Mother had cut down that little dead tree and brought it up to the house and decorated it with paper chains and things. My brother and I thought it was just wonderful, so the next year we wanted a Christmas tree again. Mother said she had no idea where we could get a tree. It was miles to the nearest tree. And we were so disappointed; I can remember how I just longed for a Christmas tree.

A month or so before Christmas we were out playing in the snow, and mother had a garden that she watered from the horse tank. Well, down at the foot of this garden some big horseweeds had grown in the fence. They'd gotten huge—six feet tall—just great big old horseweeds.

The leaves had frozen and fallen off, but they had a stalk about two inches through. When I saw that row of horseweeds, then I thought, "There's my Christmas tree."

So we pulled the biggest and dragged it up to the old soddy, which was still standing.

On Christmas Eve, Mother brought it into the house, and wedged the bottom end of it into the hub of an old wagon wheel, to make it stand up. She put a cowhide robe around it, to cover the hub. It spread out on the floor and looked so pretty.

China head dolls were a treasured possession of many little girls, usually reserved for special times. The less breakable rag dolls were taken with the owners everywhere. Picture taken in 1917.

My brother and I had been making paper chains ever since we stored the horseweed, so we had yards and yards and yards of paper chains. And then we strung popcorn and wild rose hips. We had a pretty tree; we just decorated it up so fancy with all of those things.

Nellie Yost, 76, Nebraska

Do you save your Christmas decorations?

Oh, yes. I've got decorations that were on the tree when I was a child. I have given my daughters some of these decorations to put on their own trees, because they need to be handed down. Some of them are the little German blown glass things. They weren't expensive at the time that we had them, but they are now. They are worn, but that's part of their charm.

Henrietta Phillips, 69, North Carolina

Mother always managed to buy us gifts. One particular time she ordered our gifts from the mail order catalog. She supposedly had them sent to a neighbor, but while she was gone one day, the order came to our own address.

Us four girls opened the box and looked at everything we had. She managed to snatch it away when she got home, but we had had a ball picking out who got what.

Edith Finnell, 68, Missouri

At Christmas we didn't have a lot of money to buy gifts, but usually we would make each other something during the year. When I was small, my mother would always make me some new doll clothes, or I would get a new dress. And I would embroider little things for my sisters.

On Christmas morning, we would come downstairs and around the dining room table was a soup bowl, and in that soup bowl was an orange and some mixed candy and nuts. That was a treat for us, because we didn't get that very often.

Then for Christmas dinner our mother almost always would have a nice baked chicken. Turkey was unheard of then, but she was a fabulous cook and she always had everything fixed nice.

Dorothy Tolley, 67, Arkansas

We had our own Christmas rituals. One was firecrackers. It was great fun for my dad to take a shovel full of coals out of the stove and go out and shoot off the big firecrackers to wake up the neighbors. Lots of people use them for the Fourth of July, but in our particular section firecrackers were for Christmas.

Frankie Carruthers, 76, New Mexico

Now this is looking through old lady's eyes, but I think (pause) they go a little bit too far sometimes in their celebrating. There is an awful lot of commercialism. I think that the holidays are a little bit abused. But, as I said, I'm looking through old eyes.

Beatrice McCann, 82, West Virginia

Being raised in a camp with so many different nationalities and so many friends amongst all the different people, we were lucky, 'cause we celebrated everybody's holidays.

The Filipinos celebrated their fiestas and they had their dinners, and the Japanese, when it came to New Year's. And us Portuguese, our two main holidays were Easter and Christmas, so the Portuguese women all made bread—the sweet bread which was traditional for Easter and New Year's—and all of the Portuguese style of roasting pork and meats, and Portuguese stewing chickens. And we shared all this with our neighbors.

We had a Puerto Rican neighbor next door and she kept us supplied with the Puerto Rican food, the Filipinos would bring us food, and the Japanese would bring us food. I love every kind of food. I mean I can eat every nationality's food, because we were raised on it.

Julia Souza, 62, Hawaii

My mother was Hawaiian and my father Chinese, so in addition to Christmas and New Year's, we had Chinese New Year, too. We really celebrated Chinese New Year. When we had the regular New Year, we had Kalua pig—Hawaiian style pig. We had tables brought into our house, and lots of chairs, because everybody came to our house. We were the only ones that had Kalua pig. As long as I can remember, Mother would make cake. We had the traditional Hawaiian luau.

Then on Chinese New Year, we would have Chinese food. Then my father would roast the pig with a stick over charcoal. This charcoal was made from corn cobs. Then in the early part of springtime, the Chinese had this festival—they call it Bai San, where they go to the grave for Chinese decoration.

Mary Soon, 60, Hawaii

Our little community of Japanese had their traditional ethnic holidays celebrated. So New Year's Eve the young people of the community would get together, and at the midnight they would serve noodles and soup. Another holiday that the Japanese community celebrated was the birthdate of the emperor. Those are the outside holidays I remember, besides the traditional big holidays of Thanksgiving and Christmas.

Kazuko Kurose, 65, Hawaii

One of the first things I remember about Thanksgiving, I was about 12 years old. And I remember my mother and father were picking corn, and it was Thanksgiving, and it was beginning to snow, so they had to get the corn in.

So I proceeded to go out and get a chicken and fix it up and then I baked some bread, and I made Thanksgiving dinner.

That was quite an accomplishment for a twelve-year-old. When you say you went out and got a chicken, do you mean you killed and butchered it?

Yes. I did. Evidently I had helped before.

Gussie Mumey, 67, Alaska

At Easter time, we'd go to my grandmother's house and there were

several grandchildren, quite a few of us. My aunts that were still at
home, they'd color the awfullest lot of eggs. They'd just have a great
big pan full of eggs.

They let us take those eggs after lunch and go out in the yard and
make nests, and play around with them like that.

Katherine Taylor, 84, Florida

These are Ukrainian Easter eggs. They are symbolic of the Resurrection, with the Resurrection bringing new life and new hope to
Christians, and that is exactly what these eggs are all about.

These eggs are raw. Eventually, if these eggs are kept over a period
of years, the white will form a powder and almost disappear, and the
yolk shrinks to the size of a small pea. These are heirlooms that are
kept for many, many years. If they're handled properly, they can last
indefinitely.

The eggs are color-dipped, just like any other Easter egg. You begin
with your white egg. We use beeswax and a tool called a stylus. The
basic part of the design is placed on the egg with wax while it is white.
The egg is dipped, and the wax is applied again to make other sym-
bols, and the process goes from the lightest to the darkest colors until
it is all finished.

The Easter egg in the Ukrainian language is called a "pysanka."
**You have been very kind to share your eggs at various Extension
Homemaker programs, and the entire county has been most grateful
for your classes and your sharing.**

Dorothy Tyrawski, 58, Delaware

Our family and our neighbors would get together on the Fourth of
July in this front yard and set up tables for food on sawhorses.

A Mr. Pryer lived kitter corner about a mile over there on the other
road. He had a flat-topped house, and he would shoot fireworks off of
his house at night on the Fourth of July. We had a windmill and my
brothers and the hired men would shoot fireworks off from there. We
would take turns so that they could see the ones over there; the ones
that were here, we could see the ones over there. For about two hours
the fireworks went off. They were wonderful.

Rubie Gillion, 80, Michigan

We always recognized Decoration Day. We kids used to always go
in a gang and they would gather wildflowers along the railroad track in
great big baskets, and then Decoration Day, they'd just put them on
the graves of the soldier there. That was a tradition.

Another thing, when we lived on the farm yet, there was a cemetery
back at the end of the farm, so when we kids didn't have anything else

to do, we used to go back there and hunt up a grave that nobody took care of, and we'd clean it off and keep flowers on it.

Estella Myers, Michigan

Mother's Day, it was special. We'd go to church and we'd come home, and then we would have this dinner, and us kids would always be the ones that would cook it. Mom couldn't do anything that day; that was her special day.

Edna Dagnen, 67, Washington

Watermelon is a special treat at this Fourth of July picnic in 1921.

Birthday was a big thing, it was just automatically a big birthday dinner. You were just the fair-haired person on [your birthday]. If it was my brother or my dad, we did their work for them for the day, and if it were our birthday, they would do the work for us. We didn't do a thing. It was so nice.

Mary Raymond, 60, Wyoming

Birthdays were always special to us. On our birthdays, our mother let us choose what we wanted to eat. For instance, I always like chicken pie, so my mother would fix that. That was my favorite birthday dinner. Then she'd always make us a cake. There weren't a lot of presents; there might be something that she had made.

   Dorothy Tolley, 67, Arkansas

   We always had a birthday cake. Even though we didn't have a real big party, there was always a little celebration for everybody's birthday. So with as many people as we had in the family, we was always having some sort of a party.

   Zilphia Edwards, 63, Louisiana

Religion

As you grew up, were you interested in music or dancing or . . . ?
   When I lived in the country, I was a Methodist. You remember?
Oh, yes. That answers my question (laughter).
   My cousin lived in Pennsylvania and I stayed at her house one time for six months while my grandmother was very ill. She [cousin] gave me a pair of black silk stockings which were *wonderful*. I was there at Christmas time, and I had my first Christmas tree—the only Christmas tree that I ever had. The church that she belonged to, they taught children how to dance.
   Well, my grandfather heard about it and he came right up the following week and took me away. He was not going to have *his* granddaughter learning how to dance.
   I'll tell you one thing that made me believe in God. My grandfather was very strict, and he believed in saving. If somebody gave you two cents, you had to save one. I had a bank and every once in a while I would get a penny or two to put in.
   This day I wanted something, I don't know what, so I took a knife and I slipped out a few pennies.
   A week later my aunt picked up the bank and she noticed it wasn't very heavy. She said, "Did you take money out of your bank?" I said, "Yes." She said, "I'm going to tell your grandfather."
   I was terribly afraid of my grandfather because he was so strict. His voice alone scared me. I was so frightened that she'd tell my grandfather . . . . We had a corn crib up in the back of the barn, so I went up there—I must have been no more than nine or ten—and I got down on my knees. I sat there like this. "Please, God, don't let her tell my grandfather." You know, she never mentioned it again and she never

told my grandfather. From then on, I believed in God.
Mabel Hughes, 82, Florida

We always went to church. First I remember going to church in a wagon, but later we had a buggy and then later we had a surrey—a two-seated buggy, you know. Drove two horses to it. We went to church in that and we carried the neighbor children.

Parents who read the Bible and practiced its teachings were a strong influence on growing children.

Going to church was a must with us. We just didn't think about *not* going. We went every Sunday to Sunday School and church. It's been with me through the years, and I'm still going.
Bertha Andrews, 89, Alabama

My grandmother was very strict about religion. Every weekday morning we went to church. At four o'clock in the morning, she woke me. She lived on Upper Kula Road, and the little round Holy Ghost Church was way down on the lower road. We used to walk in pitch darkness through the fields without any light. She knew the trail, and I just used to hang on to her skirts and we'd go to church.

Julia Souza, 62, Hawaii

With distances like there were then, was there a church you attended in your early life?

No, not when we were on the ranch. There was a church in Tryon, twelve miles away, and the roads were usually very bad. Even after we got the car, it was quite a struggle to get to Tryon over those sandy roads. In the winter you shoveled snow and in the summertime you shoveled sand.

Once in a while Preacher Ware and Bishop Beecher came to a schoolhouse seven miles north of us. Bishop Beecher was well known over all of Nebraska and part of Wyoming. He was the cowboy's preacher. He would go to Preacher Ware's home, and then they would come down to this little sod schoolhouse two or three times a year— not oftener than that. We always went, and my brother and I were baptized by Bishop Beecher.

But during those years there were no church services or Sunday School. Not until I was a senior in high school down at Maxwell did I get to go to church or Sunday School regularly.

Nellie Yost, 76, Nebraska

My folks used to tell about two Danish churches here in Flaxton; the singing Danes and the dancing Danes. Which one were you?

We were the dancing Danes, but we weren't allowed to play cards. But singing Danes, their kids were not allowed to play cards and they were not allowed to dance, either. Of course they would sneak it, sometimes. They'd play cards upstairs and the old folks would be sitting downstairs. One would always stand guard. And when they'd go to confirmation, why they'd come out and they'd sit in the ditch and play a game of cards on the way home.

But after a while we got more or less united and they joined in and called it the United Lutheran Church.

So now they can both sing and dance.

Anna Sorensen, 83, North Dakota

I went to the Albright Evangelical Church. It was a one-room building. Sunday School was quite noisy, with all the classes trying to meet in different areas of the same room.

There were two coal stoves, one on either side. There were short seats next to them, and long seats in front and one long seat behind. The stoves would be heated up real hot.

We liked to sit on the long bench behind the stove, because George Julius always sat on the south end of that seat and he chewed tobacco. He'd sit there with his cud of tobacco in his mouth, and ever so often he'd spit and hit a knothole in the floor. Never saw him miss in my life.

Beulah Grinstead, 68, Indiana

Of course the men sat on one side of the church, and the women on the other. They had an Amen corner on the women's side and an Amen corner on the men's side. I never heard any Amens scarcely from the women's side.

Mostly the men.

Yes, there would be loud Amens over there.

Pearl McCall, 89, Indiana

We went to church regularly. I remember in the summertime carrying our shoes until we got in sight of the church and then put them on. Shoes were hard to come by back then and we had to conserve them as best we could. That was common practice back then.

After church, we would go to someone's home for dinner. There were a number of families that rotated. We'd have dinner, then stay and play all afternoon, have supper and go to prayer meeting that night.

We kids looked forward to that in the summer. In the winter we'd see each other at school, but in summertime we could hardly wait for Sunday to all get together again.

Nellie Frakes, 71, Indiana

The big thing when I was a kid going to church was their Children's Day programs. About two or three times a week all the kids in the neighborhood walked in to practice, and then on Children's Day Sunday we'd put on a program for the parents. That was when our little church was usually full.

Dorothy Hoffman, 60, Indiana

We would have to memorize verses. We all had pieces to say, and I remember my mother making us wreaths of myrtle and white daisies. We would have white dresses and had to recite our pieces.

Frances Harley, 90, Indiana

We always had a Children's Day program in the summer, in June sometimes. And we had singings. We used to have the all-day singing and the Dug Hill bunch would come, and from other places. There used to be about five of those Jackson boys, and they were good singers. They used to come to our singings. Seemed like we had something to look forward to most all the time.

Vivian Jefferson, 95, Arkansas

My parents' lives centered around the church when they lived in Virginia. Their entertainment might consist of singing school at the church. People walked there at night, with their lanterns casting long shadows on the road.

The singing master would have a chart of shaped notes, and he would sing them and the people would sing after him, the different notes and the different melodies. There is where I learned the scale and

Baptism in flowing water was part of the
religious experience for many newly-
converted church members.

how to read the shaped notes. They sang everything from church hymns to "Seeing Nellie Home."

Mary Graver, 80, Indiana

Camp meetings would last two weeks, and they would have ministers from everywhere. There was just about as good a sermons as you ever heard.

But as kids we were more to have fun than we were to go to church. That was one time you got to wear your nice dress, if you had one.

We'd go up there and just parade around. Sometimes the boys would play ball on the grounds.

Opal Whitsett, 84, Indiana

I joined the church at age nine and was baptized one Sunday morning in the Boquechita Creek by Reverent S.D. Hyman.

Sallie Bell, 74, Alabama

How did they baptize?
When I gave my heart to Christ, it was at a protracted meeting, as they used to call it [similar to a revival meeting]. There were 34 people united with the church at that time, including several of the girls that were my age. We went to the Rochester Baptist Church and used their baptismal.

But my older sister was baptized at Nyona Lake. After they were baptized, they wrapped a blanket around them and they went up the hill to Smith's to change their clothes.

Lois Waggoner, 76, Indiana

We always had prayers before meals. I never knew of us to sit down to a meal that my father didn't return thanks.

Margaret Butler, 87, Indiana

When my brother and I were growing up, every night we went to my father and mother—the foot of their bed—and repeated the Lord's Prayer.

Lora Torsey, 84, New Hampshire

My grandfather was a very staunch church man and had been a schoolteacher in his earlier days. My grandmother was unable to read, so every evening my grandfather would have all of us sit with them while he read from the Bible to my grandmother.

Sarah Amstutz, 81, Indiana

We always had family worship. My mother and my dad would take turns and read the Bible to us, and then we knelt down and everybody prayed on his knees.

One night I will never forget. In the fall the mice would come in, and a little mouse was playing around. My brother was the only one behaving; all the rest of us were watching the mouse. Well, the mouse ran up the leg of his pants, and he went Bam!! and he had him. All the rest of us almost burst out laughing, and Mother would have spanked us good if we had.

Beulah Grinstead, 68, Indiana

Health

I was the child that was always stepping on a nail—sticking nails in my feet. My daddy would always get a jimson leaf—we had lots of jimson weeds growing out in the barn lot—and he would wilt this jimson leaf on the stove and put it on the place where I had stuck the nail in my foot. It would draw until it would look yellow. Then he would lance it himself.

Opal Cypert, 68, Arkansas

We had a long porch which was clear across the front of the house and I ran across this porch and I ran a big old sliver of wood in the bottom of my foot. They didn't take me to the doctor. It was too deep for them to get ahold of to pull out. They used turpentine and kerosene to keep it clean, and they let it go. It swelled and swelled—well, I almost lost my foot.

Finally the time came they knew something must be done. My two uncles, my granddad and my dad held me on the porch, and my mother took one of these little long razors and lanced it. It was in there so deep.

Jessie Halsell, 68, New Mexico

I stepped on a piece of barbed wire and it ran right through my foot and I started getting blood poisoning. We had a wooden bucket and they put wood ashes in the bottom, and they poured hot water on it, and kept pouring cool water till I could get my foot in it. I sat with my foot in that for an hour or two at a time and that healed my foot.

[Editor's note: Pouring water over wood ashes was a common procedure to make lye, a component of homemade soap.]

Mabel Hughes, 82, Florida

As long as I lived at home, in the medicine cupboard we always had a puffball [dried fungus]. Then in order to stop bleeding you would just puff that puffball onto the blood. It would stop it and clot it.

Too, we always had a bottle of alcohol with Balm of Gilead buds in it. If we got cut or scratched, that was always put on.

Lora Torsey, 84, New Hampshire

Mom made quite a bit of use of her doctor book, because in them days you had to rely on a lot of home remedies.

One time she went after the cows and there was a neighbor's bull in the pasture. He started chasing her horse, and the horse turned a somersault with her on. She had a cracked collarbone. She came home and she didn't want Dad to know about it, so she got the cookbook-doctor book combination, and she found how to put a bandage on for collarbones.

She had me tear up an old sheet in four-inch strips and they were fastened together. She was holding this book and I bandaged her. It was kind of across one shoulder and around her body and back up across the other shoulder. So she didn't tell Dad anything.

About a week after, my sister got into the kerosene and drank some. So a neighbor went to the closest telephone and called the doctor. When he got there, Mom had gotten her vomiting, and she was going to be all right, but then Mom told him about this collarbone being cracked.

And I can see him yet, sitting there laughing, wondering how in the world we had got that bandage on.

Margaret Lien, 68, North Dakota

At that time if you didn't have a bottle of Watkins red liniment in the house, you were just not prepared for an emergency. You could rub it on a bad arm, or rub it on a sore stomach. Sometimes you would take a little liniment in hot water and drink it.

And if a horse had a bad knee or bad leg, they'd rub some liniment on that. So liniment was the all-around thing in those days.

Good for both horses and people.

Good all around, inside and out both.

Anna Sorensen, 83, North Dakota

Six months after my grandfather was buried, my grandmother had another child. And the people back in those days believed that a baby born after his daddy died had a way of curing thrash [thrush—a fungal oral infection common in nursing infants].

So that was the way my grandmother could make a little extra money, and she would take this baby of hers when he got big enough—eighteen months or so—and he would go and blow in a baby's mouth five mornings in a row and they thought that would cure the thrash.

Opal Cypert, 68, Arkansas

In the fall they would trap and they would get skunks. That was a smelly process. Sometimes, if they'd got their clothes stunk up too bad, they'd dig down in the dirt and bury them for two or three days, to get the smell out of them.

You would skin them and dry and sell the skins. And then you'd take the carcasses and took the fat off. It's in a layer, almost like a pig. They'd fix a tripod in the yard, and hang an old iron three-legged kettle and they'd put the [skunk] lard in that and render it. I don't know if it would have stunk in the house, but I never took chances.

And after it was rendered, you couldn't tell it was from a skunk. That was used a lot for medicine. They mixed it with turpentine and rubbed on the chest for chest cold. It was warmed and used for earaches, the same as with goosefat. And they also used it for softening up harness leather.

Margaret Lien, 68, North Dakota

An anxious mother fans a feverish sick
little boy.
L. M. Huffman, photographer

I know one time I had the earache and Mama didn't have a hot pad, of course, so she did the next best thing. She turned over a hoecake and cooked it and got it right warm and wrapped it in a napkin and put it on my ear. I lay down by the fire (laughs).

That afternoon, a lady came in to visit Mama and she brought her little grandson. I was lying near the fire on a pallet, and that little boy said, "The cat's eating a fritter!" That tickled me, and sort of embarrassed me, too.

So if you don't have a hot pad, you can just cook you a hoecake.
Bertha Andrews, 89, Alabama

The extended family of parents, grandparents, aunts, uncles and cousins was part
of growing up. Most families had a
particularly appealing member, such as
this, whom the children admired and tried
to imitate.

I was real sick one time and my mother said, "I'm going to put some
onions in the hot ashes and I'm going to put some onion poultice on
you." And do you know where she put them? On the bottom of my
feet.

How did you keep them there?

Well, she put the onions inside of a little thin cloth and put that on the bottom of my foot and then put on a sock. Well, I was on the verge of pneumonia and she said, "She's just not getting any better," so she called Dr. Reid.

There was only one doctor in Matthews and he was getting up in years and he traveled with a horse and buggy. She called him in the morning, and he didn't get there to right down in the night. So when he came, I still had the onion poultice on my feet.

And he said, "Well, you needn't call me. I see you've done got her fever broken." And she said, "What did I do?" and he said, "You put those onions on her."

I expect he wanted to back out the door. You couldn't go in the house hardly when you used onions.

Letha McCall, 91, North Carolina

I remember that my Grandpa Adam had rheumatism in his back, and he would lie on his stomach and ask my brother Oliver to walk his back. It was fun to us to hear him yell, "Ouch, ouch!"

Grandpa told us that he came from North Carolina, which means that he must have been the son of an immigrant from Africa.

Sallie Bell, 74, Alabama

If you get snake bit, slice the bite with a pocketknife and soak the wound in coal oil [kerosene]. The poison will come out and float. It will come to the top of the oil, turning green.

Billie Jones, 72, Louisiana

What about folk cures?

We had one famous cure in the family that was handed down to us. A doctor gave it to us to cure rattlesnake bites and blood poisoning. He gave the ingredients to the family.

My littlest brother, LeRoy, was following Father as he was plowing in the field, and a rattlesnake bit him. My father unhitched the horse and rode to Holmberg and got the ingredients to make this medicine and gave it to the boy. In about a week he was coming out of it, and the medicine had cured him.

Also, my uncle was in the hospital for operations, and he was being sent home to die. He said the cloud was coming down over his eyes when the family arrived with the medicine. They gave him a few drops and he recovered and lived for several years afterward.

Eva Gill, 80, North Carolina

One remedy was a bag of asafetida and they tied a string around it and you had to wear it around your neck. You wouldn't get any diseases at all when you had that smelly thing hanging on you.

Edna Wood, 77, Nebraska

My dad's favorite croup cure was to rub Vicks Salve on the throat and tie a wool sock around the neck.

Whiskey was used often as a medicine. For a bad cold, take a toddy of one tablespoon whiskey, one tablespoon sugar, and a cup of hot water. Drink as hot as you can and breathe the fumes. Go to bed and cover warmly.

Mrs. Jones, reckon that same remedy wouldn't work today?

Sure it does (laughter).

Billie Jones, 72, Louisiana

The neighbors depended on my mother when they had a family crisis or sickness in the family. I think she was considered a levelheaded person and they wanted her thoughts. My mother had a tenth-grade education—she never graduated from high school—but she had gotten a lot of education from the school of hard knocks.

She never feared going into a home where they had even a communicable disease. I can remember her coming home and coming in the back door and stripping down and saying, "Throw me some clean clothes." I don't think she ever drug anything [disease] home to the family, but she certainly went a lot of places where they had sick people.

And also, people didn't go to the hospitals, and a lot of deaths occurred in the home. She would be called to sit with the sick in their last few hours. I remember one time taking something that she had wanted me to bring, in such a case. And when I got there, she was sitting beside the bed aholdin' the lady's hand. She was sort of talkin' to her, tellin' her not to be afraid. It's pathetic as I think of it, but that was the kind of person she was.

I suppose if she'd been born fifty years later, she'd have been a nurse, but all that [training] wasn't a necessary thing. What they needed, more than anything, was just encouragement and soothing words.

Mildred Weaver, 64, Indiana

We had a country doctor named Dr. Austin, and my mother was very anxious for her family to be healthy, so every time one of her children got real sick, she rang Dr. Austin on the party line phone.

He lived eight miles from us, and you could hear him coming down

the road, [with] his old horse's hoofs going clap, clap, clap.
    Ruth Irwin, 83, Mississippi

The sound of the hooves of the doctor's
horse was welcome, but his black bag
carried most of the limited amount of
medicines then available.

It was the popular thing to have a family doctor, and he would go
out in the country to call. I know when my grandmother lay on her
deathbed, he was as attentive as though it had been his own. It was
wintertime, 1912, when we had that terrible winter, and he came to see
her on horseback.
    Sophie Bigge, 82, Kansas

There was a hospital up over the Merrill Store. The doctor had his patients up there, and he operated on some of them. I guess it wasn't exactly what you'd call a sterile place, but he got by with it. He operated on them for appendicitis and things like that. He was a great hand to operate on people's neck. If they had a little lump, he'd cut open their neck and take that out. I know now that never should have been done. It was just a gland that belonged there.

Anna Sorensen, 83, North Dakota

Did you go to dentists then?

No, not really. My dad was the main one that did the tooth-pulling. 'Course, there wasn't any fixing our teeth. It was just if you had a bad tooth, the tooth needed to come out. And they [neighbors] would come over. My dad would pull teeth without any shots, or anything. The way he did, he would set them in an old-fashioned cane bottom chair, and they would hold on to the rim [edge] of that chair. He would get these pliers and he would pull their tooth out without any medicine or anything. They'd get up and go on home then, and probably plow that afternoon.

Opal Cypert, 68, Arkansas

You started as a health club?

Yes. Miss Arts was our county health nurse at that time, and she came probably four times during the summer and gave us lessons in first aid.

That was in the summer of 1921 and then we became an Extension club in 1922.

Christine Gaffin, South Dakota

I've made much use of the lessons on nursing and health care.

Eva Gill, 80, North Carolina

Death

What were funerals like back then?

My mother and daddy would go and sit up with the sick. They [the sick] would either get well, or they might linger a long time. And then Daddy would just keep sitting up night after night. Then some of the people who weren't able to sit up at nighttime, they go in the daytime.

My daddy would go sit up, and then he'd come home of a morning and he'd hitch the team up and he would plow. It was my chore to go to the field and tell my daddy if this person had died.

I well remember how he wouldn't plow back around to the gate if he was on the far side of the field when he saw me coming. He'd stop his plow and he'd unhitch his horse from the plow, and he'd go right out of the field right then. He didn't go back in the field anymore until the person was buried. But that wasn't long. They had to make the casket. They felt like it was bad luck to make the casket for anyone and have it extra, so the men of the neighborhood made the casket. And the women of the neighborhood would come to my mother's house and they would make her burying clothes.

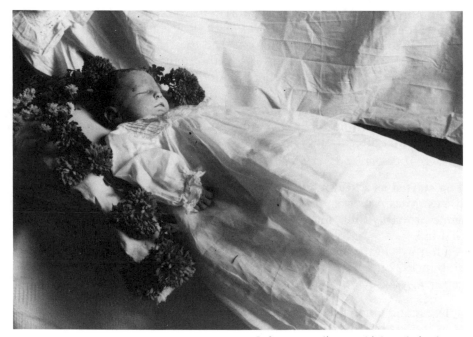

Infant mortality was high early in the century. Pictures of dead babies, such as this one taken about 1910, were requested by grieving parents who had no other pictures of the child.

Usually they died early of a morning. They'd make these clothes and get them ready. They would bury them in the afternoon, because they couldn't hold them out if it was hot weather. Now in the wintertime, they had more time, but they really had to work and work fast. While some of the men was making the coffin, some of them was at the graveyard digging the grave. It was a pretty sad situation. They loved to do it for them, but they was really saddened by those things then.

Opal Cypert, 68, Arkansas

Mother's baby, who was only six months old, got very sick with what they called "summer complaint" at that time. Now they call it dysentery. And by the time Dad come home, he died shortly thereafter.

And that was a very sad thing. My mother could never get over it, 'cause she couldn't nurse the baby and had no place to keep the milk cool, and she thought the baby got sour milk, possibly.

And when the baby died, there was no cemetery, no doctor close by, so my uncle he had built a little casket out of some new board, and lined it inside and out with some white cloth and the neighbors helped dig a little grave about ten rods from the house. There was no cemetery to take care of things like that then.

I remember Mother telling about how they picked wild flowers and made sprays and put around the grave.

Anna Sorensen, 83, North Dakota

When somebody passed away, they were always kept at the home, and different neighbors would come and set up all night with the body. The body was never left alone, until they were buried.

Estella Myers, Michigan

In my younger days, everyone in the neighborhood attended the funerals to pay their respects. Everyone attended the services—young, middle-aged, and old alike. I think this was a good custom. It let the children know dying is part of living and is sure for everybody. It helped them to cope with the inevitable.

Billie Jones, 72, Louisiana

What was the custom with the funerals?
The funeral would be in the home with your favorite preacher. When my daddy died, we couldn't get his favorite Missionary preacher, so Uncle Jess Childress, the hard-shelled Baptist preacher that just lived across the river, we had him to have the funeral. Dad had tried to convert him over to the Missionary. He was very nice and very sweet, and he loved Dad, too.

Dad had made the arrangements for us and had wrote them out before he passed away with T.B. He had everything down.

We had the funeral in the yard, and we had some nice plants that we set out on things, on chairs or something. We had lots of people. That yard was full!

Then we took him over on a flat car on the railroad. It was a narrow-gauge of Ritter Lumber Company. We took him to Grundy and buried him from that flat car. There was plenty of neighbors and things, and the flowers were out of their yards.

Corria Ratliff, 82, Virginia

Not long ago I attended a lesson at a mortuary that our Extension agent had set up, and I asked the question, "Should children be shielded from death?" Because I was accustomed to death. If anyone died, we went [to the funeral] with the family from the time I can remember, and I've accepted it.

Frankie Carruthers, 76, New Mexico

Values

I [have] thought since maybe children of my time should have been allowed to talk and speak their mind more; that people would live easier if children were allowed to live rather more naturally.

Nona Berry, 81, New Mexico

Dad and Mother always had a way of bringing us in to the family group. We were never allowed to sit back in the corner and listen—we always were with the family.

And Dad and Mother and my older sister [and me], when anything of real seriousness came up, or if they wanted to talk money matters—they would get around the table. Dad and Mother would say, "Now we have so much money, and we have to pay our taxes, and we have to have certain machinery, and then our groceries. And we'll put back a little for illness." And we were taught from the time we could understand words that these had to be cared for.

So we were actually taken into the family group, really as a grown up.

Elsa Skiles, Washington

I had the misfortune of losing my mother when I was four years old, and I don't think anyone can take a mother's place.

Florence Reed, 64, Delaware

I see how very hard it is on children. My mother went into the hospital in Charlottesville, and was away from us and had an operation. I can remember asking, couldn't I just go to see her, and they kept saying that she would come home. And I kept thinking that she's never going to come home. And that was very traumatic for me; they kept telling me she was O.K., but yet I didn't get to see that she was all right. It seemed like forever, but I think it was only a couple of weeks.

Constance Anderson, 28, West Virginia

This is a memory that's run in my life for a long time, all my life. When I was just a little child, I had a very good little friend that lived about a quarter of a mile up the road from us, and we played together a lot. Well, on this particular night, I stayed until it was getting dusk to go home. Well, with this high hedge on one side and the weedy fence on the other, I tell you I was scared. But, through the dusk, I saw my mother coming and she took my hand and we went home.

I hope that my family each can have as good a memory.

Nona Berry, 81, New Mexico

I enjoy thinking back over the years that I lived out on the farm. I think I'd like to go back just for one more day and listen to the old red rooster crowing from the top of the garden fence. I'd like to hear the old henhouse come alive, and I'd like to hear the cowbell tinkle as she comes up the cow path every evening with our daily milk. And I'd like to lay in the old loft in the hay, and listen to the raindrops on the old tin roof while I read a book and dream away the day.

And I'd like to go with my mother one more time down the cow path and pick a gallon of big ripe juicy blackberries and eat the cobbler she'd bake in the big old family baking pan. And I'd like to go back to the schoolhouse and I'd like to play the games we'd play at the school when we were little kids. I'd like to go to a taffy-pulling once more, and I'd like to have the old-fashioned husking bees where we gathered around in the evening, and what a time we had!

Alvah Watson, 97, Indiana

EDUCATION

Early Schools

Were there any schools and churches at that time?

No schools—that was the worst of it. My mother went around with a petition to get signers to get a schoolhouse built, but she never heard from them. She got signers—[there were] just three that didn't sign in the whole township. But then she didn't hear from them for a whole year. That's when we had our school in our house at home. Home-made desks—and she had to have some children come from neighbor townships so that she could have school, because we had to be six and we were just four.

Did your mother act as teacher then?

No, they hired a teacher and she boarded at our place all the time. We had a two-room house, and an upstairs. We all slept in one room upstairs, but the teacher had a curtain around her bed (laughs).

Cora Lykken, 89, North Dakota

Mother had been a homesteader's daughter and a schoolteacher. She taught us at home. We didn't have a school to go to until I was ten, but I could read and write and figure well enough that the teacher put me in the fifth grade that first year in school, so I wasn't behind other youngsters my age.

Nellie Yost, 76, Nebraska

I went through elementary school in a sod schoolhouse. That was quite a few years ago, of course. I was fortunate in that our house happened to be one of the closer ones to the school. For years we boarded the teacher, and that was really an advantage—it was a prestige thing.

Marjorie Pontius, 65, South Dakota

I like to talk about my school days because they were happy days. I went to school in a one-room schoolhouse. All eight grades were there, from the first through the eighth. The little children had small seats, and they would be at the front of the building. Then, as you'd go farther back in the schoolroom, why those seats would get larger.

You always had a partner to sit by, and you kept your stuff in your desk. We could whisper, but could just whisper so many times during the day.

We didn't have hot lunchrooms then. We had a wood heating stove and each child would begin taking a potato, or some beans, or something, and we got to making soup in the wintertime. There wasn't any food restrictions back then; we could just cook in this great big pot. Each child had their bowl.

And in the warm days of school, why we'd take our lunch in a bucket—a lunch pail—and we'd sit it in the back of the schoolroom. We'd sometimes have different children that didn't maybe have as much lunch as we did. They would slip in the dinner buckets, and a lot of times you'd go to get your lunch to eat, why your cake and some of the things that you had would be gone.

But we'd all take our lunch pails and go sit out under the tree, and eat our lunch. Then we'd go get a bucket, and two of the people would get to go to the spring. We had to carry the water from a spring across the field from the schoolhouse. We set that bucket on the shelf in the back of the schoolhouse. We had a dipper and everybody would go get a drink. We wasn't afraid of germs back in that day.

Was the length of the school the same as it is today?

No, we only had three months. We really did study, though, and we learned a lot in those three months, because we didn't have any ball games, or any activities that took up our study time. It was strictly school. We had one recess of a morning, 15 minutes; 30 minutes at

noon; and 15 minutes evening recess. Other than that, it was study.
Opal Cypert, 68, Arkansas

We went to school with coverall aprons, even with sleeves in them. When we came home from school, we had to take that off and get our school dress off, 'cause that school dress had to last all week. We wore an apron to school to save our school dress, so it'd be clean enough to wear a whole week.
Lennie Hern, 90, Indiana

I began school at four years old, with a country teacher that would take you if you would only spend the day. So from that I had a good beginning.
Julia White, 61, Tennessee

My older brother started school, and I cried every morning; I wanted to go to school, too. So finally the teacher said, "Well, *send* her to school then." So we had a great big mare that we had to ride horseback, and my legs were so short, and she was so broad across the back that every time I'd get on, I'd fall off. We tried me sitting in front. That way he put his arms around me so I wouldn't fall down. But he had to put the lunch pail around the horse's neck. We went to school for two years on that mare, with the lunch pail hanging around her neck.
Mary Mootz, 76, North Dakota

Even before we went to school I used to go to school with my brothers, and Mrs. Dupont was the teacher there. I loved her classroom, because she had a beautiful dollhouse, all with this homemade furniture. You could take off the roof and there was a hanging basket of the little plants. I used to just *love* to be in her classroom. She didn't mind [having] me in school, even though I was not technically in school.
Julia Souza, 62, Hawaii

I was born on the ranch on May 13, 1894, and started to school there four years later. The neighbors were all very much incensed at my mother for sending me to school at four years. She said, "Well, she might just as well sit at school and read, as to sit at home and read." So I can't remember when I started to read, but it was quite early in life.
Jennie Williams, 89, Wyoming

One old lady, Mrs. Watkins, she let me read books from her house, and I would take them back. She would loan me books of any kind, and I learned to read. My older brother, that was two and a half years older than I was, he taught me how to read before I ever went to school. The sad part about it, I never had a primer. I used to cry for a primer, but nobody bought me a primer.

Corria Ratliff, 82, Virginia

Scene in a very early school. The desks, as seen in the rear, are handmade, and the school room is very small.

Describe the inside of the one-room school in the wintertime.

There was a big stove in the middle of the room. There were little cloak rooms on each side of the door. One for the boys and one for the girls. There was generally a bucket of water there with a dipper in it for us to get a drink.

It wasn't always the warmest place to be. Our fathers generally kept the school in wood. They all took turns cutting wood for the wood-house which was close to the school door.

Was that part of the student's chores to bring in the wood and the drinking water?

Yes, there was a pump right there. There were blackboards at the far end of the school. The teacher's desk was up there.

Iva Crouse, 85, Indiana

The first school I went to was a little one-room country school. I was so interested in what everybody else was reciting—everybody would come up before the teacher and recite—that when I'd get home at night, I'd know a lot of what all the rest of the grades had learned that day.

Dorothy Tolley, 67, Arkansas

I liked the one-room schoolhouse. When you were maybe in the sixth grade, you had learned all the things that were going on in the seventh and eighth grades, so you knew what you were going to be taking the next year. I think that's one reason why sometimes the children advanced and skipped a grade, because they had already learned a lot from the students ahead of them.

Luella Hamilton, 71, Michigan

I don't think many young people now know that when Oklahoma Territory became part of the state, or even before, there were rural schools every three miles. And they, I think for the most part, had really good education.

They used to have county tests and then they had a county graduation, and I felt like they had had a real good education, for not only our children but nearly all the valedictorians and salutatorians were children from rural schools.

Sarah Ball, 74, Oklahoma

When I started country school, in 1953, there were four of us in the first grade and about six or seven eighth graders. [No grades in between] We had a man who probably had a high school education plus one year normal school. He was coping with four six-year-olds and about six or seven 13 to 16-year-olds.

Eighth graders didn't necessarily always get out at the end of their thirteenth or fourteenth year. Some of them stayed, and stayed, and stayed, because they would be taken out in the spring and be out working on the farm, and they would flunk, and they'd have to start all over again.

When I got to be second grade, this is when we were an exclusive class. The teacher had so much time with us that she could give us separate instruction. We had an unstructured school before it became popular again.

Then when we got to be fifth grade, we merged two schools and all of a sudden there were seventeen of us in one room. I tell you, it was excitement, plus.

When I got to the eighth grade, that was the last year we went to country school. Then we went to town school and I was faced with 32

kids in the same room with me, in the same class.
    Karen Retzlaff, 34, North Dakota

When I started to school, there were three children in my class, including myself. That went on till the fourth grade, and from the fourth grade to the sixth grade, I was the only child in my class. I went at my own pace. I graduated from the country school with three of us

A later school room. The seats are manufactured, with fancy ironwork on the sides.
It is a graded school, probably seventh and
eighth grades.

in the graduating class. Then I went to high school at Rozel and there were fourteen in my class. The rival school was Burdett, and the man I married was going over there. Shortly after we graduated in 1964, we had the consolidation. By that time the little country school that I had gone to had been closed. I was really sad to see it close, because I felt like the smaller the school, the more individual attention the child got. I was always glad that I had gone and graduated from the little country school.

Were the people bitter when they had to consolidate?

It was a hard thing for two communities to come together, since they had always been rivals in sports and academics, and it took several years. Finally the people began to come together. Now we are a very strong community. We have a wonderful school system, and everyone gets along really well.

Brenda Van Meter, 36, Kansas

Fun at the Schoolhouse

Usually the big holiday of the [school] year was the last day of school. The whole neighborhood would turn out.

Marie Brown, 64, Oregon

Did you have the big dinner at the very end of school?

Oh, my, yes. That was the highlight. The school board bought great big five-gallon containers of ice cream and we could have all the ice cream that we wanted. Everybody that had children and people in the community came. It was a big covered-dish dinner. We played games and everything.

Brenda Van Meter, 36, Kansas

There were pie socials, spelling bees and ciphering matches held three or four times each year at our school.

The girls would decorate the boxes that held our pies with crepe paper, ribbons and roses, each hoping our favorite boyfriend would buy ours.

There was one boy who always bought mine. I thought he really liked me very much, until he told me he always wanted mine because my mother baked such good pies.

Violet David, 79, Indiana

They used this money to buy maps, and globes, and that sort of thing so that our education was a little more complete.

Sophie Bigge, 82, Kansas

You had recess and played games, I presume. Do you recall some of those games?

We played stick base. If you got caught, you had to stay on a base until somebody rescued you. We played Annie Over the Schoolhouse with balls. We played Bear. Somebody was the bear, and he had to catch the rest of them. Like children do.

Frankie Carruthers, 76, New Mexico

We used to play Drop the Handkerchief, Merry-go-round, and London Bridge is Falling Down, games like that.

In the wintertime, they would throw snowballs and some of them would get under the water they pumped and made snowballs so they were like ice. The teacher made them quit that because they would hurt.

Frances Hurley, 90, Indiana

Recess time at a one-room school.

The teachers played with the children at intermission. Some of the favorite games were: Bear; Stink Base; Rover, Rover; Move Up; Blind Man; Anti-Over; Drop the Handkerchief; Crack the Whip; races, spinning tops, marbles (both indoors and out), rolling hoops, hoop races and blackboard games.

Snow was always welcome. Then we enjoyed Fox and Goose, coasting, snowmen, snow angels and snowballing.

Essie Rumble, 78, Indiana

One of my teachers weighed over four hundred pounds. She was light on her feet. [Three of us pupils] were nine years old and she could run in games with us and run as fast as we could. We couldn't beat her.

What kind of games were you playing?

The Last Couple Out and Drop the Handerchief and all kinds of games where you did a lot of running.

We had a pond between her place and our place that froze up in the winter. I don't know how she made it, but there was a pole in the middle of the pond, and from there was a long, long stick with a sleigh on the end of it. We'd pile in that [sleigh] and her and some of the bigger kids would push. They would walk slow around, but, boy did we ever go, because we was way out on the end. That was fun.

One time she forgot her key, and she told us kids to go on the other side of the schoolhouse. It was an old-fashioned window and she took the whole window out and crawled through and got the door open. She was tall, she was awfully tall. She had to order her shoes, or otherwise she had to buy men's shoes, because she couldn't get ladies' shoes big enough.

But she was a good teacher, and could she ever play the piano! But you should have seen her piano seat. It was *really* braced.

Minnie Ness, 81, North Dakota

The girls at this school, come recess time, we would go outside under the trees. We would build our playhouses and there we'd play. The boys and girls were not allowed to play together. There was a division line, and you did not dare step over this line. You were completely separated.

Jessie Halsell, 68, New Mexico

It was a good mile and a half to walk, but we were kids, we didn't care. One way we would go across a brook. My brother would always try to get a water snake and he would put it in [his] school bag. When we would get in school, the first thing you know the kids would be squealing, and there would be a water snake running over the floor (laughter).

Mabel Hughes, 82, Florida

The big boys would get mischievous. [We had] big double seats, two in a seat, and they had an inkwell, a little hole where you got your ink out of. The boys sat behind the girls, and they would stick their hair in it. They would write notes and throw them across to people and then the teacher would hit you and make you read the notes.

They would stand them in the corner with a dunce cap, too. The boys would put frogs in the teacher's desk. There was a little drawer in the desk and sometimes she would open that, and out would jump a frog.

Frances Harley, 90, Indiana

Maybe I should tell about my boys [sons]. I never knew the rascals they were until [now] they're grown up. That Harlin decided at recess that he should catch a gopher. They all helped with that, I guess. They put a string on it and had it ready.

Miss Spoonheim went outside to ring the bell at noon for the kids to come in, then he was supposed to stand by an open window and jump in through there and stick this gopher into her desk, and then cut off the string. Then he'd go sit down in his seat, as though nothing had happened.

And they all came in, these kids, all waiting to see what'll happen when Miss Spoonheim opened up that drawer. Of course, the minute she did, the gopher jumped out and pretty-near scared the daylights out of her.

Now if his brothers had come home and told on him, which they never did, he would have gone to bed without supper that night.

Anna Sorensen, 83, North Dakota

I remember we chewed gum, and the teacher would say, "Mabel, put your gum out of the window." I would take my gum and stick it on the window sill on the outside. Somebody else would be chewing gum, and she'd say, "Ruth, put your gum out of the window." She would stick her gum out on the window sill on the outside. At recess time we'd raise the window, pick up our gum, and start chewing it again.

Were you sure you got the same one?

Mabel Hughes, 82, Florida

When we stayed at my grandparents in Spreckelsville, we were put on the train [to go to school] at the Spreckelsville store. All of these high school kids were on that [train].

If you talk about *kolohe* [mischievous] kids, that was the days of *kolohe* kids. They cannot say that today's kids are naughty, because they were naughty from the old days, too. They used to stop at the Spreckelsville store, and they'd have certain girls that would go in and they would take hold of the manager's attention, probably buy something, and in the meantime the other girls were raiding the jars, big glass jars on top of the counter with bubble gum and the dry abalone. They'd do that just about *every* day. Then they'd go up and down the train, passing these out to anybody.

Mary Soon, 60, Hawaii

We didn't have any chewing gum like we do now. There was a great big sweet gum tree in the creek bed. There was one girl that could start the chewing gum off of this sweet gum tree. She'd work all recess starting different ones of us, chewing the sweet gum. I look back and wonder if that wasn't why we shed our teeth at such a young age—because it really stuck to our teeth. But we loved it.

Opal Cypert, 68, Arkansas

School Attendance

We worked when the fields opened up until we took the last stuff out of the fields. We weren't kept in school. [We had] to work in the fields. In those days, in our community, in the schools we attended this was an excused absence. We could miss school for whatever was necessary. It gave me a great sense of responsibility of the job, and I feel a better person for it.

Mary Raymond, 60, Wyoming

I attended elementary school in a little small country school. Very often the boys, the older boys, did not attend school until after the corn was shucked and in the spring they quit when the farm season opened. The girls attended the entire year, and many of the older girls were wonderful in assisting the teacher in the instruction of small children.

Floy Chapman, 80, Illinois

Johnson Mesa had summer school. We began in April and ran until Christmas time. Then we just lived and kept care of the cattle and kept care of ourselves.

Was that because of the winter conditions that you had school in the summertime and dismissed in the winter?

That's right.

Nona Berry, 81, New Mexico

My father was a trustee of the school in that area. He was always a leader in seeing that schools were kept open the four or five months of duration of public funds, and supplement five or six weeks during summer months, for children to get at least six months' schooling in one year.

I always made good marks in school, which kept my parents happy. My goal was to become a teacher.

I remember my father going before the county board of education to ask for a longer term and some equipment for the black children's school. They had done all the assignments for the white children; and had appropriated money for building shelters for the children standing on the side of the road.

Then when my father's name came to say something, they say,
"What do you want, boys?"

Sallie Bell, 74, Alabama

In those days they had graduation at the end of the eighth grade,
because girls weren't expected to go on to school. What was the use of
going to school? They were just going to get married anyway. So we
weren't encouraged to go beyond the eighth grade.

Neva Schlatter, 79, Indiana

I was supposed to go from the fifth grade to the eighth grade. They
wanted to skip me to the eighth grade. I came home and told my
mother. I think I was only eleven years old. My mother said, "Oh, no.
Your father's not going to let you go to high school."

Mrs. Kalmis, who was the principal, had made arrangements for me
to stay with one of the teachers at Maui High School, and she was
gonna pay my board and my tuition at Maui High School. But my
father wouldn't hear of it.

So my mother said, "Don't you jump grades. You go right back to
school, because if you don't, you're going to go right out and work
full-time." So I continued on to the eighth grade. I graduated valedic-
torian, and that was the end of my education.

Some of my brothers and sisters were allowed to go to high school
after . . . and some of them that could go, didn't want to go. It just gets
me so angry when I think about it. How much I loved to go to school
and I didn't have the opportunity.

Julia Souza, 62, Hawaii

My dad never would let us go to the library for books, and he never
wanted us to take books home to study. We had to sneak them in.

Why was that?

He [said he] sent us to school to study and that's where we were
supposed to do our learning.

I wonder why he felt that way.

I guess he never had any schooling to speak of himself. He left home
when he was twelve years old.

Estella Myers, 80, Michigan

My parents were very limited in their education, but they wanted
their children to have the best education they could receive. That was a
guide for me.

Eva Gill, 80, North Carolina

My aunt wanted me to go home with her and go to school in

LaFayette. Well, I didn't want to go, because that was leaving home. I love my aunt, but I didn't want to go home with her and stay.

But Mama insisted. She got me off in there and she said, "Now, you can go to school up there with your aunt, and you can get you an education. Or you can stay on here and chop cotton, just whichever you want to do."

So I went on up there. I enjoyed school. I always loved school. We studied at home and was always encouraged to do our best in school.

Bertha Andrews, 89, Alabama

I wanted to go to college to be a teacher, but because of the economic factor, I realized that was the next thing to impossible.

I did resolve that if I ever had any children, they would go to college if I had to take in washing to pay for their tuition.

Billie Jones, 72, Louisiana

Getting To and From School

One time we were stranded there all night because it stormed so bad we couldn't get home. The smaller kids stayed close to the stove that was in the corner of the building, and the rest of us, we had to run around the schoolhouse [room] to keep warm. We couldn't sit down very long at a time because it was so cold.

How long did you have to stay there in the school?

Well, about noon the next day they came and got us. We was pretty hungry by that time.

Minnie Ness, 81, North Dakota

When I was old enough to go to school we were about five and a half miles from a school and across prairie, with no road, of course. So it was too far for me to go to school. Dad didn't want to take a chance of even going across there in the winter, on account of storms.

When I was going to be eight, Grandma Adamson had moved to Coteau, because Grandpa Adamson had passed away. So I lived with her then to go to school.

Margaret Lien, 68, North Dakota

I can remember very well my first day of school. I had ahold of the teacher's hand. I had on a little polka dot dress and I was so proud, but we had to walk two and a half miles through the mountains to the first school.

Frances Mathews, 72, New Mexico

I remember that first year that I started to school. My brothers and sister that were older than I went on to school. We could see the schoolhouse, it was a half a mile. And they left me the lunch to carry.

Mama fixed all our lunch in one market basket, a little market basket, and they left that for me to carry. There was ice on the ground, and I can't stand up on ice—never could (laughs).

So I started with the lunch, and it was rolling land. I could walk up the hill, but it was going down that I couldn't stand up. So I'd sit down on the ice and give the basket a shove and shove it on down in front of

Mules pull out a hopelessly mired car.
During muddy weather, early roads
became almost completely impassable.

me, and I'd slide down to the basket. Then pick it up and walk up the hill, get to the next litle ridge, I'd do the same thing.

Did you get to school safely with the basket, that's what I'm wondering?

Oh, yes.

Letha McCall, 91, North Carolina

When we first went to the city school, my daddy bought us a brand new buggy—a rubber-tired buggy—and we drove a horse. We rented a stable in town for us to put our buggy in, and when we came home in the afternoons, he was there to meet us.

There was a great big rock which my father kept by the fireplace all night. In the morning, when we were ready to go to school, he placed the rock in the bottom of the buggy, and he wrapped us and tucked us in, and we stayed warm until we got to school.

Then it was a cold buggy to get into in the afternoon, but coming home he always met us. He would take the horse, put it up, and when we went into the house there was the aroma of baked bread and maybe a big pot of vegetable soup. I can still smell it.

Elizabeth McAdams, 69, Alabama

When I was 17 years old, I drove the school bus, and I drove it two and a half years. Drove a horse bus, and many is the time in the spring, when we had what we call the spring thawout, and the bottom would go out of the road, I would take my kids within a half mile of school; tie my horses to a fence post; and walk the kids to school. Then in the evening, I tied my horses at this corner and walked down and led my kids out. I think I had 16 or 17 on the bus.

Edna Winter, 84, Indiana

We had more fun when we was going to school. If it would be bad weather, my mom would hitch up the horse and come over and get my brother, sister and I, and we brought our two cousins along home.

We were all in the buggy, and it was muddy as all get out, and when we went by, some of the kids throwed stones at the horse and hit it. So away we went, just a-sailin', and we had to go over the railroad track, and a train was coming.

My mom tried to slow the horse down, to let the train go by, but that horse, she couldn't hold him. She'd keep a-sayin' "Whoa, Jimmy! Whoa, Jimmy!" and us kids was all hollering and laughing. We just went over the railroad track a-bouncin' and the train went by.

And Mom says, "I'll never come after you any more." She says, "Just walk home, it's only 2½ mile." So after that, we always had to walk home.

Masa Scheerer, 82, Indiana

About the time I was a senior, my father bought a brand-new Model T Ford, which was really something at that time, and I drove it back and forth to school with my sister.

Ruth James, 78, New Mexico

Did your boys go by bus then?
Yes. The bus man, he'd haul the kids in the morning and then he'd go and haul coal all day in that same bus, and in the evening he'd haul the kids home. Boy, were they black with coal dust! They had to

change everything they had on and wash up before their supper.
   Minnie Ness, 81, North Dakota

   I rode the very first school bus in Stoddard County. My dad just
thought his little girl could not go to town and stay with an unknown
family, out of his sight. The superintendent of schools said, "Well, Ed,
if you will get out and make up a bus load, I will buy a bus. I think
that I can support the bus on two dollars a month for a student to ride
it."

An early motorized school bus. Note the
"windows," which are hinged wooden
shutters which go up or down.

   My dad was run out of a few people's yards for even mentioning
high school to them about their children, but he did get a load, and I
went four years to high school in Dexter.
   The school bus was a long dotty thing that had seats down like each
side, and a straddle board, we called it, in the center. If you weren't
lucky enough to get a side seat, you had to ride the straddle board. The
only heat in the bus was an ordinary car heater, which didn't near heat
the bus. I've walked into school a lot of mornings when I couldn't feel
the floor, my feet were so cold.
   Edith Gladden, 63, Missouri

I can remember when I drove the school bus, lots of times I'd get stuck in the sand and the children would have to get out and help me to push to get it out, because we didn't have paved roads at those times. Sometimes my husband would drive. We had to cross a little creek. When we had rainstorms, that creek would rise and he would have to take the little children over piggyback, to get them across the stream.

Elsie Gould, 87, Florida

I started school while we were living at the farm, and I had to go a mile to the interurban, and then I had to go about three miles on the interurban and another half a mile to school. I remember once that I didn't get off at the right station, and there was no telephone and there was quite a bit of problem, because I had to go to school alone that day.

Violet Cottrell, 69, Washington

In the early 1940s our children were attending a rural school, and the highway was so bad in the wintertime. Lots of times we'd hook a team onto the car and pull the car out to the road. Then we'd leave the team there—they were real good—they'd stand there as long as we had the singletree behind them. Then we'd take the kids the other three miles up the highway to school, and then come back and hook the team back on to the car and pull it back in home. Our youngest daughter was born in 1936 in August and that winter the older kids were going to school. So Alice, little as she was, she'd be with us in the mornings. There was days that probably it was forty below, but we were out there getting the kids to school.

Now when Doris, the oldest one, first started then we had a hand sled. Ben nailed a wooden apple box on that and put a horsehide robe in there. Doris would get sitting down in there and he'd cover her up, just her nose sticking out, usually. Then he hooked a rope on to the sled and on to the saddle on his horse and away they would go across country to school. Sometimes she got tipped over, but she didn't seem to ever get cold.

Margaret Lien, 68, North Dakota

We moved to the Haliimaile [plantation] and [they] took us kids to school in a truck. In those days it rained just every day, just rain, rain, rain. So we always rode with the truck covered with a tarpaulin.

Julia Souza, 62, Hawaii

When I started at Maui High School, we had to pay tuition, ten dollars a year. My father was out of work, so we had to raid my piggy bank. I had about twenty dollars, so there was enough to pay my tuition. Lunches were cheap, about ten cents for a lunch. So that wasn't too bad.

We rode to school on a bus. It rained [a lot] and if the plantation road was flooded, or the road was slippery, then we had to go all the way to Paia and go up the Paia Road. There we'd see the train coming with the kids from Wailuku. The down country kids would come to Hamaopoko on the train, too.

I belonged to different clubs and whenever we had activities, I'd have to stay. There were a couple of boys who were also active and good students. They would bring their father's pickup truck, and there would be three or four Kula kids and we were able to go to the activities and come home on the truck.

But if we didn't have that, we'd walk up the main road and catch a ride to Makawao. Then I would sleep at my uncle's house in Makawao and the next day I'd catch the bus and go down to school the next morning.

It was really hard. Even when I was a senior, I had to do that. I missed out in lots of the social activities in high school.

Mary Soon, 60, Hawaii

Food in the Schools

We took our lunch. I have seen others come in with lunches that didn't look too attractive. I have seen lunches brought in a syrup pail with a lid on them. Biscuits soaked with sorghum molasses, which never looked very appetizing to me.

Frankie Carruthers, 76, New Mexico

We carried a dinner pail. In the wintertime they froze, too. We had to thaw them out before we could eat.

Minnie Ness, 81, North Dakota

Did you have a hot lunch program back then?
Oh, yes (ironically). In the bucket you carried (chuckle). Packed your bucket before you left [home]. If you didn't get what you liked it was your tough luck, or you traded with somebody. I can always remember if I got to school and somebody had a boughten bread sandwich, it was "Will you trade with me?" because I was so sick and tired of homemade bread.

And what you'd do now for homemade bread and usually homemade jelly.

Dorothy Hoffman, 60, Indiana

My oldest daughters started in a one-room school. We started a little PTA there, and also thought it would be nice in winter, at least, if the children had hot lunches.

So I volunteered to bring enough for the whole school, which wasn't as big a job as it sounds. I think there were 14, including the teacher.

We would bring a casserole-type dish and the other mothers would do the same thing. So we had our own little hot lunch program going, with no additional charge to the students. The mothers just took turns.

Marjorie Whitney, 69, Illinois

Older students serve cocoa to elementary students in an early attempt to cook something at school to go with cold lunches brought from home.

We cooked school lunches at that time. You wouldn't be able to do that today, because of the health rules and regulations.

At that time through the summer about five of us mothers would buy peaches and we would have our own tomatoes, and [would] can through the summer in our homes, helping each other. Then in the fall when school started, we would provide free lunches for the school children.

We had a neighbor lady across the street from the school building.

We hired the use of her kitchen. She helped us prepare the lunches and carry [them] across the street and serve them. [We would] carry the dirty dishes back and wash them at her house. And we provided free lunches for the school.

We had lots of fun doing it. It was a lot of work.

What would be a typical day's menu you had then?

Meat, and we always had some kind of soup, tomato or vegetable or

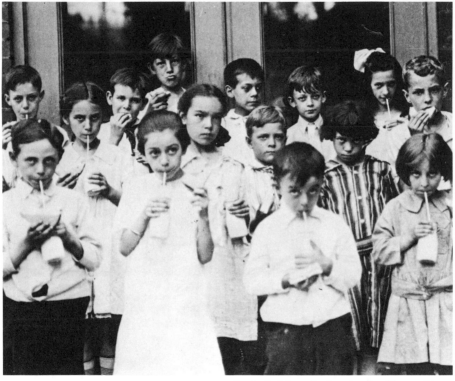

A sandwich and a bottle of milk provide a
nutritious meal supplement at school.

chili. Always milk. Always a dessert, [maybe] fruit with a cookie on the side.

Lots of work and dedicated people.

You didn't think about it. It was part of life.

Pearl Sollars, 70, Indiana

Can you tell me some of the projects your club did in the community?

Well, in the early days there was a new school built in our little town. The school board didn't have enough money to finish it, so the

EH clubwomen got busy, and their husbands, and they put the ceiling in the auditorium and they bought the stage curtains, and we started a hot lunch program. We just helped in any way we could.

Edith Fennell, 68, Missouri

High School, College and Continuing Education

When I finished the eighth grade in the country school, then I went to high school, and I stayed away from home. I had to board with friends who lived in Boswell, Oklahoma. I would come of a Friday afternoon and then go back on a Sunday afternoon or early Monday morning for the week of school.

I remember it was very difficult. People were very poor. I remember one time when my dad in the fall of the year sold a big load of corn and received only enough money from this load of corn to pay my rent for the month—rent and board. This was $12.50. It was a real sacrifice for my parents to send me to school. Years later, when my brothers were old enough to go on to school, they had a bus service, and they could go to school and be back home every night.

My dad had bought me a horse to ride, and I would leave the horse at my grandparents who lived in town. I'd leave it with them in their barn, and then, come Friday, I'd come home. Other times, when I didn't have the horse, maybe there would be neighbors who would be coming in to town and as they'd go home, they always remembered that I would be needing a way home, so I would go with them.

Jessie Halsell, 68, New Mexico

I lived all my life on a farm northwest of Rush Springs, until high school days. Then Mother moved into Chichasha, so that we could be put in high school.

Had your father died?

No, he still stayed on the farm.

Zelma Wood, 77, Oklahoma

When I was ready for high school, I went in to Cape Guardo, and we did our own cooking. We took food in from the farm. Had to buy milk and bread and things of that sort, 'cause we did our own cooking.

Frankie Carruthers, 76, New Mexico

I started to school in a one-room school, but we moved back to Clay Township and I attended school there.

Gee, what a big school. One room was bigger than the whole school-house at Dongola. There were four big rooms downstairs and a hall-way going in all directions. I was lost for three or four weeks. I didn't know for two or three years what was up the big stairway on the second floor. I would see a host of big boys and girls go up and down the stairs.

Marjorie Malott, 70, Indiana

For two years I played on the girls' basketball squad. Well, then

Bloomers and middy blouses were standard attire for most girl's athletic teams at schools.

somebody got the idea that girls' basketball was too hard on the girls, so they quit on it for a while. But now it is quite a sport again.

Margaret Lien, 68, North Dakota

My sister was a great runner when she was a young girl. The uni-forms that they had to run and jump in then was white middies and black sateen bloomers.

The first year that my sister entered in the races, my parents wouldn't let her wear those black sateen bloomers—she had to wear her dress.

She just run clear off and left the girls that she was racing with. So when we got home that evening, my daddy told my mother that she just must get some material and make Inez a middy and some black sateen bloomers because any girl that could outrun that many girls as far as she did, they deserved to have a uniform, too. So the next year when my sister run the race, why she got to wear the black sateen bloomers.

Opal Cypert, 68, Arkansas

I guess that's why I decided in my later years now to take up running again, because I used to win some races. I have a few pictures of those big, black bloomers. Then my mother made us wear straw hats when we were out running, because she said it wasn't good to get sunburned too much—we'd get freckles on our faces. So we had to wear straw hats and those bloomers and white blouses, if you can imagine that.

Pearl Mehl, 67, Colorado

My parents were very limited in their education, but they wanted their children to have the best education they could receive. That was a guide for me.

Eva Gill, 80, North Carolina

After I was through my sophomore [year] then I was married. But I didn't finish my education until after all my kids were grown up and away from home. I took supervised study through Fargo, and in 1962 I went to Fargo for graduation.

Margaret Lien, 68, North Dakota

You told me that years later you went ahead and got your high school diploma. What made you do that?

Well, that was after I had been in the Peace Corps and came back home. And I had been in VISTA for six months. And my kids all had a high school diploma, and I read of this GED test, and I figured that I could pass it. So, I went and took it and did.

And I went to the alumni banquet once, just because I was qualified to do so (laughs). But I missed something that happened that night. We were all sitting up in the bleachers, and they called for the classes to come down in the year they had graduated. And I got a standing ovation, and I didn't even notice it, because I was watching the steps so careful to come down off those bleachers.

How old were you at that time?

Well, I was 69.

Neva Schlatter, 79, Indiana

I graduated in 1913, the 29th day of May, and I decided I wanted to teach, so my mother—we never had a lot of money—so she said, "That's O.K. We'll see that you have enough money to go to Terre Haute [Teachers College]." So she sold a Jersey cow and got $60 for it, and that was all I had to pay my room and board and buy my books and pay my transportation to Terre Haute. On $60.

Pearl McCall, 92, Indiana

They only had eleven grades in Maryland schools at the time.

That was the equivalent of a high school education?

That *was* a high school education. And I wanted to go on to business school, so we scraped up the money somehow and I went to Beacom, and they didn't have dormitories. The girls worked in homes of people and did work such as washing dishes and taking care of children and being a built-in babysitter. That's what I did while I was there. And I have walked 24 blocks to Beacom in the morning and at night to save carfare, which was only ten cents.

Florence Reed, 64, Delaware

My father was a factory worker, a shop worker and [his] wages didn't cover college. I didn't expect him to send me to college. But I found out I could work it. I got a job in the Building and Loan in Alliance, and I worked for the full sum total of thirty dollars a month. I thought I was just richer than rich, and I was. It was a lot of money in those days, and I went to college on my savings. Miami University at Oxford [Ohio] had me the first two years. Ohio State graduated me. I was graduated in 1922 from Ohio State.

Cecilia Lamb, 87, Michigan

My mother was very firm in her belief that an education was pretty necessary for her children, so I did go on to the university and graduated. When I went into the School of Business at the university, my father was very happy, because he thought I could be of help in the store for the bookkeeping.

One day afterwards when I was doing the bookkeeping he came in and said, "What's the bank balance today? We've got some bills due."

I could not tell him what the bank balance was. I shuffled through papers trying to find it. He says, "For heaven's sake, girl! I could keep it in my head better than you can with a degree from the University of Kansas."(laughs)

And yet I have been voted as one of the distinguished graduates of the alumni of Kansas University (chuckle).

Evelyn Alden, 74, Kansas

Teaching School

About 1910 to 1913, I taught in a rural school—eight grades—for $35 a month. Built my own fires and did my own janitor work. And I just loved it!

How many students did you have?

Forty-five the first year and I was only eighteen years old, too. Boys that were almost as old as I was. I see them now, their hair is just as gray as mine.

Some of the other students kept saying, "Wait till Harold Hanson

Ages in one-room schools ranged widely.
The teacher on the right is surely not much
older than some of her pupils, and may
have been a fellow-student a year
or two ago.

starts!" He wouldn't come, only just in the fall when there wasn't any farm work to do. He seemed to have a name for causing trouble. I never had one bit of trouble with him. Not a bit. I said, "Harold, I'm going to trust you to kind of help the little first graders out here on the playground. That'll be your job, to kind of look after them a little bit. Don't let them get in any quarrels or fights." He did a real good job of it.

Josephine Nixon, 90, Wisconsin

That was about the only alternative that the girls had, was to become teachers. We didn't have a business course in high school at that time.

Before I was out of the school where I grew up, one of the board members said, "Now, we're planning for you to teach our school." I said, "You know the recommendation that our Normal training teachers give us is not to get into a school where we are known, or go home to teach." But there was no problem, we didn't have any controversy with anything. And I knew the kids, all of them.

Sophie Bigge, 82, Kansas

Did the older ones help the younger ones?

Oh, yes, some of the older ones would help. Some went to school until they were 17 or 18 years old [in the eighth grade]. I remember when I was in school there were seven from one family, and the one girl was like 17 years old. And Jake Shipper, I think he was 17 years old.

So when I came back to teach there, I had about six pupils I had gone to school with, and I was their teacher.

Florence Phillips, 90, South Dakota

The first job [teaching school] I got was in the rural schools. I had a job in the middle of Carter County, about ninety miles from any bigger city.

I had a horse, and I rode this horse each day. It was a seven and a half mile round trip, and ten miles on a bad day.

Oh, you had to go a different route?

Yes, then I had three creeks to cross, and two gates to open on the way.

Quite an experience for a young person from a small city.

Then I had to unsaddle him and put a halter on him in the barn. At noon I had to put a feed bag on, and then when I went home at night, I had to saddle him and put a bridle on him.

Did you live with somebody in Carter County?

Yes, I lived on a sheep ranch at that time. They had about four cowboys (chuckles) and a sheepherder. Of course they all liked to give the teacher a hard time.

I had five children [to teach]. Then the snow got so deep in 1935 that we had to close school. She [landlady] said, "Do you want to work for your room and board this month, while you're not doing anything?" I says, "Yes, what doing?" She said, "Well, you can melt snow for the milk cow."

Do you know how much snow it takes (laughs) for a milk cow to drink a tub full?

Pearl Herndon, 67, Montana

You must remember then that it was all right that a teacher be married and teach school, though they always preferred a single teacher.

But if you were married and you were pregnant, then that stopped your teaching school. There was no more of that when I came pregnant. I no longer was a teacher.

Jessie Halsell, 68, New Mexico

I found teaching a pleasure, but one that took everything that the teacher could put out. I'm glad that I had the experience and I loved those children as if they were my own. I still do (laugh of joy).

Floy Chapman, 80, Illinois

When you're married and you don't go to school any more, you don't pick up a book and study or anything. You listen to this [Extension] and you go home and practice it. It's a form of education and, oh my, I don't think I could measure the benefits I've gotten out of it and the friends I've made. Oh, my, I wouldn't take a million dollars for it.

Mary Jonas, 81, Ohio

I married young, and I had high school, but no college. I think that's one reason that I have felt that I got *so much* good from the Homemakers organization, because of working with the Home Demonstration workers They *were* college graduates, and I felt like a little bit of it rubbed off on me.

Beatrice McCann, 82, West Virginia

I have always been one for education, and I didn't have a chance to go to college. My father was one of those that felt you went to college to get a man, and he thought I could get a man without going to college.

I could never have done all the things I have without the Extension Homemaker opportunities. The chance for the formal education that I never had a chance to get.

Donna Agness, 61, Indiana

We have a program where we can get credits for different things we attend. They call them CEC credits, Continuing Education Credits. And these can be applied toward a Board of Regents Degree. And that's what I'm currently working on. I'm going to get a Board of Regents Degree with all this acquired knowledge that I've gained through Extension Homemakers, all these lessons and workshops I've attended and finish up some schooling that I gave up to get married.

Deanna Cook, 31, West Virginia

I have said so many times that I could almost have a college degree on what I have learned from Extension. Now maybe I am biased, but I can't think of any organization that a young woman can join that would be of any more benefit to her.

Beatrice McCann, 82, West Virginia

Our State Leader [of Extension Homemakers] said to us one time, "Don't you know that this Extension is the broadest and the best adult education program in this country?"

Evelyn Alden, 74, Kansas

COURTSHIP AND MARRIAGE

Dating

We went together in flocks; (laughter) the whole neighborhood kids went together. The young people went to dances. We got into whatever cars that were available and we went together—brothers and sisters, and brothers and sisters of other households—and went to the dances. Our brothers were there and carried on the martial law (laughter). They saw to it that nobody bothered their sisters. So there was a feeling of protection and good will among each one.

Finally, couples paired off. If they did, why it was almost with intent of marrying. It was a courtship.

Rubie Gillion, 80, Michigan

When I was growing up, Mama said, "No courting alone, until you're eighteen years old." Well, I had a few dates before then, but was *always* in the company of someone else.

I remember my husband came to see me, before we were married. He wanted to take me to an Elks entertainment. And Mama insisted that my younger sister ride with us in the horse and buggy over there and stay with my other sister who lived in Raleigh [until the entertainment was over] and come home with us.

Theo Hammond, 82, North Carolina

I'll tell you the first date I had. A neighborhood boy wanted to carry me to church one night. They was having protracted meeting. So my mother felt like I needed a chaperone, so my brother went behind in another buggy and chaperoned.

When we got to the church that night, it was filled to capacity. The usher found me a seat, but he didn't find one for my date. I was disappointed—first date I had, and I didn't get to sit by him in church (laughs).

Bertha Andrews, 89, Alabama

Did you get to go to dances when you were young, or was that against your father's belief?

I remember one time I wanted to go to one and he took me. When

Young couples enjoy a picnic spread out on a white cloth in a meadow, with a rail fence in the background.

he would take us to play-parties or anything, he always sat right there where he could watch his girls.

Edith Finnell, 68, Missouri

We used to take walks. We didn't call it anything else. After chuch was over, maybe two or three couples of us would walk. Maybe we'd stop and have ice cream some place. Church was out and it was still early—nine o'clock or something, and we didn't think we wanted to go home yet. So we'd walk.

Cecilia Lamb, 87, Michigan

I was not allowed to single date until I was sixteen, but young peo-ple had their ways of getting together. A date consisted of going to church together. When I was dating, my husband rode horseback to church. We led old Fred home. Old Fred—I don't know how he could walk that slow, but he did.

    Edith Gladden, 63, Missouri

The neighbor boy that lived right close by wanted a date one night

A posed humorous shot, probably taken
on a summer Sunday afternoon.

and carried me to a party. I had never been out with him on a date, so we went on to the party. But anyway, when we started home he went to sleep.

    I thought that was a sign that I was pretty bad company, if he went to sleep on me (laughs) coming home. So I just punched him in the side and told him to wake up. I said, "I don't want to ride along here by myself in this dark night." I said, "I want you to be awake so you can scare the buggers off if any comes along." (laughs)

    Bertha Andrews, 89, Alabama

I'm going to say this—my father and mother—it was a peculiar household, I know. Wasn't like any of them back then, I'm sure. We just went wherever there was a party and we was invited. Mother would say, "Now you girls cannot go. You've been out already this week one night, or two nights. You can't go." And Daddy would say, "Mother, I believe I'd let them go." Well, anyway, we'd get to go.

Now let me tell you what. Then we'd come home, they [parents] had a kerosene lamp. When they'd hear the first one [come in], they didn't turn it out. They'd turn it up, and we'd go in and we'd sit down on the bed. Directly the rest of them would come in, and we'd all be sitting there on the bed, and we'd all be telling everything we done—whatever it was, good or bad. They'd be sitting up in bed just laughing, and we'd be having the best time you ever saw.

Eunice Cameron, 80, Florida

We went to parties when I was a young girl. We'd go to different houses—there was no public places where we met—and have parties. My sister loved to go to parties. If she got to go, why I had to go with her. She was teaching school, but still she wasn't allowed to go alone with the boys.

She told me if I'd go with her to this party, she would buy us both a dress. The materials back in those days were so different. We called this material crepe de Chine. She had her a navy blue crepe de Chine dress, and she got me a turquoise-colored crepe de Chine.

We just had one boy in the crowd that had a car. That was our daddy's greatest worry. He did not want us to get in a car with a boy. He told us, whatever we did, why we was to walk.

While we was at this party, why it began thundering and lightning. I told Inez we had better go—it was going to start pouring down rain. But she was having a good time; she was enjoying the party. She was dressed up in her navy blue crepe dress, and she wouldn't go.

So it did begin raining, and we had to start home. This boy that had the car asked us to ride with him, and she wouldn't, because our daddy had told us not to get in the car with a boy. So we started walking.

This was how material was in those days. We hadn't gone very far up the road till we got wet. I looked down and my dress had just drawn up, and Inez's had drawn up. We looked like we had blouses on, and our legs was all colored with that dye. So by the time we got home, we was a pitiful sight to look at.

I told my sister when I got home that I was going to ask my daddy which would look the best—to ride in a car, or come home looking like that. Back in those days when they got ready to punish you, they didn't ground you or anything. They just gave you a whipping, and I got lots of whippings. My sister told me, she said, "You'd better not say that to him. He'll whip you." I said, "Well, I am."

So, sure enough, when I got home, I asked my daddy. I said, "Which do you think would look best—riding in a car, or walking and our dresses doing like this?" So he did. He gave me a whipping.

Opal Cypert, 68, Arkansas

My husband often told our children he could date for twenty-five

The Circle Theatre advertises photoplays and promises an inexpensive evening of entertainment.

cents. Take his girl to the movie, buy a ticket for ten cents each, and share a five-cent package of Wrigley's chewing gum.

Billie Jones, 72, Louisiana

I didn't know any people in the neighborhood, but I went to an ice cream social. My brother and a close friend of his had brought my sister and me.

So when we started out to go home, my husband [to-be] stepped up to one of the boys standing there and said, "Introduce them girls to me." This fellow said, "Yes, this is Maggie and this is Katie." I never thought any more about that.

The next night—Sunday—they had services at the church and we went down there. While we was waiting for the service to start, my sister said to me, "That guy keeps a-lookin' at us." So after chuch went out, he walked up to me and asked if he could take me home in his buggy.

He had his younger brother with him, and he made him stay down on the corner [of the road] until he came back. He [younger brother] was so mad at him for making him wait. He wanted to go home (laughs).

From then on we went together, and married in three years. He was so reserved and quiet. But if you knew him, he wasn't so quiet, either (laughter).

Katherine Taylor, 84, Florida

Where did you meet your husband?

He bought a farm not too far from the folks, and was farming.

Where were his parents from?

Norway. He came here when he was only fifteen years old.

Why did he come here?

There was a man in this country and came back to Norway and was telling how wonderful it was. He was only a kid, and he thought this would be fun. He came alone. He was the only one here, except he had uncles and aunts in Minnesota.

I suppose that the courting was done by horse and buggy?

Oh, yes. He used the horse on the plow and the machinery all day. Then he'd feed it good and put extra feed in the back of the buggy, so the horse could stand and eat while we was in dancing and having a good time.

Minnie Ness, 81, North Dakota

Weddings

Was there anything different about the weddings than the way they're conducted now?

I think there were a lot more home weddings—at the home of the bride and occasionally the groom. Then they would have a dance afterward. The ones I remember were always in the home, with big eating, dancing and playing games afterwards.

Mary Mootz, 76, North Dakota

We had an archway in my home and I remember my older sister decorating it with roses. We were married on June 15, 1910. We stood in the archway when we took our vows. And I had an organ in my home and my husband's sister played the organ for us. We spent the night at my home. The next day we went to his parents' home and we

A newly-married couple.

had what they called an "infare" dinner and they had relatives from my side of the family and their side of the family for a big dinner.

    Edna Vandenbark, 91, Indiana

I didn't have a big wedding. We went up to Torrington, Wyoming, and got our license and from there we went to the Presbyterian minister at his home, and we were married there. The minister's wife and son were our attendants. We went to Scotts Bluff and had our dinner. From there we went home, and my mother had a big supper for us.

Tootie Johannsen, Nebraska

The Vo[cational] Ag[riculture] teacher of my school, Choctaw Training School, and I fell in love after a few months of courtship. We married secretly and he went back to school to continue his education. Three years later, we announced our marriage. We began housekeeping, but we were teaching in different towns. A son was born to us. I carried my son and hired someone to keep him, while I worked. During World War II, my husband was given a job in a high school in Crawfordville, Georgia, so the baby and I followed him. That was the beginning of our housekeeping together.

Sallie Bell, 74, Alabama

We got married at four o'clock on Sunday afternoon, October 16, 1921. Jim had four neices and they had gone out and found autumn leaves and flowers, and decorated the whole house. The women of the family had cooked a wonderful wedding supper, and they had invited the family.

Jim's father said to me after the marriage ceremony, "Jim was married on the exact same spot he was born." He was born February 22 when the house was so cold they moved Ma Simmons' bed near the fire. The girls had decorated the fireplace with all this beautiful foliage.

And that was my wedding.

Essie Simmons, 81, Arkansas

I was married at home, and we didn't have any such a thing as buying all this folderol for a wedding. I wanted it to be just real nice. I was quite interested in handiwork. I liked to work with cane and raffia, so I made the baskets. Then I made the flowers to go in them. I made flowers from crepe paper and dipped them in paraffin.

I made my wedding dress. I made the cake. We cooked the dinner for the wedding—for the few people we had there—and baked the rolls that morning and had them for supper.

We didn't tell that the wedding was going to be that day, only [to] the people that were to be there. We had courted for five years, and people had kind of given up on us, but they were curious because I didn't sign a contract for [teaching] school again, so they thought it was coming sometime that summer.

That little house—we had to move out furniture to have a place for this wedding. But we moved furniture back into the house for sleeping. We supposed we were going to leave right away the next morning for

[our honeymoon]. But I had some cousins that were kind of sharp, and
so they got around my mother [and found out].

We were married at five o'clock, and about eight, here they all come.
They had that worked up pretty good. There was two of them brought
shotguns with blank cartridges in. They got on either side of our small
house and somebody gave them the cue when to fire, and they fired
both of them at once. Honestly, you would have thought the top was
a-goin' right off.

A courting couple play with a couple of
puppies in the hammock.

We were a little wary of it. My husband had gotten treats. We talked
about it—what he should have for treats. The custom was cigars; well,
he didn't smoke. He said, "What do you think?" and I said, "Well, you
don't smoke, so I wouldn't." That was quite a point with me. So he
bought oranges and those chocolate star candies—a whole gob of
them. I know there were over a hundred, because he had more than a
hundred oranges.

Now would this be what we call a chivaree?
Yes.

Did they wheel you around in a wheelbarrow, or anything else? Did they stay very long?

No, they just got their treats and we visited and fooled around, and then they left.

I'd like to know the date you were married, to tell the folks what era this was.

July 22, 1924.

Sophie Bigge, 82, Kansas

The bride and groom move into their new
home together, and household
chores begin.

Setting up Housekeeping

Where did you go to live after you were married?

Well, you always go—back then—with the in-laws a while. Now with my first marriage, we went to his home to live. We stayed up there a few months, and we had ordered furniture to come to the station at Sword's Creek. We had a house that we were going into, and he died before we had time to go get the furniture. He just lived five months and a week.

That was a custom in those days, to move in with the in-laws, wasn't it?

Till you'd get straightened out, you about had to. When I married Dewey Ratliff, we got to courting. We had been raised up together on each side of the road down there at the mouth of Little Prater. So we were courting, and we married and went up to his house and stayed till time to move out. Then we moved in our own house.

Corria Ratliff, 82, Virginia

I met my husband when we were both students at the university in the thirties. He was two years ahead of me, so he had a job as an accountant. We were thinking about marriage and when we could do that.

One time a call came for me. There was a bad accident. Vern's mother had been severely burned and had died from it. After that, in only two weeks, his father suffered a stroke from the pain and shock of that loss. Another call came for me; his father wanted our marriage. We were married at his bedside in the farm home, and he passed away during that same night.

Oh, my! That is quite some way to be married, and to start your marriage off.

And to start our marriage. Then, as my husband was an only child and the heir, there was the responsibility of the family farm—with an inexperienced non-farm background bride.

The decision was soon made afterward that together we would make the farm our home and future. With advice and help from the Cooperative Extension Service, we made it through the Dirty Thirties.

Evelyn Alden, 74, Kansas

I guess you learn a lot of manners in some of your Extension Homemakers lessons. I remember when we first got married, my father and stepmother came to eat at my first meal at my table. We had some kind of dessert—I believe it was pears or something that had juice on it. My husband, after he finished eating, he turned up his bowl and slurped that juice right out of the bowl, and I kicked him under the table because I was so embarrassed. Then, instead of making amends or anything, he said, "What did you kick me for?"

Phyllis Sullivan, 49, West Virginia

What prompted you to join an Extension club?

Well, I hadn't been married much over a year, and I just felt there were a lot of things I could learn through Extension club work about homemaking. I had always helped my mother, so I knew how to do all the household duties, but I was always eager to learn new ways and new methods. I thought that would be available to me in Extension club work.

It was also a social club for the neighborhood—a good time for the women to get together and visit and just enjoy each other. So I was much interested in the whole project.

Nellie Yost, 76, Nebraska

Values in Courtship and Marriage

I had boy friends, but I never thought that I cared enough for them to marry them. Then my mother—if we ever heard of a girl that had had a child out of marriage—my mother thought that was the worst thing that could ever happen. She *never* wanted her girls to come home with a baby. Which we never did. I don't know whether she frightened us so much that [that was] why I didn't get married. My two sisters got married, and my brother's been married more than once (laughter).

Lora Torsey, 84, New Hampshire

I never picked up with boys very good, because my mother was always a-tellin' me to watch it. She was always scaring me of the boys, so I didn't pick up with boys very quick.

Lura Hess, 90, Ohio

How has your life related to these far-reaching social changes in courtship and marriage?

It's altogether different to what it used to be, and I believe the old way was the best. I don't believe in permissiveness.

I never let my husband kiss me till he married me, and that's a common thing with young folks these days. 'Course I can't change it, but I still think to be virtuous and not be so permissive with the opposite sex is the best for everybody.

Bertha Andrews, 89, Alabama

Do you see any difference in marriage when you took it on as a responsibility and the attitude today?

Yes, I certainly do. When you and I were married, you figured it was for life, and now I don't think they think that when they get married. I was always under the impression that if you got married, that was it. A lifelong commitment.

Florence Reed, 64, Delaware

There was never any divorces in our family. In our seven brothers and sisters, there was no divorce. Absolutely, that was not the thing we did. We was taught that we could get along, for the sake of the children at least, if there was any differences. 'Course, everybody had their quarrels and what not, but they were solvable.

Rubie Gillion, 80, Michigan

The thing I can remember is that one of my mother's brothers got a divorce. Oh, there was so much talk going on about that couple getting a divorce. His name was Byron, and her name was Ethel. Of course, all the relatives blamed Ethel; they never blamed the brother at all. But

A buggy ride on a nice summer day, with the top tilted back to let the sun shine in.

Ethel was a lovely woman, and as I look back, I don't think it was Ethel's fault at all. But that is the first thing I remember, because they didn't condone divorce in those days. It was very rare to have one in your family.

Dorothy Tolley, 67, Arkansas

I think when I got married, the young people were more for making it last, regardless of what. Trying to get by. But now, so many of them go through [the ceremony] with the idea, "Well, if I don't like it, I can always get a divorce." But it didn't seem to be like that among my friends when we were getting married.

Edna Dagnen, 67, Washington

You indicated there was a problem with your family when you married Dick?

Well, during the olden times and days, people did not believe in their children marrying men who had been married before. That was their belief—that they were disgraced if they were married to a man who had been married before, and my husband had been married before. When we [got married], why they disowned me for seven years.

But then there was a reconciliation?

My mother became ill, and my father sent for me. So that was the beginning for me to be back with my family again.

My father and mother had been very good to me, and that was their belief and I didn't hold it against them, because they thought they were doing best for what they thought was best for me.

There was eight of us children and you can imagine me being alone then by myself, away from them. It was quite trying.

But I had the companionship of my husband, which was very dear to me. We loved each other's ways, and I think it was good for me. I learned how to sacrifice and to save and to get along with what I did have.

Elba Johnston, 79, Oklahoma

There's been a great change, and maybe not all for the bad. I feel like in my day everybody was kind of chilly and distant. Maybe if we'd been raised freer, everything would have been easier. But at the same time, everything's gotten to be so permissive now that I really look down on it. Now they just move in and live together.

Nona Berry, 81, New Mexico

I was brought up strictly. Today that isn't true, and I think the pendulum swung a little too far the other way, now. There ought to be a happy medium in there somewhere. All in all, I prefer the way I was brought up, than the way things are happening in many homes today, with teenage pregnancies and all.

Theo Hammond, 82, North Carolina

CHILDBIRTH

My father homesteaded there [Idaho] in the early days. I was the oldest one in the family and I was born with a midwife. They only had one doctor then, in either Moscow or Pullman. Our doctor was sick in bed and the other fellow was gone someplace.

They thought my mother was dying. She was only seventeen years old. I was slowly dying myself, too, and so was my mother.

There was an old lady in the neighborhood who had been around births and she knew something about it. Finally she heard about it and

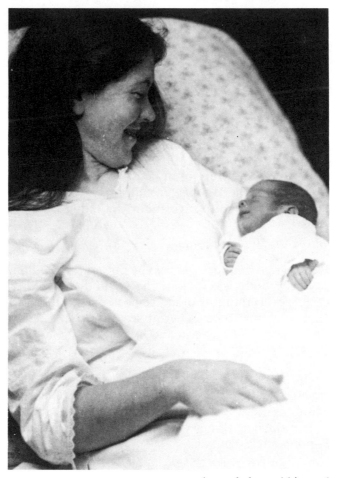

A new baby and his mother rest
comfortably at home.

here she come. She walked several miles. She said, "We're gonna get that baby." She got busy, and I was born.

Lora Foster, 100, Montana

I was born in the state of Arizona before it was even a state, back in 1908. I was born right out of doors, with a number of Cocopah Indian women standing by to offer Mother encouragement. I had a Cocopah

Indian nursemaid when I was a baby, and I started talking the Cocopah dialect before I could speak English.

Bea Cochran, 67, South Carolina

Where were the doctors? How far was it to a doctor in those days?

At that time there was a doctor in Portal. A little boy was born in March, and my mother always had a hard struggle. She always had one of the neighbor women to come in, and like [be a] midwife.

We finally decided to get a doctor, so my dad drove the team of horses and the sled up to the Portal doctor. And when he come out of Portal, heading home, it blew up a terrible storm. He couldn't see where he was, and there was no lines, fence lines, no roads or anything. Finally he let go of the horses' lines [reins] and just sat there, and pretty soon they stopped right in front of the door to home. Now you see how smart a horse can be.

Anna Sorenson, 83, North Dakota

You delivered right in your own bed. Chloroform was the only anesthetic you could use in the home, and I couldn't take that, so I delivered without anything.

Beulah Grinstead, 68, Indiana

What was childbearing like, in comparison to now?

I don't know as it was much different to what it is now. You still have to suffer pain to bear a child. It might be more bearable now. They do give, I think, some [medication] to help you through the pain. But all of mine, I bore them just naturally. It's a painful experience, but it's a very rewarding experience—to think you can bring a life into the world. It was something that I was always proud of.

I had six children, and they were all born at home. I never had any trouble. I got along fine with bearing my children, every one of them.

Did you have any family planning? Did you want to have a large family?

I didn't have any family planning at all, and I don't think six children was too many. Most families don't have enough. I don't think you should raise up one child by itself if you can have more.

Bertha Andrews, 89, Alabama

My husband went after the cows to bring them back home—on a Sunday—and I thought he'd *never* get back. I didn't know what was keeping him so long, because I was having a terrible bellyache.

So he went and got two ladies and they come back. It wasn't very long till they had a fire going, and the water hot, the baby washed and dressed, and brought back into bed with me, the cutest little redhead!

How long did you stay in bed?

Oh, my, ten days. We weren't allowed to get up out of bed before ten days, or we'd have a hemmorhage, sure (laughter). Then when you got up, you were so weak you couldn't walk.

Josephine Nixon, 90, Wisconsin

We had a lady from Bethany, a spinster lady, that came out and stayed with us for most of the children's births. Our fourth child was born at this lady's home. Her parents at that time were feeble and she didn't want to come out to my house and stay for a week or ten days, so she said, "If you will come to my house, why I'll take care of you."

Our second child, some of her [nurse's] family was sick and she couldn't do it, so at that time they had a so-called hospital in Yukon. It was a two-room thing up over a grocery story, and this practical nurse had a delivery place [there]. That was all she did, practically, was births. And my oldest daughter was born there.

It was a lot of work preparing for a birth at home. You got a government book telling you what all to fix. You would fix the pads that you'd line with newspapers, and cook them to sterilize them and have all kinds of pads. This was before the days of Kotex. Heaven help us! I don't know how we lived without it! You had to make your own things of that kind, and it was quite a job preparing for a birth at home.

And in those days, you didn't jump out in two days and do things, like they do now. The first time I heard that, I shuddered, because they used to keep us in bed quite a while, and then you'd be weak after you'd been in bed. It was quite different the way your deliveries were handled.

Sarah Ball, 74, Oklahoma

Around 1927 or so, I began caring for mothers and babies—doing the nursing care, housework, cooking. I stayed on a case usually about two weeks, then somebody else would want me. Sometimes babies came—there was once two babies came the same day. I'd get one mother and baby all washed up, and then the next one. And that day I got pretty tired.

I used to assist Dr. Palmer, mostly, but other doctors, too. I took care of over fifty babies.

Some [of the first] of them was some of my sister's babies and my sister-in-law's—and then it began to go to friends. They'd hear about it, and then they'd engage me to come and work for them. Sometimes I could work in two jobs in one month.

One mother said that I would never leave a job until the last diaper was washed. Of course, diapers were birdseye [type of fabric].

I worked once in taking care of a mother. When I went there they had no electric lights, of course. They had kerosene lamps and lanterns for light. They had to pump their water by hand, and they burned green wood. Out in the woodshed I could see one long tree being brought in. There was a grandpa there, and he would go out and saw it up and work it up and brought it in for us to build the fire to heat the water to take care of the baby.

Lora Torsey, 84, New Hampshire

What happened when a child was born?

The doctor would come to the home, and a neighbor would come in and help take care of the baby. They washed it and cleaned it up and then the doctor would come back—I guess it was the third day he would come back to see the mother.

She would have to stay in bed for nine days; the tenth day she would get up; and she wore a band around her stomach. The neighbors would come every day and look after the baby.

Did they put a band around the baby's abdomen too?

Yes, they used to call them "belly" bands. And at that time the babies wore big long dresses.

How long did they nurse the baby usually?

For a year to 15 months.

Frances Harley, 90, Indiana

As you approached your time, did you call the doctor immediately or did you have someone in the neighborhood who came and stayed with you?

We just called him and he'd tell me what to do, and as it got closer [he said] "I'll be there in a little bit." We had a neighbor that was on call, and the mother would always come.

Did you send the children away from home at the time of the birth?

They accepted birth and death as part of livin'. I never sent them away from home, 'cause my mother was here, and sometimes my dad would come and entertain the kids. I don't ever remember sending the kids away from home.

Edna Maddox, 71, Indiana

What were prices like for deliveries in those days [1920s]?

Well, the first one was an easy case, so that was only $35, but the last one was a hard case, so that came up to about $100.

Minnie Ness, 81, North Dakota

Were all your children born on the farm?

Yes, all five of them were born out there. There was the same little old lady, Mrs. Ed Barr, she was a midwife who lived about three and a half miles from us—she took care of them all. Well, she delivered four of the kids, because the doctor didn't get there in time.

Ben would go get her and bring her to the place, and then he would go down to the Flats—that was about five miles—to the nearest phone and call Dr. Hilts. If he was around, why fine. If he was out in the country, or busy with somebody else—well, we had to wait.

But he would come. If it was summer he came by car. In the wintertime he would come by car as far as Sorlie's. Then he came to our place with a team sled.

Did this engaging little fellow actually sleep in a coffee box bed? Probably not, but the photographer had an eye for a good picture.
L. M. Huffman, photographer

But I tell you, we paid a little different than what deliveries are now. The first girl, it was $35 for her. But the third one, that was in 1932. So Dr. Hilts said, well, we had some real nice young pigs to butcher—it was the last of December. So he wanted one of those pigs butchered and delivered to Bowbells. So Ben brought it in to them, and he [doctor] said, "Oh, that weighed too much!" That it was more than he thought that delivery was worth.

So he wanted to know if Ben would take that battery-operated radio he had. It was an old Zenith, and here Ben came home with the old radio. Dr. Hilts even bought a new battery. But, anyway, that was our first radio.

Margaret Lien, 68, North Dakota

Then most babies were born at home. That was just the way it was. Most of them got along all right, but there were losses that now they save in hospitals. I know my mother lost children that if she had been in the hospital in modern days, I'm sure those children would have been saved.

Sophie Bigge, 82, Kansas

I did go to the hospital for my children. I was under the doctor's care, which I don't remember my mother having doctor care before the children were born. I did go to the hospital and stayed 24 hours to two or three days, but then we stayed in bed for 10 days. On the tenth day, they always said, that's when everything went back into place. So we stayed in bed for ten days, the eleventh day you could get up. But I guess that is the only time you got any rest. It was a good thing you did stay in bed for ten days.

Dorothy Hoffman, 60, Indiana

There is one thing I was thinking of—the difference between today and in my early marriage—say twenty years ago when my family was being born—is that the fathers were not directly involved. They didn't visit the doctor during pregnancy. When your husband brought you to the hospital he brought the baggage to the reception desk and the nurse politely said, "We'll call you, Mr. Dame, when your baby is delivered and let you know that everything's fine. Meanwhile, you might as well go home, because [there's] not a thing you can do here."

Now the fathers are right in on the whole nine months' procedure, right up to the delivery room and the delivery. I think that is very important. I think our family really missed out on that.

It has to give the father more understanding of what the beginning of a family is, and what a baby is, and what a mother really is.

And what you have to go through to get it.

It's not just "There's your cute little baby all wrapped up in its bunting in the bassinette." I think that's one big thing that has changed for the better.

Carolyn Dame, 40, New Hampshire

We went through the classes, my husband and I both went through them and were looking forward to it. Then I went to the hospital and they hooked you up to a monitor, and my husband would hold my hand, and he could see my contractions coming before I could even feel them. He would squeeze my hand and he would say, "Here comes a good one." And then after it would be over with, he would say, "Boy, that was a good one." And I think it helped a lot.

A loving mother and a happy baby.

Do you think being there when the babies are born gives the fathers a closer feeling from the very beginning?

I think it makes them closer in the sense that they see what is going on and see what it is all about. I think they appreciate you for going through the pain and the discomfort, because we really had some tender moments, the two of us, because he was there.

Theresa McFadin, 29, Indiana

We were going through some old minutes from our Extension club, and in 1938 among the topics we discussed was birth control.

Clear back in 1938?

Yes, in 1938 (chuckles).

Anna Coburn, 75, Nebraska

What topics have been most useful to you, and in what way?

The cooking was helpful to me, because as a licensed practical nurse, I did all the cooking while taking care of mothers and babies. The sewing helped me, too, because I used to make the babies each a little dress when I'd get through taking care of them. Sewing and needlework, because I'd crochet a little around the necks of the dresses.

Lora Torsey, 84, New Hampshire

CHILD REARING

When I was married, with a baby girl, a leader from Purdue came to the country church near here. About a dozen interested ladies came to learn how to care for their babies.

She gave out literature with her talk. It was a book about a hundred pages long, on coarse paper with fine print, but it was my baby "Bible."

I had lived in a family with children of all ages, but I wanted to learn some new ways of caring for my baby.

Lois Waggoner, 76, Indiana

I thought motherhood was a right big undertaking, but I was proud of my child, and I felt like I had accomplished something worthwhile.

Describe the discipline of your children.

I just told them what they shouldn't do, and what they could do. It didn't take much discipline. But you always have to discipline a child, because if you don't, it's too bad for the child and for the parent, too.

A child that's not disciplined, they don't grow up to be a good neighbor, or a good homemaker, or anything. They're expecting something all the time, and there's a lot of times you don't get what you want. They want too much, too soon, and not able to get it.

Bertha Andrews, 89, Alabama

Now you said your children never did hesitate when you asked them to do a job. They knew that you expected it done, and there was no argument about it.

Yes, well, we really worked as a team. You've got to start when they're small, letting them do little things for you.

I'll give you an illustration. Cecil [my son] had to put in a new side porch for me. His little boy is four years old and his mother teaches school, so Cecil keeps the little boy. Well, yesterday the little boy had a brace and bit and hammer, and he was making holes, and he was driving Cecil's good nails in a block, just a-hammering.

Now I shouldn't have said anything, but I hate to see waste, and I said, "Honey, you're driving up Papa's good high-priced nails in those blocks." And Cecil says, "Mama, he's learning."

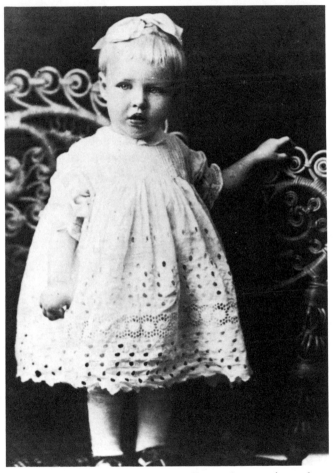

Fancy dress against a fancy wicker
photographer's chair. Note the long white
cotton stockings.

Well, I thought about it afterwards, and he *was* learning—learning to drive that nail in that piece of wood. It was in Cecil to teach him while he's little, and that's going to be a lot of help to him later in life.

Letha McCall, 91, North Carolina

My daughter was at the age where she wanted to get into cooking, and we used corn bread particularly for our noon meal. I was letting her make the corn bread, in that she poured the dry ingredients together and sifted them in the bowl, but then I took over. I didn't let her break the egg, I didn't let her put in the milk and stir, nor put the batter into the pan and put it into the oven.

And my Grandmother was visiting with me at that time, and she told me, "Let the child carry the job all the way through. Let her finish up. It doesn't matter what kind of a mess she makes. Let her finish it up, put it in the oven, cook it, take it out and put it on the table. Then she'll feel like she has had a part in this meal."

And many times later her words came back to me. For years, with all those children, I felt like that I was the only one who could decorate the Christmas tree. I knew how to put it up. I knew how to bring in the decorations and just where to hang them, handle them carefully and all that.

One Christmas it became so congested at my home that I could not do it. I just could not do it, and the children did it. What a revelation that was to me.

They did it as well. They had all that pleasure. They handled all those things so carefully. They had real enjoyment in putting that Christmas tree together and look how much better off I was.

Henrietta Phillips, 69, North Carolina

We wanted our second son to go to college, as the other boy had started, but he didn't want to—period. He said he would go to trade school. He wanted to be a mechanic.

From the time he was a kid, he tore up everything that was in the house. He wasn't destructive, but anything that would come apart, came apart. He carried a little pair of pliers with him and a screw driver. He took the little pads off the Crosley refrigerator, and he got out into the yard, and he took the bolts loose in the tongue of the rake. When his father hooked on to that rake to go and use it, he got down in the middle of the barn lot, and he didn't have anything. That kid had taken the bolts out.

So I told my husband, "If he wants to go to trade school, let's iron it out. He has learned to tear up everything. Now let's have him learn to put it back together."

Sophie Bigge, 82, Kansas

Why are young folks bored today? First, the little child has so many toys that they have no interest to build or make anything. We made doll clothes, built doll houses, used hammer and nails to build what we wanted. Now the growing boy and girl have everything handed to them.

It is amusing to see how much children enjoy doing odd jobs, and when they visit in our home, I let them do whatever work I am doing. I think that is one thing that is happening to our society, giving the children too much and not letting them work out how to work out things themselves.

Anna Evans, 81, Kentucky

We were very close to our girls, and they to us. We were a family that played together and prayed together. We disciplined them, and it was not always easy, but their daddy, especially, had a way with them. We took a keen interest in their school activities and participated in school-related activities.

Opal Price, 70, Alabama

In the wintertime, they'd have toboggan parties and skating parties and then we'd all gather. The whole family went. Then we'd gather at somebody's home and have chili and sandwiches afterwards. I know one time I had 65 people at my house after a skating party. Not one of my own kids was there, because that was after my kids were grown up. It was fun. It was something that the family did together. I never heard then of kids objecting because they had to be with their families.

One time at New Year's, a group of the kids were at our house because we had a pretty good-sized house at that time. There was some over 20, and we had a New Year's Eve party. They hadn't been there very long until they got Ben [husband] calling square dances for them, and teaching them how to do that, and he just loved it. There they were doing Virginia Reels. For music, they had one guy playing the mouth organ [harmonica] and one guy strumming on the guitar. When they [musicians] wanted to be in it, why then they had the phonograph on. The kids had a great time.

Margaret Lien, 68, North Dakota

You lived up there on a windy hill where the east wind blows and the snow drifts. I know that sometimes you are without electricity and are snowed in. What in the world did you do those long, dark winter days when you had to keep eight youngsters in the house?

That was the most exciting time of the whole year! All summer long, everyone was working, either picking berries or some other employment to help finance their education and their clothes. So, when winter came and no one could move—the drifts were too deep and the school was closed—we had a great time. That was the time when they put on their boots and their coats and went out sleigh riding, or came in and we popped corn and played games, and had a wonderful time.

We didn't even have television, but we wouldn't have missed it, even with the electricity off, because we were having too much fun. We would cook our meals on the camp stove or we'd cook it in the fireplace in the big pot. They were memorable times.

Alice Wand, 65, Oregon

A charming twosome.

Is there a difference in bringing up children now and the way children were raised when you were growing up?

Children are not disciplined as much as we were when we were growing up. We were always taught that we should be quiet and not heard. When we were told to do something, we knew we better do it.

Nowadays they use so much psychology on children that I don't think it works as well as it did years ago.

Mary Moore, 73, New Mexico

I think Dr. Spock should have been drowned in the first water he was bathed in (laughter). That's a purely personal opinion (laughter again).

Dorris Graves, 70, Oregon

I belonged to the old school of physical reminder of bad things. My children got spankings, but I didn't have to do much spanking after three years old. I still believe in a little bit of physical punishment. It has worked for me.

Theo Hammond, 82, North Carolina

Children like to know just how far they can go and if Mama is not there to tell them, to let them know just how far they can go, there is trouble. They like that restraining love that a mother has for her children.

Nobody else can give that love that a mother gives them.

Jalie Martin, New Mexico

If you can't train your children to be something, they'll never be it. I think that the mother throughout the needed years should stay with these children. I think that that's the happiest time of her life and of their child's life—the one he wants to remember. I think, too, that during the growing-up years what he gets in his head makes the man, or her the woman, what they will be.

What's your attitude toward women who go out to work and have babysitters?

I think they're the losers, and the child is, too. If you want your child to be like the babysitter, then you've got it.

Corria Ratliff, 82, Virginia

My mother had worked during the depression, and I can remember what it was like, coming home to an empty house. I said my children would never come home to an empty house the way I did. So every day there would be warm cookies, and to this day, the children say, "Mom, when we came home and got off that schoolbus, the house always smelled so good. It was wonderful."

Dorothy Tyrawski, 58, Delaware

I liked my way of child-rearing, and I enjoyed being a babysitter called "Mama."

Linnie Arnett, 65, Virginia

There's so many have to work to make a living now. Living costs is so high there have to be two in the family working. I think it's all right. But if they have a family, and they can live without working outside while the children are little, I think it's much better if they stay at home with their children, because nothing takes the place of a mother.

Bertha Andrews, 89, Alabama

The fact that I started to work probably has caused the biggest change in the way I have dealt with my children. I tried to be with them as much as I could and give them quality time while I was with them. Of course, all the modern conveniences that we have now makes it easier to have more time to spend with your family and to instill in them the values that you want them to have.

I don't think that changes have affected my values in any way. My values were set before I ever married and left home. I received them from my parents, and I have tried very hard to give my children the same experiences in their home life that I had in mine. There was love, companionship and a joy of being together. I could invite anyone home anytime I wanted to. Anybody was welcome in our home. Honesty and things like that, that I learned at home, this is the values that I have tried to instill in my children.

Mary Jo Depew, 41, Kentucky

Do you believe that your children will be raised differently than you were?

I really don't believe they will, and the reason I don't is because children pattern after their parents, and I find myself every day looking at something I've done; and I look back and see that, as a child, I was disciplined in the same way, or as a child, reacted the same way. And I feel like that they will be brought up about the same way that I was.

Constance Anderson, 28, West Virginia

I wanted to be a trained nurse, but my father and mother didn't want me to.

I bet that you have let your children pursue their interests.

Yes, anything they wanted to do. And we sent seven to college.

That is a real record.

That's why we never did get much ahead. I don't care how scarce money was, we never deprived our children of anything that was uplifting, that would help them later in life.

And what I was doing, I was doing for them. I told my husband many a time it wasn't just what I was learning from my own use in Home Demonstration work, it was what I could teach my girls, so they didn't have to go into marriage as blind as I did.

Letha McCall, 91, North Carolina

A call on the toy telephone distracts one cat lover. Note the long black cotton stockings and the supporters which the short pants fail to hide completely.
L. M. Huffman, photographer

I feel like we've done two things for them. We did bring them up in the church, and they're still attending church. And they all four have gotten their college education.

So they are prepared for life both spiritually and mentally, and if they don't make a success—well, we feel like we've done just about all we can do.

Virginia McIntyre, 63, Louisiana

They got a sermon every few days, just telling them how to live, live a good Christian life, be honest, truthful children, and learn how to work. We taught them from just little things, wait on theirselves and to help others. And they came up helping others.

Letha McCall, 91, North Carolina

I think the greatest satisfaction is in knowing that we have raised our daughter to have an active faith and to make available to them those experiences that show us what life is all about. We are very thankful for the great blessing of parenthood. Here again, the early training in our lives helped us in raising our family. We owe so much to our wonderful parents.

Opal Price, 70, Alabama

What about child raising? Do you have any words of wisdom?
Love is the best thing. I think that's the main thing, to be sure that they know that you love them. My son certainly knew that we loved him. He's a loving man himself. I can depend on him in every way. He has a beautiful wife. They live right next door, so I'm looked after within an inch of my life.

Grandchildren and great-grandchildren?
I have a granddaughter who is my pride and joy (chuckles). She is head of the math department at Corunna High School. I have two great-grandsons, and they are my pride and joy (laughs). We think they are very smart children. They mind very well; they're well disciplined. Their home life is happy. They're just as happy as they can be.

Do you think that is an accomplishment on your part?
Oh, I'll take credit for anything (laughter).

Rubie Gillion, 80, Michigan

What is your greatest satisfaction as a homemaker?
My children. They are probably not going to set the world on fire, as far as the world is concerned, but they seem to have kept the values that I have taught them, which I think is one of the most fulfilling things that I can think of in life—that they feel that my values that I taught to them are the kind of values that they want to continue having.

Vi Cottrell, 69, Washington

What would be your biggest satisfaction of being a homemaker, Priscilla?
Probably the fact that our children have turned out as well as they have—really good citizens and good family people, and have carried on the traditions that we have learned along our way, and I've been able to impart my learning all the way down through. We both have—

not just myself, but my husband. He's had as much influence as I have on the children, because he is a real fine man, and has set a very good example.

Priscilla Lloyd, 56, New Hampshire

What are your biggest satisfactions?

I think that I have helped raise these four children and they have made themselves known in the world. I'm very happy about my grand-children and the progress they've made. Now I'm looking forward to the outcome of the great-grandchildren.

Eva Gill, 80, North Carolina

What are your biggest satisfactions as a homemaker?

My husband and my children. Children are always delightful—I don't think there is ever a dull moment. They reward you more than you can ever reward yourself.

Constance Anderson, 28, West Virginia

THE HOMEMAKER
AND HER WORK

*"It is almost impossible to realize
what a changed and wonderful
world we live in today."*

Opal Amsler, Indiana

Tremendous changes have occurred in the mechanics of housekeeping. In years past, almost all housework was done through sheer muscle power.

Water was pumped from wells, lifted and carried in, used and carried out again. Each piece of laundry was handled four or five times in the process of scrubbing, rinsing, wringing and hanging out.

Food was available only in unprocessed form. It had to be grown, stored, peeled, cooked and served for every meal of the year.

Clothing was a bolt of yard goods and a treadle sewing machine. Sometimes even the fabric had been spun and woven. Socks and scarves often had a short journey from sheep to homemaker's needles to the wearer.

Cooling was by running water or icebox, lighting by kerosene lamps, heating by wood stoves, and plumbing was unavailable.

With the coming of electricity, all this changed. Those long stretches of wire running down lonely roads and into farmhouse lanes brought light, water and labor-saving appliances to hardworking homemakers.

THOUGHTS ON HOUSEWORK

You said your dad was a farmer. Did you work in the fields?

Yes, and when we was too little to work, why Mother would take us, because she had to work in the fields. And we would stay at the end of the field on what we called then a pallet.

My mother would work all day in the fields. First, early of a morning, she would get up and she would get the breakfast over with and get the dishes washed and put away. Then she would take us and go to the fields.

Then, when we'd quit to go home for lunch, why she would fix lunch. You couldn't cook anything that morning and leave it, because of no refrigeration or ice. She'd cook our lunch and then we would eat, and then she would start doing up the dishes. My dad, he would always go in and lay down and take a nap and rest a while. When my mother would get the dishes washed, she would say she was ready to go back to work.

I have often thought about how hard she worked. The rest of us, we had time out to rest for a while, but my mother never rested. Of an evening when we quit work—we worked almost to dark—then we'd go home and she had to get the evening meal. We couldn't have anything left from lunch, because it would have spoiled. But she never seemed to get tired. I often wondered why mothers didn't get tired.

Opal Cypert, 68, Arkansas

My mother was always such a hard worker. Even now, when I think back, I can never remember my mother sitting down just resting. I can always remember her either with a broom in her hand, or a dust rag in her hand, or she was either cooking, or washing, or doing something like that—even to this day. She would never just relax. There was always something that she had to be doing.

She's always been able to work circles around me, but maybe that's true of all of our mothers. They probably could all work a lot harder than we do in this day and time. Yet we stay as busy as they do. It's just a different type of activity, maybe.

I think most of us don't spend as much time doing household chores now as we did even a few years back. We are more involved in going and learning and applying our time to other things which are, sometimes, a little more important.

Ann Webb, 48, Arkansas

All these modern things have come in; it makes life easier for the housewife.

Dorothy Carlsen, 78, Idaho

Without power-driven appliances, all household work was a matter of using time and muscle to accomplish even the smaller chores.

What is your daily homemaking routine now, as compared to then?

You can get up now out of your bed and go to the bathroom and take a shower. Then you had to draw your water from the well, heat it, and bring in the bathtub. Sometimes that was [only] once a week. You washed up, but you didn't take a bath every day. My grandmother made soap, too. She even made the soap to bathe with.

Now you can go in your kitchen and turn the electric stove on. Then you had to go out and get you some wood and make your fire.

Now if you have to clean up, you can pull out your vacuum cleaner. Then, you had to take that broom, and sweep everything you had. My grandmother kept her kitchen so clean until you could eat off the floor. She scrubbed it with beat-up sand rock. She scrubbed the kitchen with that; scrubbed her table with that. Now you just go get your vacuum cleaner.

If we were going to town, we had to go out and hitch up the mule and get the wagon out. Now you just go unfasten your car and back on out of your garage. And we've got the telephone; we can call our friends. We didn't have that then. You had to go and visit friends if we wanted to talk to them.

It certainly is a difference.

Julia White, 60, Tennessee

As the years went along, and the modern conveniences did come, what do you think was the biggest help to a woman in the house?

Either the electric lights, or the water in the house—hot and cold water. Heat, you could go in the basement and fill up the furnace and have your good heat and didn't have to carry out ashes. All of those, I think.

They were all *big* things, weren't they?

Oh, they were big! You'd hear of some neighbor getting them. You'd think to yourself, "Gee, I'll *never* have things like that." (laughs) I just almost planned on it that I couldn't afford things like that. "They really must be making money."

But eventually they came to you, too.

Yes.

Josephine Nixon, 90, Wisconsin

My mother lived a more regimented life than I do. She washed on Monday—it was an all-morning job. She ironed on Tuesday; she cooked and cleaned up a little bit on Wednesday; cleaned her upstairs on Thursday; cleaned downstairs on Friday; and cooked on Saturday. Then Sunday she went to church. That was probably the only time she went out during the week.

I do not have the luxury of being a full-time homemaker. I am in our office and I run errands.

But my life is easier. I don't have to use a broom; I don't have wood stoves. Mine is all automatic. My life is easier [but] I think I have more emotional strains, but less physical work than she did.

Eleanor Whittemore, 55, New Hampshire

Can you describe a typical day?

Well, usually it was get up early in the morning and build fires. Get a child ready for school. Get myself ready to go to town to the job. Spend eight hours in the office, come home, take on the homemaking chores again. In the summer months, usually grab something I could put on the stove to cook and run to the garden and pick a bucket of green beans. String them as hurriedly as I could, put it in the cooker. I've set up many a night to one or two o'clock in the morning, waiting for the pressure cooker to go down.

Edith Gladden, 63, Missouri

How does your life as a homemaker now compare to your mother's life as a homemaker?

Well, the basic things are the same. Mother cooked, and washed and took care of the household. We do the same, and with electricity my work is so much easier than some of her work was then.

But you are still providing your family with food, clothing and shelter?

As it always will be for a homemaker. The basic needs are still there.

Hautie Nelson, 69, Tennessee

FOOD

Cooking

We never worried about calories. Calories is something new—you know, since Home Ec (laughs).

We worked, we didn't have to worry about calories. Everybody worked, from the oldest clear down to the littlest one. As soon as they could understand, they had their chores.

Edna Winter, 84, Indiana

Mother always had hay hands or some kind of hands to cook for, it seems. She would go out and kill the chicken and dress it that we were going to have for dinner (maybe three or four of them, depending on the size). Go out and dig the potatoes, pick the vegetables, pick berries to make cobbler or pie, maybe pull off a load of hay, lead the horse to the [hay] fork in between times, have dinner for hands, and sometimes for supper.

It really makes you feel like a piker, because it sometimes is a strain nowadays to open a package of frozen food.

Evelyn Rigsby, 58, Indiana

What would breakfast be like then?

Biscuits, and either ham or bacon, and eggs, and gravy. Until I got to teaching, I never thought about putting my family down to anything but biscuits for breakfast. But after I had to go to teaching, Jim got to where he'd eat light [yeast] bread. But before that, (chuckles) he thought he couldn't eat anything but biscuits.

Vivian Jefferson, 95, Arkansas

A six-burner Detroit Jewel gas stove, with warming ovens above. With a dish towel pinned on for an apron, the homemaker is preparing pancakes.

To get to school on time, we got up at four o'clock in the mornings. We children helped Mother prepare breakfast, which was a huge meal consisting of meat, gravy, oats, apple butter, biscuits, milk and coffee. My sister and I washed the dishes, while my mother prepared our lunches, which we carried to school in small buckets.

Violet David, 79, Indiana

We didn't have pie for breakfast, like one of our neighbors did. He
thought he had to have pie three times a day.

He must have really liked pie.

Well, that was his hobby, I guess you could call it.

Grace Heinzman, 84, Indiana

My mother was a great hand to fry chicken and make chicken gravy.
She would get up in the morning, and she had to dress her chicken of a
morning and cook it because of no ice. She would make hot biscuits
and gravy. Then, if she thought that the fire would keep in the stove,
she'd build a fire in the wood cookstove and she would leave some
beans on cooking. That way she kind of had a start for dinner.

She could peel her potatoes of a morning, before she went to the
field, but she always made her cornbread when we got back home.
Then she'd put the potatoes on and cook them after we got in from the
field.

Then at supper—it was more or less a short supper—maybe she
would make mush for my daddy. He was a great hand to eat mush.
Then she would make the children cornbread and milk, and that is
what we would have for our evening meal.

Opal Cypert, 68, Arkansas

I was one of seven, and there was always a hired girl in the house,
and my grandmother lived with us in the winter, and a couple of hired
men. So it made about fourteen at the table three times a day. You can
imagine the amount of cooking that went on.

Rubie Gillion, 80, Michigan

My mother, she would fry potatoes in a black skillet frying pan, and
nobody could ever do that, that would taste the same as hers. That was
about the last thing she did for my kids, before she passed away, was
she fried them potatoes in a black skillet frying pan.

And there was a green bean—my mother brought these beans from
Tennessee with her, and they're scattered all over the county. They're a
green bean, and my mother could cook those—nobody else could ever
cook them like that.

Edna Dagnen, 67, Washington

I think that all young people when they start out to learn to cook, I
think you have to learn; and when you cook for quite a few, you learn.

Living on the ranch, you would have around fifteen or twenty with
all the cowboys that they had then. I can remember funny things that
happened when I first learned to cook. I was awfully glad I had pigs

and chickens to feed, because if I had a failure, I took it to the pigs and tried all over again.

That's what I always tell young Homemakers now—well, I was better off than they are, because I did have the pigs, chickens and dogs to feed. They ate all my failures, so it wasn't entirely wasted.

Mary Moore, 73, New Mexico

And you made do with what you had. You didn't run to the grocery. We bought salt and flour and pepper and vinegar. Otherwise we had everything at home.

What about sugar?

Well, sugar, that's right. But my father had eleven working families on his place, and they raised molasses and put it in wooden barrels. As the molasses got further down the barrel, sugar would form on the sides of the barrel. A lot of times when the weather was bad and you couldn't get to town, great lumps of that rock sugar would be taken off to use.

Did you pound it up to use it?

You could melt it in an iron kettle.

Ruth Irwin, 83, Mississippi

We never had ice cream till it snowed in the wintertime and our mothers would make homemade ice cream. I could hardly wait until the first snow fell, because I was so hungry for that ice cream. We'd get real close to the stove, and we'd blow that ice cream, thinking it would be easier for us to eat if we warmed it up.

Opal Cypert, 68, Arkansas

The house [where we lived] was a tiny little house with two bedrooms and a living room and a dining room and a kitchen. But the house that we called the corn house, where they stored all the vegetables they raised, and the corn, and the sausages, and all, was bigger than the house itself.

My grandmother had a room just to make her bread, and a little portion where she stored her bread, and her cheeses, and all her flour. There was a section—they had these white crocks, with all these goodies inside—all of the sausage and everything packed in crocks along the wall, and the bags of cabbage and onions and whatever they raised. Then they had the smokehouse next to it.

My grandmother made her soup out in that smokehouse. They lit a fire every day with the waddle wood that grows up in Kula. That makes the best-tasting sausages. So that fire was going continuously, and every day we had a pot of soup. We had other foods, but that was the basic—the soup. Of course, Mama made bread so many times a week, and every time they made bread, they delivered bread to Mrs. Walker and to the Rices, and to all the Japanese—the Nakanishis who let them lease their land for raising vegetables—and to all the neighbors.

And Mother did the same thing. She never made bread or sweet bread without giving it to all the natives. So we were constantly making bread. They had the habit of mixing the bread at night, and we

Invited guests come for Sunday dinner at noon, bringing the baby and a gift of food in a basket.

were *tired* and we wanted to go to sleep, but we had to help my mother knead the bread. Then it was an all-night affair. She had to get up and pound the dough down as it got high, and then start cooking so the bread would be ready for the next day.

Julia Souza, 62, Hawaii

My mother was Hawaiian, so we ate poi. The poi was delivered to Kula from Wailuku about once a week. I learned how to make poi the right way from my grandfather—my *tutumaka*—because once a week I would take the poi down to him. Then he would sit down and he'd take a long time mixing that poi—not just put the water in and mix it, but mix it and add a little water in at a time. Even today, I take a long time to mix my poi.

Mary Soon, 60, Hawaii

Every year in the spring, I have the urge—just like when I was a girl at home when I used to carry a sap yoke made from wood that my father had hewed out, with ropes on each end to carry the pails of sap. So it was in my blood, and every year I get that urge to tap. So each year, I set around fourteen trees, and I usually make eight quarts of syrup each year.

Lora Torsey, 84, New Hampshire

We had a maple sugar tree orchard up on the hill. These trees just grew volunteer up there, but they were sugar maples. In January and February, my dad would tap these trees, and he would drive a spigot in, made out of river cane. We'd hang a gallon syrup bucket on that, and it would drip till that bucket would get full. It would surprise you how full that bucket would get, because it would be cold winters, and then when it would begin to get warm, why there would be lots of sugar water.

Me and my sister, it was our job to go—we had 42 trees on this hill—and it was our job to go around with a big bucket and take the little bucket off the spigot and pour the sugar water into this big bucket, and then take it down the hill.

Our dad had brought a sled down there with a 50-gallon barrel on it. We'd take our big bucket of sugar water down there and pour it in this barrel, then go back. When we'd get this sugar water gathered up, we'd take it up to our house.

He had built a fire the next morning early, under a great big kettle. We'd have a big fire under that and stir it till it would boil down. If we had fifty gallons of sugar water, when we got it boiled down my mother would beat it until it went to sugar in two dishpans, and they wouldn't be but just about half full.

Then she had these great big old-fashioned white cups, and she would take this syrup in the dishpan and pour it in these cups, and it would get cold and make sugar maple cakes out of it. Then she would mail those to Dallas. She got ten cents a cake for the maple sugar.

When they was having the stir-off, why my aunt would bring her children out—all this big family. I know my mother didn't leave but half a cup of sugar in that dishpan, but we'd all get us a spoon, and we was going to scrape the sugar out of that pan and eat it. It would sound like a band, when we'd get our spoons and go to digging in that dishpan, all of us getting some of that sugar. It was a great evening when the stir-off was to be.

Opal Cypert, 68, Arkansas

Do you remember how hominy was made from corn?

I don't know whether I could make it today, but I remember taking the ashes from the fireplace and taking them out in this barrel and let-

A family gathering around a Sunday dinner table. The cloth is white linen which must be laundered, starched and ironed with each use. They are enjoying fresh strawberries and cream, after a bountiful main course.

ting the lye drip out of them. That lye was what we made our hominy corn out of. We would put it on the corn and let it soak, and it would eat the husk off the corn. Then you would have to wash it and wash it and wash it some more. It was good.

Was that served for the family?

Oh, yes. We grew the corn and then made it into hominy and we would eat it. If you made more than you were going to use, then you canned it. You could open it up later and eat it.

Jane Morgan, 63, Mississippi

Can you tell me something about the ethnic foods of the German-Russian people?

Oh, they were nice solid foods. If you couldn't make your pie crusts with lard, you did not make pie. If you couldn't put in a lot of sugar, you didn't cook. They used to take watermelons, if they had a surplus, and boil them down to make a syrup similar to the pancake syrup you buy in the stores. The sugar content in that stuff was unreal.

They're very big on dough products—bread, *fleisch keuchla*, which looks like a pocket bread. You take the dough, and you put a mixture of pork and beef, and onions and salt and pepper into this dough, and you cover it up, and you drop it into good hot lard. You let it fry until it's a deep golden brown. Your pork and beef is cooked inside, and all those lovely juices are soaked into your dough from the inside and the outside.

Strudla is another example that is just loaded with calories. They would take this dough, and they'd spread it with sugar and butter—not margarine—and the dough was rolled thin. They'd roll it up into a pan, like a cake pan only a little deeper. And you'd pour good rich farm cream over the top, and sprinkle a little more brown sugar on top. It was delicious.

But if you take a look at a lot of the German-Russian women, the older women, especially, most of them are pretty square, literally. If you want to keep your figure, you don't start indulging in that stuff without working—shocking your bundles and threshing, to get the calories off.

My dad's favorite, after having had his pork chops and potatoes and vegetables, his favorite addition to this would be to take a thick slice of homemade white bread cut good and thick, spread it with butter and jam, put it in a plate that had sides on it, and pour cream over the stuff. It's a little much for me, but for my grandparents, that was the best treat in the whole world. Then, after that, they would have their pie or cake.

Karen Retzlaff, 34, North Dakota

I know you made a lot of Scandinavian food. Did you make *lefsa*?

Oh, did we make *lefsa*! A lot of *lefsa*.

How is *lefsa* made?

You boil and mash potatoes, and you put in a little sugar, and a little salt—not much—and a little butter or lard and cream. And then you use half as much flour as you do potatoes. You roll them out real thin, bake them on both sides on the top of the stove, or on your *lefsa* iron, whichever you've got. They're good.

Now, before electric grills, what did you use to cook them on?

Well, we washed the top of our [wood-burning] stoves with soap and water, and got it good and hot, and that's what we used—right on top of the stove.

Minnie Ness, 81, North Dakota

Dairy Products

At that time nobody had real big herds of cattle, because the cows were milked [by hand]. And you turned the separator by hand.

Did you sell the cream as it was, or did you churn the butter and sell the butter?

When I was a small kid, Mom would churn the butter, but when I was getting a little bigger, then we would sell the cream. We'd bring cream into one of the towns that had a cream station.

The first churn that we had was a dash churn—a stone crock with a cover on, and then there was a wood handle with a crossbar of wood at the bottom that you used as a dasher and went up and down with it. Later we got a barrel churn that we turned. But lots of time, if we needed butter, why it was nothing to see somebody take a syrup pail or a glass jar, and shake that to get butter out of it.

Of course we didn't have refrigerators to keep the cream cool, so we'd hang the cream down the well—have something to hook it onto with a rope and drop it down an old shallow well and hope that nothing got into it. Unless we had a real cool basement, then we'd keep it in the basement.

Margaret Lien, 68, North Dakota

With a dasher churn, I've counted up to a thousand strokes it took to bring butter. But you didn't think about that. You thought of poetry, or you tried to read, but you kept the old dasher going.

Dorothy Personette, 77, Oregon

The thing I didn't like as a kid was churning the butter. I had an old stone churn when I had to do this, and I sat there and I'd churn and cry, then I'd churn, then I'd cry. 'Cause the butter wouldn't come.

Opal Becker, 78, Indiana

I'll tell you about old Shep. He was kind of a blooded dog and he was a smart old fellow. We taught him to run this dog power[ed apparatus]. It was longer than this bed and a little bit upgrade all the way.

We'd tie him in, and he'd paddle away and turn this big barrel of cream to make butter.

Once in a while he'd get tired, and he'd lay down, and everything stopped. He'd watch up the cellar steps, and when he'd see me coming—I never scolded him—he'd get up and start paddling (laughter).

Well, then he got to hiding from me. He knew when I was going to churn—when I'd bring the cream up to get it warm—and Old Shep

A friendly cow stands in the barnyard to be milked, and even the cat gets a squirt of fresh milk.

would disappear. I found out right away he always hid in the same place out back of the barn, and I always went out there.

When he saw me coming, he'd get down and come to the house and go down in the cellar, and he'd be paddling away when I got back up there. He'd be churning (laughter).

Lora Foster, 100, Montana

I did make cheese a lot when we had lots and lots of milk. I had a recipe that called for skim milk and you had to clabber it and get it sour and then heat it at a certain degree—always had to have my dairy thermometer. And then drain it and put it through a bag and then after that, you had to put it on and heat it again. And put some butter and salt in, and that made a really good cheese, like brick cheese. We liked that.

Anna Sorensen, 83, North Dakota

Do you remember uncolored margarine?

We had to let the margarine get warm enough, and then break the little capsules that came with them, and stir them up with a fork or your hands.

My kids had a plastic bag. The margarine came in a plastic bag and they busted the capsule and done it that way.

Nowadays a lot of dairymen sell their milk to the processing plant, then buy margarine themselves.

Luella Hamilton, 71, Michigan

Bread

Did you bake your own bread?

Oh, yes, we baked all our bread. Of course, the early years we had yeast foam. So in the evening it was to make a sponge and put it in a container, and wrap it up real good to keep it warm overnight. Then in the morning, make your bread.

Margaret Lien, 68, North Dakota

A funny thing came to me. They put out a recipe for sourdough bread and it went the rounds. I thought, "I don't understand that." So I went digging into what sourdough bread was, and it's nothing except the starters that we used to have. And we was so glad when we didn't have to use that, and could use granular yeast.

And now they think this is something new.

It didn't have to be sour, because in a family where they baked two or three times a week, that bread was lovely.

[There was] a funny thing on that starter—one of my aunt's neighbors, she was kind of forgetful. You kow, if you dump it [starter] all in your bread, you're done. "Well," she [neighbor] said, "I put all my starter into the bread, and I've got to have some more."

My aunt said, "I just mixed mine up fresh, and I'll see that you get it. I'll send it by mail." They were on the same mail route and the fellow came by my aunt's first.

So she put her wad of dough in a baking powder can and put the lid on and Mrs. Gump's name on it, and took it to the mailbox. By the time the mail carrier got around there, he had his wagon full of dough (laughs heartily).

Oh, it had raised!

Yes, it pushed the lid off.

Homemakers, cooking on coal/wood
cookstoves, turned out enormous meals
with lots of baked goods and
did canning, too.

I never heard of sending bread dough in the mail like that.

That's quick thinking.

Sophie Bigge, 82, Kansas

Did you grind your own flour?

We used to. My dad used to grind our dark flour. But the white flour, we'd get that from a mill. You took your wheat in there and got it ground. It come out pretty cheap to get a few hundred pounds [of flour] that way.

Anna Sorensen, 83, North Dakota

We would get from 800 to 1000 pounds [of flour] ground after our family was getting bigger. We'd always see that we had some flour left from the year before when we got new flour, because [with] the new flour, the bread got dark looking. It wasn't as good as after the flour got to be a little aged.

Margaret Lien, 68, North Dakota

We had Portuguese neighbors and every week when our neighbor made bread, she'd come down with one or two loaves of Portuguese bread, and it would be hot! We always enjoyed it. Even after I had children, I used to go to my mother's and old Mrs. Furtado used to walk down with a loaf of sweet Portuguese bread, and my children always looked forward to it. It had to be hot, because you had to cut it and spread it with butter and eat it.

So finally she taught me how to bake Portuguese bread, but I could never bake a bread as good as she did. Even her daughters couldn't make bread as good as she did. Those were such pleasant memories.

Mary Soon, 60, Hawaii

My grandmother used to make the biggest, fattest, lushest baking powder biscuits. That was her specialty. I would eat breakfast with her on Saturday and Sunday morning, and that was what I would wake up to, was the smell of those biscuits.

Edna Dagnen, 67, Washington

We were big bread eaters, so I used to bake about once a week, sometimes eight loaves.

Did you measure by pinches and handfuls?

Oh, yes, I never used to measure when I baked bread.

I hear that you used to fry bread. Tell us about it.

I'd take and make a ball of it [bread dough], then I'd pull it to make it flat. Then I'd have good hot butter in the pan, and I'd put it in there. I'd fry it on one side brown, then I'd turn it over and fry it on the other side.

Cora Lykken, 89, North Dakota

We had the big old-fashioned cookstoves with a huge oven, with a rack in the center. You could put a pan of loaves on the bottom and one up on the rack. We baked bread every other day. Each pan held six loaves, so that was 12 loaves every other day. We were feeding ten children, Poppa and Momma, and Grandpa always stayed with us. That was 13 people in our family—that took a lot of bread.

I'll bet a lot of good smells came out of that kitchen.

Agnes Bell, 85, Indiana

I was going to stay with a family in Maine when the wife had a baby, and they came down and got me. Hackettstown, New Jersey, was where we stayed overnight. That was where a Negro came in with a great long whip at this place where we stayed overnight. I couldn't think what he was going to do with that whip, but he was driving the cats out of the restaurant where we were going to eat.

Lora Torsey, 84, New Hampshire

Did you have flies and pests?

Yes, that first year, right after this house was built, in 1909, we had well drillers here, and my mother had to cook for them. And we still hadn't gotten screen doors on at that time.

And the flies!! It was the time of year when the flies were so bad. My mother, poor soul, she'd stand with a willow twig that had a lot of leaves on and she'd try to chase the flies out, so they wouldn't swarm all over the table. The next year we got screen doors and screen windows put on.

Anna Sorensen, 83, North Dakota

What is your most-liked aspect of homemaking?

Cooking. I love to keep house, bake pies. Nothing makes me happier than for the family to come in and I can cook a big meal for them. That's one of the happiest times, when the girls say, "Grandma, I'm coming home," and I can get them around the table.

Clara Ashcraft, 70, Indiana

My love of cooking started my cookbook collection. If I find a new cookbook, I take it to bed with me and read it just like a novel. Other people can't understand that I can read a cookbook and enjoy it, but I do.

Helen Weigle, 77, Indiana

Food and Extension Lessons

We studied very basic things. Some of the women when we first started had not finished high school and had not studied nutrition, so I think the food and nutrition was very important those early years for people who had never studied. At that time the women were deeply interested in it for their family's health, and we had many lessons on nutrition.

We had, we have always, and we still have lessons on food, but it's an entirely different angle now on foods. You have more on diets and tastiness and the way you serve now.

Sarah Ball, 74, Oklahoma

The first lesson I can remember, the Home Agent taught the women how to use a measuring cup and a measuring spoon (chuckle) and we think that's funny now, because that's one of the lessons that we teach 4-Hers in their first lesson in cooking. But in those days, many people didn't have standard measuring cups and measuring spoons, so this Home Agent was showing them how to use one and also what to use if they didn't have one—how to measure in just an old coffeecup or just a table spoon.

Sue Moman, 55, Alabama

They started with basic diets—with the basic food values—and they were very thorough with it. It was something that was absolutely new to the women. They always knew that they set a balanced meal, more or less, on the table—green and red and yellow vegetables, and meat, and a certain amount of sweets—but they never knew why, or how much was enough, or what they lacked. In this way they became very proficient in preparing their meals.

Rubie Gillion, 80, Michigan

One lesson showed us how to make dry cereals. Dry cereals were very inexpensive at that time, but in the depth of the Depression, you just couldn't afford anything, there was so little money to go around.

So this lesson showed us how to mix grains together—rye, wheat and graham flours—and make a thin dough that we rolled out like pie crust. Rolled as thin as possible and then baked it in the oven. Then, when it was baked hard—very hard—you broke it up with a hammer. You could crumble it or roll it as fine as you wanted to, like Grape Nuts, say. You'd use a rolling pin to crumble it that fine.

It made a good substitute dry cereal. We made quite a lot of it and it was quite a little cheaper than buying the manufactured cereals.

Nellie Yost, 76, Nebraska

When we went to meetings at a person's home, they had one special thing. And I remember this one woman, she made apple pie. And it was so good.

When her husband came in, he said, "Well, it ought to be good. She made three or four and threw them out before these." (laughter)

Mabel Hughes, 82, Florida

What has your favorite project been through the years?

I think the cooking. I didn't know a lot about cooking. On the farm we always had a lot of meat and things, but everything was fried. They [Extension] made me aware of better ways of fixing it, broiling and such. I can make better tasting and better flavored meat, and that's an expensive item.

Winifred Thrush, 70, Ohio

The women that had big kitchens learned to make their kitchens over. I remember they put islands in their kitchens and that took away so many steps. They put all their cooking area in one end, and it kept them from walking all around in these great big kitchens.

Mary Jonas, 81, Ohio

I remember one program that was very popular when Extension first started. They used to demonstrate how you could reorganize your kitchen so that you wouldn't have so much walking to do.

There was a club out north that had an all-day meeting, and after luncheon in this woman's home, they reorganized her kitchen. After they had all worked all afternoon, she looked it over and said, "I'd druther have it the way I'd druther have it." But most people were very much pleased with this sort of help.

Jennie Williams, 89, Wyoming

My family always got a kick out of the new Extension dishes that I tried to fix, except my son. He was never one to try anything new. He would say, "Mom, couldn't you just do the old stuff, instead of trying to do all this new stuff?" (laughs)

Dorothy Hoffman, 60, Indiana

FOOD PRESERVATION

Early Methods

We raised what we ate, and ate what we raised. You didn't go into town and buy it, so it really was important to put your garden out and really take care of it, and take care of it when it was ready to harvest.

Beulah Rawlings, 76, Indiana

Then Dad used to dig a hole and put straw in it, and you always put vegetables in there. We had cabbage and turnips and potatoes, and that's how we kept our vegetables through the winter. That was our cellar at that time.

Estella Myers, Michigan

Gardening to grow food for use in the
summer and to be preserved for
wintertime.

When I was a girl up North, before pressure canners, we never canned much vegetables because it was all put in the cellar. We canned fruits and tomatoes, but that was about the only thing we canned, mostly fruit that you don't have to put in the pressure cooker.

In our cellars we put in our carrots and potatoes and onions and turnips and we even had a big bin fixed up for celery. We'd store apples and pears.

Elsie Gould, 86, Florida

We usually had a good apple orchard. And Dad, he'd bury those apples in the oats bin, in lard cans—50 pound lard cans. There might be as many as 15 cans buried down in the oats bin, and they'd be just like out of the refrigerator now, when you'd take them out. They labeled them and even marked up on the wall in the bin where they were buried, so that he didn't make a mistake a-bringin' them in. Then we'd put them in the basement, we called it a cellar, it had a dirt floor. We'd put them down there until that can was used.

Mildred Weaver, 64, Indiana

You mentioned salting vegetables?

You cut up green beans and put a lot of salt with them and put them in a big jar and put a weight on top of them and let them stand in the basement where it was cool.

And whenever you wanted to use some, you took some out and let it soak out, and boil it in two or three waters, before you could use the beans. They really weren't as tasty as they could be. But they were filling.

Anna Sorensen, 83, North Dakota

We even put down corned beef in a bit earthenware [container]. We put it down with saltpeter and salt. You'd put a big stone on it to keep it down in the liquid.

Elsie Gould, 86, Florida

Butchering

We'd start about February to butcher. They would butcher about two hogs at a time. They would heat the water on the big coal range in the house, and they would take it out to the platform and put lye in the barrel. Two men would have ahold of the pig and they would put it back and forth in the water. They would turn the hog and scald the hog on the other end. They would get it out and scrape it. They would cut it up.

They rendered lard, and they fried down sausages. They made soap out of the cracklings. Nothing went to waste.

Edna Wood, 77, Nebraska

Then when the time of the year came around for killing the pig which they raised the whole year, before the pig was killed we had to get ready the onions and the parsley. They would kill the pig and then [you had] to get all those intestines clean. You didn't buy clean intestines; you had to do it yourself. We used to go get this little blue grass that grew in the fields, and square it off like chopsticks. We had to wash it [intestine] with Hawaiian salt and scrape it with lemon juice. Use those sticks to just pick up all that slime, until we got the intestines all ready.

A butchering scene. Seven very large hogs
will soon become ham, sausage and bacon.

We'd fix all the different types of sausages. They made so many types of sausages in those days. Not just blood sausage and Portuguese sausage.

They would clean the skin of the pigs as clean as could be and get rid of every hair. Used to chop that off into tiny little pieces and made a certain kind of sausage with that. That was the sausage for the soup. It was delicious; it had a little crunch to it. They made milk sausage. I mean just all kinds of sausages.

It was a weekend affair. It was a time of fun. The children used to come and we used to play. Everybody used to wait for the pig's bladder. That was the only ball we had to play with. So, once a year, you looked forward to that bladder to play with. We used to have a rollicking good time.

Then the following week the same thing happened at another neighbor's. They used every part of the pig. They didn't waste the pig. So when you eat a sausage, just appreciate it, because it takes a lot of work and a lot of cooking, especially in the old days.

Julia Souza, 62, Hawaii

The neighbors would all meet at a certain place, usually at my uncle's place, because he lived near the creek. They'd have these big barrels of water and they'd get them boiling hot, and they'd all bring their hogs to this one place on a certain day. They would butcher their hogs after they got there, and then they would scald them in these big barrels, and then they'd all help scrape and all help cut up.

A real problem in food preservation. Photo of whale submitted by Alaska.

The way the people did their meat then—if somebody run out of meat before it was hog-killing time again, they just waited. They didn't want [to butcher] and have meat left over in hot weather, because it wouldn't keep. So if somebody run out of meat, why they'd loan them a ham or a shoulder, and then when they killed their hogs, why then they'd pay this back. So it was quite interesting to see them when they butchered and cut up their hogs. They hadn't forgotten; they'd go paying back what they had borrowed.

Opal Cypert, 68, Arkansas

As soon as the entrails were emptied and brought in, three or four of the women, with their little scrub boards, would clean and scrape the entrails until they were clean. To clean the casings [entrails] wasn't always the most pleasant odors, but you had to put up with it, because it was necessary that they be clean. Then, if the hogs didn't have worms, you had good casings to stuff your sausage.

Alma Knecht, 79, Indiana

When I was first married, we had to do all our own butchering.

Your home demonstration agents helped you learn how to do some of that, didn't they?

The Home Agent came and helped to improve on seasoning your hams and bacons to cure, and that's when they had the new system of pumping the hams, instead of just putting them into the salt brine. You would pump it in along the bone, and that helped cure the meat.

Mary Moore, 73, New Mexico

The other day my daughter called from Burns and she said, "Give me your mincemeat recipe. I've got some beef and I want to make some mincemeat."

I said, "First, you get out the wash boiler and you take six hogs' heads and split them and cook them." She laughed at that. But you utilized everything.

Dorothy Personette, 77, Oregon

We made ham and bacon out of our pork that we butchered. Salted it, and put it in brine and then we put it in the smokehouse and smoked it.

We ground meatballs and put in a jar and covered with lard. We made roasts and put in butter jars and covered that with lard, and put cloth and paper over it and kept it in the basement.

Then we made dried beef; we put that in salt and then in brine. Then, when it had been in brine—three or six weeks, I forget—we took it out and then we dried it. Then we wiped it off real good and we'd put a lot of pepper on it to keep the flies off. Then we hung it up in the attic. When the crows come around in the spring, then we knew the dried beef was ready to eat.

You put pepper to keep the flies away?

Then they were so bad in the house that we'd open the door, and we'd take our towels, and we'd wave towels and get the flies all out of the door. But it wouldn't be long until they were back in, and we'd have to chase them again. We chased and we chased flies.

Minnie Ness, 81, North Dakota

When we lived on the farm, we just had wonderful neighbors, and we'd all get together for picnics. At the time when they would kill hogs, that was a big event in the life of the farm. All the neighbors would come, and we'd have a great big feed, and have a big time. The kids really looked forward to that.

Dorothy Tolley, 67, Arkansas

Canning tomatoes outdoors, using both glass and tin cans. Notice the soldering iron in the hands of the woman in the middle of the picture. The women in the foreground are ready to lower cans into boiling water in the tubs.

Canning

I raised a big garden. I loved to garden, that was one of my joys—to work in the garden and raise the vegetables. And I loved to can them. It was a great satisfaction to see a whole winter's supply of canned vegetables ready by the time the garden season was over.

Nellie Yost, 76, Nebraska

About your participation in Extension Homemakers Clubs—what club activity was the most helpful to you?

I really think that the canning and preserving of food was one of the best things.

Margaret Lien, 68, North Dakota

What incidents do you remember best in those early [EH] club meetings?

Well, I guess the most outstanding one that I've remembered just what we did was the summer that Mrs. Covington was the agent. We did some canning vegetables and fruits that afternoon in my grove below the house. It was just above the spring, and we could have the fresh spring water to use.

What kind of stove did she use or what equipment, to can out in the open like that?

We had a little gas burner on a table. And a friend of mine, a real close neighbor, had a water canner that you could fire up and can about 50 or 60 quart cans at one time.

Fruit carefully packed and canned wins a prize for the proud homemaker.

Did other people use that equipment?

No, didn't any of the rest of us have this canner like Mrs. Little's, but we did it on our stoves in our own kitchens. She was just showing us to how to prepare the fruit and how to can in tin cans. We canned in tin cans that afternoon.

Today, do you still can in tin cans or do you use glass?

Tin cans got so expensive, and we couldn't find them, so we had to go back mostly to glass jars.

Letha McCall, 91, North Carolina

Mother attended an Extension lesson that taught her how to cold pack fruits and vegetables. They blanched the fruit or vegetables, cooked them and packed them in cans, sealed the lids, put the wash boiler on the stove with a wooden slat false bottom, put in the 11 cans (I think Mother's boiler held 11 cans), went to the pump outside, pumped water and brought it in to fill the boiler to one inch above the cans. Then we fired the wood stove until we boiled this water for three hours. Sometimes we gathered corn cobs in our aprons to finish firing the stove to keep the water boiling.

Lois Wagoner, 77, Indiana

That was a slow way to can, but after a while they got these pressure cookers, and that didn't take so long in there.

Anna Sorensen, 83, North Dakota

Way back in the early days, before agents were here, there was no way to take care of meat excepting to salt it away.

So Miss White told us there was obtainable home tin can sealers. So most of us homemakers bought a small home tin can sealer and we went to work! We canned meats and we canned all kinds of vegetables, and our fruits.

We got a barrel—a 50-gallon barrel—and my husband went out back of the house and set up a little place where he could build a fire between rocks and set the barrel up on top. And he filled that with water and heated it until it was boiling.

As I sealed these tin cans, I took them by the panful and carried them out to that barrel and dumped them into that boiling water and they were processed there for three solid hours. And we would do as many as 50 or more cans of meat or corn or whatever, in that barrel.

How did the meat taste, canned?

It was *wonderful.* And Miss White also taught us the different cuts of meat. We would cut the meat that way and get the larger size cans and put that meat in a fry pan and brown it nicely and then layer it in those bigger cans and put them in and process them, and when they came out, *oh,* they were just marvelous.

Elsa Skiles, Washington

We had a great big cooker that they used to cook the pig feed in. My husband and I scoured that out and set it in the milkhouse. In the fall we would butcher about 89 chickens and I would can them out in the milkhouse. We'd kill them and cut 'em up one day and throw 'em into the cooker and put ice water in them overnight. Then the next day we'd go out and dress them out. I'd do 148 quarts of chicken at a time. I'd have four cookers full.

Evie Foster, 70, Alaska

Canning in a canning kitchen. Note the
very early pressure canners.

One thing I remember, was when I first saw a pressure canner. Dr. Dean from Stillwater and Miss Martha McPheeters came out and gave a demonstration on meat canning, which we thought was wonderful. It was so much easier to preserve canned meats than it was to fry them down and store in the cellar, that we had done in the past.

Then, during the Depression years, when we had the government program of killing the cattle, why this came in handy. We spent days and days going from one neighbor's to the other with our pressure cookers. I think we only had about two or three in the community. But we'd go and spend the whole day canning beef and pork.

You learned by doing.

Zelma Wood, 77, Oklahoma

About the time I went into Extension, which was in 1928, pressure cookers were just becoming commonplace, and that was a wonderful benefit to people, to be able to preserve things.

It would have so much better taste, and you could preserve things out of season. We all had pork, because we could preserve it by brining and smoking. But we couldn't have beef, except in the winter, and we liked to eat beef.

My husband got me a pressure canner for Christmas and shortly after that, our Home Demonstration Agent—as she was then called—Irene Hanna, got up a canning school. We met at a lady's house and everybody brought their pressure cookers. The men killed the beef and the men cut it up, and we canned all day long. The smell was horrible—I do hate the smell of opening pressure cookers. But we got it all canned, and we were proud of ourselves. We really had learned a new skill.

It was great to be able to have meat during the summer months. You didn't have any refrigeration to speak of in those years. Electric refrigerators were not available, and not many people kept ice in their iceboxes in the wintertime. This was really hard times by then, and you couldn't buy much. You had to can a lot, or you'd starve.

For many, many, many years I canned meat—sometimes four or five hundred quarts a year, and an awful lot of vegetables. We also had demonstrations on canning vegetables and fruits.

We canned chickens, too. We canned lots of chickens. We really used our pressure cookers an awful lot in those days.

Sarah Ball, 74, Oklahoma

[I had been going to houses to help them can] and I thought, "There's got to be a better way!" So that's when I started a canning kitchen. I got myself a gas plate off the trash pile in front of a restaurant there in town. I carried it home, cleaned it up, and we put it up and used it. That was the first gas plate we had.

I had a couple of pressure cookers that I used for demonstrations. We bought a can sealer, and we charged ten cents to use it. So that's the way we paid for it.

Ten cents a can?

Ten cents a use. They paid ten cents for the privilege of using it. You could seal a thousand cans if you wanted to. [Narrator is a retired early Extenstion Agent.]

Pearl Laffitte, 80, Florida

They had a canning process—that was the first time I ever knew of them canning in tin cans. They had a large canning place that two women took care of, and they canned it. We took whatever we had—surplus fruit . . . But you had to help them prepare it to can it.

We had a cannery where you could take your fruit and help them prepare it and then you'd have it in the tin cans? That was a pretty good method to use.

Oh, it was wonderful. Of course, you had to leave early in the morning. It would not only be you, but several people. They'd be night getting through with it, sometimes. The earlier you got there, the earlier you got yours prepared and canned.

But it was a wonderful thing to see them, and how they prepared it.

Did you ever have any problems with the keeping of the food that had been canned in tin cans?

No, never! They knew just exactly how to do it, so we never did have any trouble with it.

Elba Johnston, 79, Oklahoma

What did you join the club to learn, particularly?

I really joined the club to learn everything that I could. When we first started out, it was food preservation, and we were taught how to preserve and can.

At this time you canned in tin cans rather than glass jars, didn't you?

Yes, we had to solder them to seal them. Used a hot solder iron to solder the top on, just like you would solder anything.

That would be a tricky method of canning.

I was reading in connection with the [county home economics] camps that one lady wondered how she could keep the moths out of her wool bathing suit, and somebody told her to can it. Put it in a jar and can it to keep the moths out. We sent our boys in the army canned pecans and goodies in cans.

Mrs. B. N. Simrall, Sr., 87, Mississippi

The County Agent would go with the canners, and they used the canners in the school. You would go every so often and can food for the school cafeteria. That was an interesting program that came through Extension work. You would carry your produce to the school. The county would furnish the cans and they would allow the canner at the school at a certain time, and you would can soup for the cafeteria.

You would give one out of every four [cans] to the school, and you'd have the others.

It was a lot more fun too for everybody to get together and can, than to just stay at home and can.

Ruth Irwin, 83, Mississippi

Do you still do your own canning?

Yes. Last year I canned over a thousand jars, and I divided it. I have three married families and then myself, and I divided that four ways.

I always have a supply on hand. I try to see that no one goes away from my house empty-handed. They always have something to take with them.

Essie Simmons, 81, Arkansas

You can get most any kind of vegetable any time of the year that you want at the grocery store. But I still believe in canning and preserving my food as much as I can. It saves money, and you know it's good when you can it yourself. It's fresh when you put it up, and it's very nutritious. So I still can most of my food.

Bertha Andrews, 89, Alabama

I think it's a wonderful heritage and helps to teach the children some of the good ways of life. To see the beautiful canned goods that's on the shelf, and say, "Well, I grew it, and I preserved it, and now you're eating it." It's great.

Emily Harper, 60, Florida

Jellies & Pickles

In berry season I would take boxes or a pail and I'd go out and gather wild berries and bring them in. I would go out every morning and I'd get elderberries and blackberries, or whatever we had. I made so much jellies.

I learned to make jelly in Home Extension. You know, really, you get so much out of Home Extension that you can't start to tell all the things.

Mabel Hughes, 82, Florida

I learned to make jelly years and years and years ago, because our agent taught us. I'm still using the same jelly book. It's just an excellent guide to making jelly.

Virginia McIntyre, 63, Louisiana

Usually every year I make about ten gallons of saccharin pickles in crocks down in the cellar. I've got at least fourteen quarts of dill pickles, and I haven't counted all of the other relishes that I've made.

You might say, what do I do with them. Well, every time there's a big Grange meeting, they look to me for some pickles. Church suppers, well, they look to me. Then I used to give a jar of pickles to every man in my family at Christmas time.

Lora Torsey, 84, New Hampshire

These beautifully ripe peaches will be in a can before evening.

We picked wild fruit and wild berries. We had Juneberries nearly every year for many years. Sometimes they were mixed with rhubarb to make a sauce, and I made jam out of them with pineapple and things. And then we had a wild raspberry patch and we picked some wild strawberries and there were gooseberries.

Margaret Lien, 68, North Dakota

I got out and picked my own blackberries and made blackberry jelly. After the boys got a little older, they'd get out and hunt green grapes, and I made green grape jelly, and ripe grape jelly. These were wild grapes.

I used to make candied peaches and candied melon rinds and candied all those things and made my own fruitcake.

Vivian Jefferson, 95, Arkansas

That's what Extension Homemakers is all about, using something you already have saves money. We have fruit trees.

You do can, don't you?

Yes, jelly, jam, preserves and can. It saves on the grocery bill.

Geneva Slaton, 82, Georgia

I always wanted to make jelly that would be nice, so I worked on that till I had it pretty well perfected. Then, at our fair, they offered the prize for the one that had the most kinds of jelly from Rooks County. I said, "Oh, my, there wouldn't be very much." About all I knew that grew was currants and plums. But my husband was working for the Soil Conservation Service, and he was out over the county, and he said, "You might run into more than that."

Well, I started in and I think the first year I had seven different kinds, and I got the blue ribbon. So from then on, I started adding to. I got kind of ashamed of myself. I think the last bunch I took in, I had 24 kinds of jelly.

Then I read in some farm paper about the pioneers making syrup and jelly from corncobs, so I got corncobs and I cooked them up and strained the juice out and I biled it down, and I made corncob jelly. Oh, it was lovely. And I had a friend that worked in the newspaper office and I took her a little jar of this corncob jelly, not thinking any more about it. Then, wouldn't you know, here was this little article about Sophie's corncob jelly.

Well, it come out in the Salina paper, an Arizona paper. It really got around.

Sophie Bigge, 82, Kansas

Freezing

We canned hundreds of jars of fruit and vegetables and meats over the years. We never let anything go to waste. We always preserved it. Now, of course, we freeze food.

Marjorie Brookshire, 60, Kentucky

Sometimes the lessons were geared toward gardening, canning and preservation. About that time freezers came along. Until then you had your freezer or locker in the cities, and then you took your food in there and had it frozen, and then you had to go and get it out.

But the homemakers started having their own freezers, and so you had all of the new training on how to prepare your foods for freezers.

Luella Hamilton, 71, Michigan

Something I really enjoyed learning more about, and that's freezing. Now we freeze more than we can. Most of the things I put in the freezer and I learned that through my Home Demonstration work.

Virginia McIntyre, 63, Louisiana

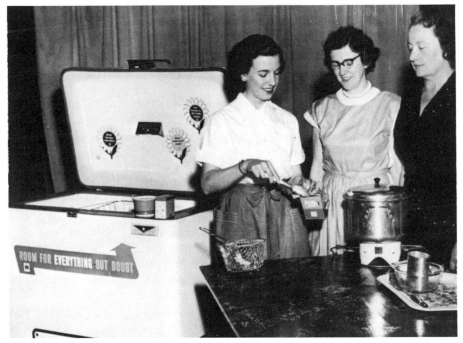

A Home Demonstration agent gives a
lesson on the new technique of freezing.

I buy meat in quantity. I buy other food in quantity and keep them in the freezer, besides some of the things we raise. I fill my jars and my freezer each year.

Vi Cottrell, 69, Washington

Finally I bought a freezer. I used to bake nine loaves of bread three times a week and put it in the freezer and have to start over again the first of the week.

Evie Foster, 70, Alaska

The first luxury item we bought when we first married was a freezer. I enjoyed having it to take care of the food from the garden. I baked a lot and would freeze it. I had no problem when guests were coming. I could always go to my freezer. We butchered our own meat, our beef and our pork. We were able to save money that way.

When we were first married, Bob gave me an allowance of $10 per week, and I was able to buy our groceries and get my hair done at the beauty shop and then have money left for other little things that I might want.

I have often said that if I had to give up every bit of furniture in my house, the last thing I would let go would be my freezer. This is simply because it's one of the most convenient appliances that you can have, and it's the most timesaving. Many times I prepare meals ahead of time and freeze them. Really, it's one of the most rewarding things I've done since I started to work is to be able to go to my freezer, get a meal out, put it in the oven, and in just a little time have a good appetizing meal.

Mary Jo Depew, 41, Kentucky

SEWING

Did everybody used to make more of their clothes?

We didn't have boughten clothes, unless it was a coat. They made their own clothes. Some made the men's shirts and gloves and their overalls.

Was it heavy denim like it is today?

Oh, yes. It was good denim. All the material was better than it is now. They made all their dresses, nightgowns, underclothes and about all they bought was socks and shoes. Some of them even knit their own stockings.

Edna Wood, 77, Nebraska

What kind of a sewing machine did you have in the early days?

My mother, she had a treadle machine she brought with when she came. She had learned dressmaking in Denmark, and she had worked out before she got married and earned some money, and she bought herself a sewing machine. Not a brand new one, but a pretty good one. And she brought it up here. It surely got put to work here, 'cause several of the women in the community didn't have any sewing machine. There were about two of them that had these that you set on the table and you sat and cranked with one hand and guided the material along with the other hand. Slow way to sew, but a whole lot better than sewing it all by hand.

But that old treadle machine, it kept a-hummin'. The one I had would patch binder canvas on it. And that takes a sturdy needle and a sturdy machine to do that. You try to patch binder canvas on some of these new-fangled electric machines, you'll have an awful mess of it.

Did you sew for the boys?

Yes, I did. I sewed a lot for them. Mostly out of old things that were given to me. Coats, and men's pants and suits and so on. And as far as

This homemaker is spinning flax into linen thread which will be used to weave linen material for clothing, or to weave coverlets. A larger spinning wheel would be used to spin wool into yarn for weaving or knitting.

patterns goes, we didn't have too many patterns. You just measured a little here and there and made a pattern out of newspaper and used that.

After a while they had patterns advertised, even in Sears, Roebuck catalogs. You could send for patterns for about 12¢ to 15¢ apiece. And then the women would exchange with one another when they needed a different pattern.

Was the material readily available by then?

Yes. There was always yard goods in every store. Big bolts of it. You could always get gingham, calico and percale. But all of that would fade before being washed too many times. It isn't like what they got now. And most of it, to look real nice, it had to be starched and ironed good. And it was discouraging sometimes to have starched and ironed, and as soon as somebody put it on and sat down, it was wrinkled again.

It wasn't like that wonderful material they have now. Oh, the homemakers should be so thankful for that good material they have now. Wash it, and you don't even have to think of ironing it.

Anna Sorensen, 83, North Dakota

When I was a child, my father used to go to Valdosta, and he would go and buy three or four bolts of cloth. You see, there was twelve children in our family, six girls and six boys. And we all had a dress off the same piece of cloth.

My mother had a cupboard, and that stuff was on the shelf there. She and Daddy would go off to church, and I'd get me a bolt of that cloth out. I would see something I wanted to make, and I would cut me a pattern and I'd cut me a garment, and I would make it. If it turned out all right, I'd show it to my mother. If it didn't, I'd put that piece of ruined material down in the bottom of a big chest.

When I was fourteen years old, we boarded the schoolteacher for three years, and I cut patterns and sewed for the schoolteacher. I cut the dress patterns, using newspaper.

I can remember some of the dresses that I made for her. I can see one of them just as plain—it had a big bertha collar that came over thisaway, and a slot that went under here, and a tie that went and tied in the back. I cut every piece of it, from scratch. But that's the way I learned to cut.

Eunice Cameron, 80, Florida

My mother would leave us and say, "Now don't you bother the machine." She wouldn't be out of the gate till I had the machine out sewing, breaking all her needles, because the boys would treadle for me and when I got ready to stop, they wouldn't stop—they just kept on treadling. I'd pull it out and break a needle. But I have sewed ever since I couldn't sit down at the machine. I stood up and sewed.

Mary Skelley, 76, Oklahoma

I remember one time my sisters wanted to sew my mother a blouse. She went to town, and us girls were home alone. We couldn't find no material to make it from, so we took a curtain that hung in front of one of the clothes closets, and they cut the blouse out, by [a pattern made from] a blouse they took apart. But when they sewed it together again, they had one sleeve for one of the front pieces, and the front piece for a sleeve. So it didn't fit very good, and it didn't look very good, either (laughs).

Mother laughed. She thought it was a pretty good thing for them to try.

Minnie Ness, 81, North Dakota

Then the cleaning of our old treadle sewing machines. We had a [Extension] lesson on cleaning them. Everybody took the tops of their old sewing machines off. We had a big washtub and we used a solvent

Early treadle sewing machines were powered by the steady back-and-forth motion of the operator's foot.

that smelled like kerosene and fuel oil. We'd dunk that machine down in there with some brushes. If you were real daring, you'd take a screwdriver and take it apart and clean it. If you didn't feel quite so smart, you would brush it and dig out the dirt. You'd be surprised at the lint and oil and stuff you could dig out of there.

You don't think we ought to do that with our modern-day sewing machines?

I doubt if they'd zig or zag if we tried doing some of these.

Nellie Frost, 80, Missouri

I sewed most of the children's clothes and I did not have new fabric to sew these clothes. I would go down to the Salvation Army and buy an adult person's second-hand coat, take it apart, wash the fabric, cut them out and make the coats and things for the children.

Vi Cottrell, 69, Washington

We didn't have much money, and there had been a circus come to town. When they left, they had left all of their heavy clothing, because they were going south.

My husband went to the thrift store in town there and he got a beautiful tomato-red coat trimmed in fur and brought it home to me. I made my oldest daughter a snow suit out of it, and a little bonnet, and she wore it until she outgrew it. Then my second daughter wore it. When she outgrew it, I gave it to my nephew who was just a year younger, and he wore it until he wore it out. And my husband had paid 25¢ for that coat.

Evie Foster, 70, Alaska

Well, our sewing was making over clothes. You were very lucky to have a new piece of material once in a while to use.

When my oldest boy was in the first grade, he needed a pair of long pants for the Christmas program, and I didn't have anything for him for pants, and I didn't know just what I was going to do.

One morning I was going down to feed the pigs, and I walked by the kids' playhouse. It was the body of a 1927 Chevrolet. And I saw—oh, my, there's some nice gray pinwale corduroy in that thing. So I went back to the house and I got a hammer and a plier to pull tacks with and I ripped that all out of there. This was early in the forenoon, and I took it to the house and washed it. I had some dark green dye, so I dyed the material and got it dry in the house before the kids got home from school.

Next day I made him a pair of long pants. I had enough for a short Ike jacket. Boy, he thought he was really somebody. He had this here new outfit for the Christmas program.

Well, next spring when they were getting their playhouse fixed up again for summer, why he noticed the upholstery was gone. He came to the house and he said, "Momma, is that where my pants come from?" Which it was, but a person had to make use of everything you had. I learned back then that there was a good reason why new homes didn't have big closets, because people just didn't have enough clothes to fill them up anyway.

Margaret Lien, 68, North Dakota

I used to get a dollar bill to take a mother's old coat, turn it wrong-side out and make her daughter a brand-new looking coat. I'd line it, and everything, and boy, I hadn't sewed hardly at all. But I was on top of the world then. Many a mother that couldn't afford a new coat brought her old coat to me.

Corria Ratliff, 82, Virginia

During the hard years, my boys wore short pants made from the legs of men's pants. And my younger boy, he had his corduroy overalls and they were his Sunday and everyday clothes. And my girls, lots of times, had garments made of feed sacks, which you could get in very pretty colors at that time. I even had a dress myself, made from feed sacks, and went to college with it one summer.

I remember they were real comfortable.

That's right. And we had a cow at the time, and we had to buy feed for the cow, and we'd try to buy two sacks the same color because it would [be enough] to make a garment.

Theo Hammond, 82, North Carolina

The first things I had was bloomers and slips out of flour sacks that they bleached the names off of. Mom was good at that. She didn't leave parts of the name. Some people had Pillsbury on their seat.

Margaret Lien, 68, North Dakota

Didn't you used to give demonstrations on feed bags, on what to do with them—making dresses and everything out of them?

[narrator is a retired Extension home economist] Sure. They made some nice things. The only fault I ever found with it was on washday. You had to starch and iron them. You couldn't wear it without.

Pearl Laffitte, 80, Florida

I had to do all the sewing in the family at that time. Ready-made clothing was not available much around in the stores, and we didn't have any money to buy it when it was.

But we were fortunate to have feed sacks, and our Indiana feed sacks were among the best in the nation, because they were made with a linen-look weave, and they were printed material. We made everything from them. We made shirts, dresses, men's shirts and all sorts of clothing with them.

This linen-look weave washed; and after it was washed, starched and ironed, it just looked like linen, and it wore well, too.

Was this when you went to the elevator and bought your feed? How did you get the sacks?

We got chicken feed and hog feed in them. And at that time you could go to the elevator and buy feed sacks for a nickel apiece. And four feed sacks would make the size of a tablecloth or a sheet, and one pillow case could be made from each feed sack.

I made sheets for a lot of people. They would give me their plain white feed sacks and I would sew with felled seams—sew four together and make a sheet. And then we talked about it and soon everyone was making feed sack sheets.

Did it have printing on it?

No, it was plain. You could get plain white.

I thought they had the feed company's name on it, that you had to wash off.

Some of them did, and some of them didn't. That was a selling point with some of the companies—they found out we wanted them without names on. But even if it had lettering, that lettering wasn't hard to take out.

And you made other things out of feed sacks?

We made practically everything. Another thing that made lovely table covers at that time was the seed corn sacks. That was a little heavier sack, but four of them made a nice square for a square table or a card table. We put them together with single tatting or a little crocheting, then around the edge put an edging on to match. And they made beautiful covers.

Virgie Bowers, 81, Indiana

I remember one lesson that was especially useful to me. I had a sewing machine with this little box of accessories in it. Had no idea what to do with them. We had a lesson on sewing machine accessories. I never had anything to help me so much as that did.

Edith Gladden, 63, Missouri

We learned how to make drapes. Another project was how to make slipcovers for davenports. That helped many women at that time, because that was around the Depression times, when they couldn't afford to have them recovered.

We were taught how to cover lamp shades, probably forty years ago.

Alice Wand, 65, Oregon

We learned to clean and oil our sewing machine. Each one brought her sewing machine head along to the meeting. This lesson lingers in my memory, as the country roads were very rough and three of us ladies were pregnant. We were concerned that the bumpy ride, with all those sewing machines, might bring on labor (laughs). All went well, though, and in a few months all three of us had healthy baby boys.

Marcella Meyer, Minnesota

What has been the most outstanding lesson [to you]?

I always thought that the sewing lessons, in my younger days when I was making things over for the kids, and sewing something new for myself. One of the agents was so good at showing us how to fit clothing in the shoulders.

Anna Sorensen, 83, North Dakota

I still use the Homemaker's method of putting on patches on overalls. That was the easiest way of doing it that I ever found.

Margaret Lien, 68, North Dakota

One really fun thing we've done recently is a fashion show for home sewers. We have about sixty models and it's all home-sewed fashions. It's really, really sold the program to home sewers. We have quite a turnout at our Extension meetings on sewing now.

Brenda Van Meter, 36, Kansas

We were trying to get the county to give a third of the expenses for a county agent. You know the county gives a third, and the state gives a third, and the federal government gives a third. So we were appearing before the council, and they advised us to wear things we had made ourselves.

I happened to be attending a hat class and we took old hats and worked with them. So I had taken an old straw hat and I painted it bright red and put new ribbons on it. And I had made a dress that had a little red in it.

When they got to us, we were each one talking, and someone said, "Well, YOU didn't make your outfit," and I said, "Oh, yes, I did! I even painted my hat." (laughter) And we were able to convince them.

Eileen Moon, 62, Maryland

Weaving and Quilting

Did you ever card wool?

Yes, you'd get wool from those that had sheep. The cards were just like two boards full of little nails. You had to do it careful—roll it back and forth, back and forth, until you had them in nice little flat cakes. You rolled them so they stuck together nice.

Then my grandma had a spinning wheel, and we spun the yarn on there. They spun a lot, because all our mitts were made of that, and some of our sweaters, and scarves, and caps. I know my grandma even wove a rug for our front room on there. They made good use of it.

Minnie Ness, 81, North Dakota

My mother would help shear the sheep that my father raised. Then she would wash the wool, and then she would spin the thread. Then, when she got the thread spun, she would dye this and she'd weave it into cloth. And she would knit it, too. She'd make sweaters, and socks, and caps. It was all hard work, but it was cooperative work. They helped each other.

The women would gather at certain places. We had to grow the cotton then, and we'd gather the cotton and then all got to a certain house where they was a-gonna take the seed out of the cotton. They'd

Stitching quilts was a highly creative process, and many different patterns were original designs.

seed the cotton, and then my mother would card the cotton. The way she'd do it—she'd lay it on the lining of her quilt as she carded it in great big rolls, and then she'd spread the top down on it, and then it's ready to quilt.

The women would all come in—whoever had the quilt up, they would all come to her house and quilt it out.

Opal Cypert, 68, Arkansas

When my children were growing up, I think I pieced a quilt about every winter, and then as soon as the heating stove was taken down, I put a quilt up and quilted it. So most of my quilts were handmade. I

gave one last year to one of my granddaughters, and she seemed very proud of it because I had made it and quilted it years ago.
I'm sure she was.
Vivian Jefferson, 95, Arkansas

My mother used to make quilts with wool, and then we tied them. Of course, the wool didn't wash, so we had to open them up when we washed the quilts, and take the wool out, and wash the top and bottom, and put the wool back in and tie them all over again.

In the wintertime that was something I did all the time, I made quilts. Made a lot of quilts.
What did you use for filling the quilts?
Cotton batting. Towards the last, we got that good stuff—real quilting filling like Sears, Roebuck used to have—some they called China cotton. That was very nice. When you washed it, it never matted. It stayed nice and fluffy.
Were your quilts tied then, or did you stitch them?
I stitched them by hand. I never tied them. I just stitched them.
Minnie Ness, 81, North Dakota

My mother did quite a bit of quilting—Hawaiian quilts. She made several Hawaiian quilts, and we always had a quilt in the living room. As children, we used to play house under the quilt.She also had quilts going at the church. We belong to the Mormon Church and the church is several hundred yards away from our house, and she always had a quilt there, and the other Hawaiian women would quilt.

We slept under Hawaiian quilts. One of my chores was to wash the quilts, which we did by filling water and making soapsuds in the bathtub, then stepping on the quilt with our feet. We had to wash our feet clean.
Mary Soon, 60, Hawaii

We were talking just the other day about people quilting back in the Depression days and before, and comparing it with today.

Now today a woman quilts because she wants to learn the art of quilting and have something for decorative purposes, maybe for the wall, or for the bed, or a keepsake.
Luella Hamilton, 71, Michigan

Our [Extension Homemakers] Unit sponsored the first quilting demonstration at the fair. We put a quilt in the frames and we had needles there. Everybody that wanted to quilt a little did. We had quite a variety of quilting! But we got that quilt quilted and sold it, I think it was something better than $200.

Sophie Bigge, 82, Kansas

In 1976 we asked each county [Extension Homemaker organization] in the state to make a block representing their particular county and we made this into a quilt for our Bicentennial project.

First we had a showing, and asked Mrs. Thurmond [senator's wife] to come. And she was so impressed with the quilt and the history that she talked to her husband and he came and saw it. Then he paved the way for us to get it into the Smithsonian.

In fact, he hand-carried it, because we didn't want to mail it. I'll never forget that morning. We took that quilt over to him at the airport and he personally carried it aboard the plane. He says, "Here I go. I'm going to hand-carry this right into the Smithsonian." Which he did.

Pat Gates, 55, South Carolina

WASHING AND IRONING

Washing by Hand

The washboard, tubs, hand wringer and clothes boiler greeted me every Monday morning, until motor-driven machines lightened the task.

Lillian Eckert, 70, Alaska

My mother used a scrub board and three big tubs of water to do the washing with. I'm talking about a zinc tub of well water that we had drawn from the well and heated in a wash pot. Of course wash day was an all-day affair, usually on Monday.

Jane Morgan, 63, Mississippi

You had three tubs. You washed in one, rinsed in the other, and blued in the third one. And you washed on the board. I used to wash two or three times a week, because I had the babies.

Dorothy Personette, 77, Oregon

My mom could put out white clothes and she could make a washboard sing, just sing. She had a knack. That old washboard would just sing.

As she rubbed it?

She had a rhythm, just like someone a-strummin' his guitar for a rhythm. She had a rhythm on the washboard when she rubbed 'em.

Edna Winter, 84, Indiana

We had to rub, you know. My dad had long woolen underwear and they were so heavy to rub. And their overalls—we used to have to lay

Scrubbing clothes on a washboard. Note the homemade lye soap she is using.
J. C. Allen Collection

them on the washboard and take a brush and dig down in the water to rub them. You could hardly wash them, they were so stiff.

Did it take all day to wash clothes?

All day. Sometimes till five o'clock.

Cora Lykken, 89, North Dakota

We wore wool stockings that she [mother] had knitted, that she used to scrub on a washboard with our clothes. She was usually still scrub-

bing the clothes when we would get home from school. I know she scrubbed till her fingers would bleed, from one week to another.
Lora Torsey, 84, New Hampshire

Wash day, that used to be the day [that] all of us kids looked forward to, us kids and her kids—all of us kids. Old Emma would come, and we had to cut wood for the fires, to get the wash pot boiling. But we ate good that day, and they ate good, too. We'd eat peas and rice like you wouldn't believe.
Pat Gates, 55, South Carolina

Did you wash on a scrub board?
Oh, yes. I drew water up out of a cistern with a pulley up over the cistern with a wheel with a rope over it.
But when we could, we always had what we called a washerwoman. She came on Monday, generally, and washed our clothes, came back on Tuesday and ironed the clothes with an iron heated on a coal furnace. They would be starched just as stiff.
Ruth Irwin, 83, Mississippi

We had to wash all our clothes on the board, we washed them, and we boiled them, because you couldn't have [really] hot water when you washed on the board. Then we rinsed them, and then we blued them, and starched them and hung them out on the line.
When did you get your first washing machine?
My boys was in high school in the late '30s.
So you rubbed on the board a *long* time.
Yes.
Minnie Ness, 81, North Dakota

Hand-Powered Washing Machines

My father later bought a washing machine. The gyrator was wooden pegs, and a wheel you turned round and round. This would make this gyrator go round and round, and switch the clothes somewhat.
Lora Torsey, 84, New Hampshire

I was quite fortunate. I had one of these hand-powered washers. The house wasn't very big, so it stood outside in the summertime, and I could stand out there and wash my clothes. I had to keep it full of water, or those wooden boards it was made of would fall apart and get leaky.
In the wintertime I had it in by the stove and pulled it. As the boys

got big enough, they had to help me with it. One had to do it five minutes, and the other had to do it five minutes, and they all watched the clock. But it helped some.

But I tell you, what was dirty, you still had to rub on the board. Shirt collars, and shirt sleeves and towels and so on.

Anna Sorensen, 83, North Dakota

We had one of those stompers. It would stomp the clothes up and down. It looked a whole lot like a bathroom plunger. It forced the water through the fabric.

Alice Guyer, 68, Indiana

I remember Mother had a washing machine, not like the ones we have today. It was a tub-like affair, oval, with a cradle-like affair made of slats to look like a washboard. With the aid of a handle, this cradle was rocked back and forth over the clothes in the lower part. It was a little easier than doing the rubbing by hand.

Ruth Snyder, 83, Indiana

I started out when we were first married, I was washing on the board, but when our baby was born, my husband said, "Well, you've got to have a washer."

There were a lot of different types of washers that you used by hand power, and they had different principles. The one we had, you pushed the stick handle back and forth, and it was much harder work than on the board. I never could do it. I just simply couldn't last more than one batch, so whenever I washed, my husband would stay out of the field and help me wash.

Sarah Ball, 74, Oklahoma

Wash Water

On wash day my older sister and I would have to get up while my mother was getting breakfast. We would have to carry water out to the big iron kettle and start a fire and put the water on for wash day.

We would have the fire going real good, and while we were eating breakfast the water would get hot, and we would do our washing.

Verona Lemmon, 65, Indiana

We didn't have running water, and we would go to the well and pump it and bring it in, put it in a copper boiler [on the stove], heat all the water, then dip it out into a pail and take it over to the washer.

Marjorie Whitney, 69, Illinois

My husband, when he went to the creamery, would bring home hot water from the creamery in the milk cans for me to do the washing with; I didn't have to heat the water.

Florence Reed, 64, Delaware

When I first started out in married life, I would have to heat water on the stove and carry it to the basement to a wringer-type washing machine.

Then my husband bought what they call a monkey stove. That was where you'd put in a little kindling and a little paper and make a little fire. It had a water tank attached to it, and it was just something marvelous. We thought it was almost a miracle.

Well, after that, we graduated to what they call the gas hot water heater. It was a spiral affair, and you'd have to go light that. Then you wanted to be sure you went and turned it off, or it would blow up. Then we got a heater similar to what we have today. But it has certainly improved.

Dorothy Tolley, 67, Arkansas

And they boiled all their clothes. Had a big boiler, filled it with rainwater and put all the white clothes in it and boiled them about twenty minutes. They were snow white when they came out.

Virgie Bowers, 81, Indiana

Sometimes a cake of [lye] soap was rubbed on an especially stubborn stain or extra dirty clothing. More of it was shaved in the hot wash water in the copper boiler.

The white clothes being boiled were occasionally stirred with a smooth stick to be sure all dirt was removed from the clothes. It took a steady hand to lift out the boiling hot white clothes from the boiler and to put them in the tub to be rinsed.

Lorene Shirk, 65, Indiana

Making Soap

My mother was a great hand to make soap. For a while they didn't have the lye that they bought in cans, so they had to make it out of ashes. They would have what they called an ash hopper. They would pour all the ashes that they took out of the wood stove in this big hopper. Then they'd pour water down through those ashes, and they'd have a trough down below and it would catch this lye water out of the ashes. Then she'd use that in her soap-making. She'd put grease in with that, and it would make soap. She was a great hand to make soap.

Opal Cypert, 68, Arkansas

Then later they got to where they used canned lye, and they could make the bar soap, cut it up and make bar soap out of it.

Vivian Jefferson, 95, Arkansas

I liked the soap made with a lot of lard in, better than using too much tallow. I'd get the lard clear, so that it didn't have any settlings in it.

It was heated to a certain degree and lye water added in it. Then it was stirred and stirred till it was getting thick, and then put into a form. I used a wood box with cloth inside. Then it was put in there to kind of age.

I got a recipe—I think it was from some Homemaker material—that told how to make toilet soap. That had quite a lot of borax in it, and that would even float. It was so nice and white, and it was not so strong, because there wasn't as much lye in it.

Margaret Lien, 68, North Dakota

In the grocery store you could get Ivory soap and that would be the only detergent [or soap] you could get. Now you have a hard time deciding which one you want to buy, there's so many of them. **I think detergents came in during the war [World War II], didn't they? The government, or somebody, discovered them.**

Thelma Barnes, 61, Florida

I still make homemade soap today. People give us fat and I renovate it, take the salt out, and then I make soap. I've got a big tub of soap now upstairs that I've made.

And I use it. I made a cotton bag with a zipper in it. I unzip the bag, put in a cake or two of soap, and put it in my washing every week. I've washed that way with that soap for many years.

Lora Torsey, 84, New Hampshire

Wringing Clothes

And you wrung them all by hand. That's what makes big arms and big muscles. I guess that's the reason my arms are so large. I wrung clothes by hand for years.

Beulah Grinstead, 68, Indiana

And I was still having to wring, which I thought was the hardest part of washing, was wringing out by hand. My wrists weren't all that strong. The first wringers, you had a little handle, and you'd put them through and turn the handle and wring them. It didn't get them really dry, but it was so much better than wringing them by hand.

Hanging out freshly-laundered clothes to dry on a rope line which would be taken down and rolled up until next wash day when the laundry is dry. Note the wooden clothespins in the homemaker's pocket.

By the way, those old hard wringers, they were wonderful for shelling peas. We used to have an immense garden, and shelling peas takes forever. Well, you could shell peas with those hard rollers, but that didn't work good with the later softer rollers, because they would smash them.

Sarah Ball, 74, Oklahoma

Do you recall anything humorous in your study group or Extension program?

Probably the most humorous one was the project where they taught us how to shell peas in our old wringer washing machines. We were supposed to put a sheet all around the wringer. And I just had the most awful mess, trying to put those peas through that wringer. There were peas all over the basement.

Alice Wand, 65, Oregon

That old wringer-type washer split so many sheets. Oh, you had to watch that thing, because if you didn't the sheet would be going both directions, and split before you could stop it.

Ima Fairly, 76, New Mexico

Gasoline Washers

I believe our son was about six months old when we got our first washing machine—a gasoline motor. It was something to own the first washing machine in that little community. A number of people come in to see it work—to see if it *would* work. Frankly, I hoped it would, and it did.

What a blessing for someone to have. Of course, we had no running water. That water still had to be warmed in the big old black wash pot outside and carried in in a bucket. But, oh, we was glad to do that. I got loose from that old washboard.

Jessie Halsell, 68, New Mexico

I had a washing machine. It was the first one to come to Grenada that had a gasoline motor on it. My husband bought it for me, and it was a lifesaver. And we put it out in the yard. We put some planks down and put it under the shade tree in the back yard and that's where we'd wash, out there. We had a sheet thing we'd put over it when we'd get through. I tell you, it was a lifesaver.

Orrie Little, 78, Mississippi

We were very modern with our washer, however. It was a Maytag with a gasoline motor. You kicked it until the motor started up, and then it would smoke so that the neighbors thought I was burning the house down.

Marjorie Whitney, 71, Illinois

Then, after a while, we finally got a washing machine that ran on a gasoline motor. Because we didn't have electricity in our area until about 1945. The only thing was, with that gasoline motor, I never was a mechanic, and it never would start for me.

I could kick at it till doomsday and it wouldn't start, and all I'd do was lose my temper. Then my husband would come in and put his foot on it one time and it would start right off.

Sarah Ball, 74, Oklahoma

Wringer Washers

You would pour your heated water into the washing machine and carry cold water for your rinse water. That was the two tubs that you set on a bench up next to your washing machine.

You had a routine. You put your whites in first and let them go through your washer and run them [through the wringer] in to your rinse water. Then you put your colored clothes that weren't soiled too badly in, and your overalls that were really dirty went in last. Can you imagine that, all in the same water? You didn't have fresh water every time, like they wash today.

Betty Alvey, 60, Indiana

We had a huge basement, and doing the laundry was like having a picnic. I had the old-fashioned wringer washer with the double rinsing tubs, and the basement was warm and cozy. The children would come down and play in the basement while Mother did the laundry and hung the laundry in the basement. So it was a real special time, doing the laundry.

Dorothy Tyrawski, 56, Delaware

We would put the water in the tubs to rinse the clothes and then we would put so many drops of blueing in it. Then we would stir it around and then put the clothes in it. It would settle, if you didn't stir it up good, and maybe get some blue [spots] on the clothes.

We used to make our own starch, too. We got lump starch and we would dissolve it in cold water, just like you would take flour and mix it up for gravy, now. And we would take and boil water and pour that over the starch and stir it until it was stiff enough.

Frances Harley, 89, Indiana

You starched the things, then dried them, and then sprinkled them down and then ironed them. It took an awful lot of energy.

Jane Morgan, 63, Mississippi

Drying Laundry

How did you dry your clothes?

Well, we hung them on the line, all our clothes.

How about in the wintertime?

In the wintertime, we had a room upstairs that they hung in; and we had lines in there. Sometimes take a whole week before they'd be dry.

Cora Lykken, 89, North Dakota

You were ashamed to hang a dingy wash on the line?

Oh, that was one of the things you could tell a good housekeeper. I heard my mother say if anyone was really inspecting washings, trying to find someone who didn't have a white wash, they would stand on the opposite side and look through the clothes toward the sunlight in the morning. If they weren't snow white, they wasn't a very good housekeeper.

Virgie Bowers, 81, Indiana

When it was wintertime and very cold, the clothes would freeze as we pinned them on the line.

Irene Clause, 66, Louisiana

Used to hang the long underwear on the line in wintertime and they'd just freeze stiff. They'd come in standin' up behind the stove to thaw out.

Edna Mattox, 71, Indiana

They would hang in the wind and rip and tear, particularly the sheets. My sheets, there were four holes all the way along, where I had pinned them to the clothesline. In the winter we would go and break loose the old frozen sheets, bring them in the house, and hang them over the furniture to finish drying.

Mary Raymond, 60, Wyoming

One of the things that I hated worst of all was hanging up the clothes, with the mosquitoes biting you. I used to hang clothes up at night even.

Zilphia Edwards, 63, Louisiana

One of the lessons—and it seems to me they have come full circle on this—they were stressing that every lady should have a clothes dryer. That hanging the clothes on a clothesline, they would get germs on them, and the sunshine wasn't as good for them as drying them in a clothes dryer.

Now, since they've had this energy conservation program, they're telling us to start hanging our clothes back out on the line. It's kind of been amusing to me, because for years I hung out clothes.

Defending myself, I love to hang out clothes, and I love to listen to the birds sing, and be out when the sun was coming up and it was such beautiful weather, and all that.

But now that I've gotten used to my clothes dryer, they're trying to convince me to start hanging my clothes back out. No way!

Ann Webb, 48, Arkansas

I'm a firm believer in that there are basic programs and they're always needed. Just like there's always going to be a need for first grade, and there's always going to be a need for a lesson on how to do your laundry. We all have laundry. There are new products on the market all the time. Even those who have been doing laundry for 20 years can certainly learn something, because of all the changes.

Carolyn Dame, 40, New Hampshire

Ironing

When my girls were at home, we ironed with the old black irons in front of a wood fire. They would build that fire of a morning in the summertime when they were going to iron. One of them would be going to build a fire before we ever got breakfast to get the irons hot.

One would really be ironing all day long, but they'd change off, the other one would take it later on. And we would be ironing a lot of times when the sun went down. We ironed all day long.

We had three boys. Back then the menfolks in the summertime wore white duck pants. And mine had to have two pair apiece, usually. If they went to anything during the week and wore a pair of those pants, then Sunday morning they had to have a second pair. And it took a long time to iron six pairs of duck pants.

Do you know why there were called sadirons?

No, I don't.

Well, I believe after I had been used all day, like you told, from sunup to sundown, they really were sad irons.

Letha McCall, 91, North Carolina

Ironing was an all-day affair. You had a little round furnace of coals that you heated the iron on, or you used the fireplace, or the wood stove to heat the irons. You had to keep the fire going, as well as do the ironing.

Jane Morgan, 63, Mississippi

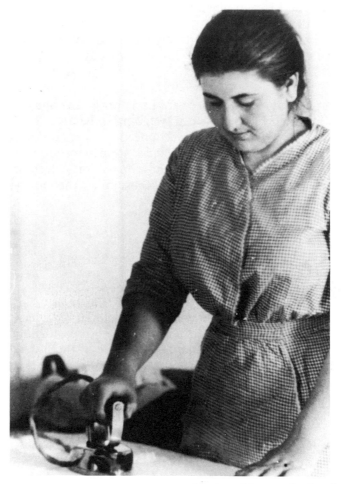

Ironing with an early electric iron. Although heavy, these irons made Tuesdays much more enjoyable. It was no longer necessary to maintain a fire in the stove on hot days to heat the irons, and the even heat did away with scorching and burning.

Before you fired up that stove, you cleaned it out. You had scrapers that you scraped out above and under the oven to get the soot out. You emptied the ash pan and carried it out to the chicken yard.

Then you split the wood and carried it in to [make the fire]. Then you heated your irons on top of the wood stove.

Dorothy Personette, 77, Oregon

We raised our own sweet potatoes and our own Irish potatoes, and when I'd be ironing, I'd have that old wood cookstove's oven full of sweet potatoes to bake. I tried to make use of both the oven and the upper part of the stove, too.

Vivian Jefferson, 95, Arkansas

Black iron on a wooden ironing board. Such irons were heated on a wood or coal burning range and then used until they cooled; then they were reheated. Two to three irons were kept heating to insure a hot iron at all times. Care had to be taken that the irons were not overheated, as they could easily scorch the materials being ironed.

We usually ironed out in the yard through the summer months.

Orrie Little, 78, Mississippi

We thought then that everything had to be ironed. I even ironed the dish towels and the baby's diapers. Everything was ironed. I don't know why I didn't have sense enough to use them without it, but I didn't.

Vivian Jefferson, 95, Arkansas

Where did you find the time, with ten children, to do all this work?

One reason is, that is where my husband came in. I would help him in the field all day long, and then we'd come in at night and we'd get supper, put the babies to bed—a lot of times he gave the children their baths and put on their little pajamas and put them to bed, while I was doing something he couldn't do, and that's how I got a lot of it done, because of his help.

I remember, a lot of times we washed; that's before we had a washing machine—had to scrub it on a board in a tin tub. Well, we would wash the clothes and get them in the rinse water and leave them overnight. Then the next morning before I went to the field to help him, I'd get them out of the rinse and hang them out to dry. Then that evening, when we came in, I'd gather the clothes off the line.

I always ironed; I had to iron everything. I ironed even the children's little everyday shirts and things they were going to just put on and go right back in the dirt to play. I just could not put them on without them being ironed. And I ironed the pillowcases; pressed the hems of the sheets.

And he never would go to bed and leave me up ironing—I always did my ironing at night. I'd lay out, as I ironed, anything that had a little rip in it, or a button off, or a loop gone—I'd lay it out to itself, so maybe when the next night come, I'd do my mending. And he'd say, "Tell me where to get a button and a needle and thread, and I'll sew that button." And he would sew the button on while he was staying up with me.

So that's how I got a lot of it done, because he was right there helping me every minute.

Letha McCall, 91, North Carolina

I had grandparents that lived up in Kula, so whenever they needed help, my father would take me up to Kula. I used to even do the laundry up there as a real young girl. I would do the laundry and we would starch it with homemade starch and I would go way back where they had acreage and hang the laundry there. Then I had to iron all these clothes with a charcoal iron. Everything was starched. So you were going along beautifully with a charcoal iron, and when you're just about finished, the ashes come out and it gets stuck on the article, and you had to go outside and wash it again, and start all over again.

Julia Souza, 62, Hawaii

When I was a young girl and helped with the ironing, we used the old type of sadirons that the whole thing was metal, the iron and the handle built onto it. You set this on the stove to heat. In the winter, the heat felt pretty good, but in the summer, unless you got up early and did it early in the morning, you suffocated, having to have the fire so hot.

And then those irons! You would wrap a cloth around the handle to take it off the stove, so that you could bear to hold the handle, but that made not much space between the handle and the back of your hand, feeling the heat from the iron itself.

By the time I was married, most everybody had graduated to the type of sadiron that had a removable handle, a wooden handle, and

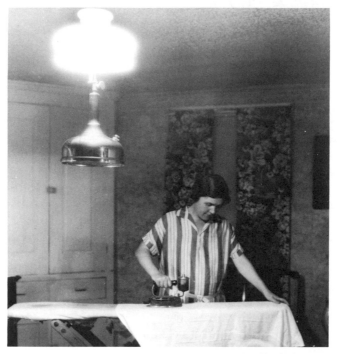

Homemaker ironing with a gasoline iron, by the light of a gasoline lamp. Gasoline irons gave a steady heat, but many women were afraid of their tendency to explode.

that was a great thing. Of course, every once in a while, when you were carrying that iron from the stove to your ironing board, it might come loose and fall to the floor, which was disastrous, but you didn't burn your hand at least.

Sarah Ball, 74, Oklahoma

After a while, they got gas irons, which I was always afraid of. My husband would always fill them, and then he'd light it and then I'd iron for dear life for a couple of hours before it went dry again, because it would only hold about a cup of gas. We thought it was quite an invention, though. You had a hot iron all the while.

Anna Sorensen, 83, North Dakota

And the first electric irons were still pretty heavy. You thought you had to have a heavy iron and use pressure, but we really had to learn that it was just the heat that took the wrinkles out.

And now, I hardly ever iron.

Sarah Ball, 74, Oklahoma

Dry Cleaning

We organized our club in May, 1931. They decided to have the next meeting in June and the County agent came with gasoline, soap and other ingredients to put on a demonstration on the how and the wherefore of cleaning clothes.

She cleaned the clothes, and being a sunshiny day, they put the clothes on the line, the fences, and all over. The breezes and the sunshine freshed and dried the clothes.

There weren't any gasoline smells left in the clothes? No danger of flames?

We used it outside, and I think that the gasoline must have been different than it is now, because we used to clean with gas and the clothes were fresh when they were hung out and aired. Nowadays, with our man-made fabrics, it isn't necessary.

I don't think they even make a cleaning gas anymore. It's been prohibited on the shelves of the stores.

Marie Carlile, 67, Montana

Do you recall any humorous incidents?

I sure do. We had a lesson on how to clean felt hats. Now you show me a rancher who doesn't wear a felt hat, and he's obviously from the city or the South—one of the two. Anyhow, we went to Mrs. Sunn's, and her husband, he had this most *disreputable* old hat. He was back in his office working and Mrs. Sunn brought his hat [out] to the Extension Home Economist who was there. She [agent] was describing how to clean hats. Mrs. Sunn said, "If you can clean this hat, I'll believe you are telling the truth."

So the agent picked up Mr. Sunn's hat and she was very busily showing how—we used cornmeal and a brush. It was working. It really was working. I mean this old felt hat—it was horrible—greasy and cruddy.

She had about half of it really clean and Mr. Sunn came to the door and yelled, "Where is my hat?" He saw the agent with the hat half-cleaned, and he came over and he said, "I'll thank you not to ruin my good hat." Took it out of her hand, plopped it on his head, and walked right out of the door—with that half-cleaned hat.

Mary Raymond, 60, Wyoming

We do have many more electrical conveniences in our homes now. How do you feel about these?

I'm pretty grateful! (joyfully). I think it's pretty fine when I can wash and dry right here in the house. I think modern washing facilities are just wonderful. I thought the electric iron and the washing machine were godsends. Sometimes I accept these things without even thinking how grateful we are. But I'm grateful, I really am grateful.

Catherine Wycoff, 90, Illinois

I just don't know; young women tell me how busy they are nowadays and how their housework takes forever, and I just can't see how, when they have so little to do, compared with what we used to do. No ironing, and just throw your things in the washer and they are washed and dried and ready to put away. It's just wonderful.

Sarah Ball, 74, Oklahoma

ELECTRICITY

Describe how it was with no electricity. How did you see at night?

Oil lamps, kerosene lamps. We had to clean the chimneys every now and then and be sure the lamp was full of kerosene.

How many stoves did you have to keep warm by?

One heater in the living room, and in the evening we left the door open to the upstairs to let the heat go from the living room upstairs. And we had a coal and wood-burning stove in the kitchen which heated it.

It kept you very warm in the winter if you were in the kitchen eating, but how about summer?

Well, they finally got to the place where they bought a kerosene cookstove, with an oven that set on top of it, and that didn't heat the kitchen up too bad.

How did you keep things cold?

Springhouse, about a hundred yards from the house.

So when you wanted milk . . .

That's where you kept it. And the butter was there, and you brought the water in from there.

Frances Caldwell, 57, West Virginia

When we were first married in 1932, we had no electricity, other than we had a light plant that had batteries and a wind charger that charged the batteries, and that was our electricity for the home.

We couldn't have any appliances of any kind, because it was only a 32 volt plant.

Mary Moore, 73, New Mexico

We had a 32 volt system, but all we could hook up to that was the iron. That was wind power. Then we had half the basement full of batteries.

Minnie Ness, 81, North Dakota

We had a Delco plant in the old house. That was a plant that had large batteries, and it had an engine that was run with gasoline and the motor charged those batteries—about twelve big batteries.

That furnished lights for the house. If you were going to have company, or have lights on all over the house, you had to run the motor at the same time, or it would pull the batteries down. But it was handier than it was before.

Agnes Emenhiser, 90, Indiana

We had our own electric plant. We put up a windmill tower. We had a neighbor and his wife come over and help us raise that tower, so we could put the wind charger up on top of it. We had 16 batteries in the basement that kept the power when the wind wasn't blowing.

So when the électricity came right up to our line fence (we were right at the city limits) we tried and tried to get our city to put a power line down to our house.

Finally they said, if you will dig the holes and set the poles, we will string the line. So my husband and I dug a mile-long stretch of holes and set the poles, and then we were hooked up to city electricity finally.

How did you go about getting these holes dug?

We had a post-hole digger and we used manpower. Art would dig one hole and I would dig the next. While he was setting the pole, I'd dig another hole.

Evie Foster, 70, Alaska

When we got electricity, that was a big step. I guess I got my stove right away, but didn't get my refrigerator. To get the electricity put in, every family had to sign up for so many appliances. So we just got what we had to have in order to get the electricity. We were so proud of TVA [Tennessee Valley Authority].

Tressa Waters, 85, Tennessee

Down at Lexington, I had everything [appliances] because we had electricity. I had a washing machine, an iron, and we had a radio.

Then when you came up here, there was no electricity in your farm?

(laughs) No electricity! Eighteen months we were without it. In November, 1937, it came through here.

What was the first thing you got when you got electricity?

I didn't get much, because I had it. I brought it from Lexington. I had lamps, I had a radio, I had my iron. I had the washing machine. I used to kick that every time I went by it, before I had electricity.

Because you regretted not being able to use it?

Yes! (laughs)

Helen Merrill, 76, New Hampshire

Lighting

Back in my childhood, we had kerosene lamps that we read by and studied by. You had to keep the chimney clean, and you had to fill up the lamps to see that they were full. That took time.

Jane Morgan, 63, Mississippi

I did my canning at night. I'd have my kerosene lamp setting up on the range top. It was all I had. I don't know how many flies we canned, because we couldn't see.

Florence LaGrange, 79, Indiana

Before we would go to school, we all had jobs to do. We used oil lamps, and we would have to clean up the kitchen and see that all of those oil lamps were cared for. We had to fill them with oil, wash the chimneys, and we made lamp lighters.

What is that?

Cut strips of paper and wind them and then you could light that in your fire, so you didn't use any matches.

Audrey Blackburn, 86, Indiana

Reading and writing by a kerosene lamp.
J. C. Allen Collection

When we first moved out here, we didn't have electricity. This town was as dark as pitch. You never will know how dark a town can be without electricity.

Mary Jonas, 81, Ohio

We had the old coal oil lamps. I remember that I decided I was going to have enough light in my kitchen. So I fixed me little brackets, and I had me four lamps in that kitchen—one by the stove, one over the sink, one by the table and one over by my cooking.

Then when we got an Aladdin lamp, that was wonderful. The only trouble was, if you didn't watch, the flame would creep up and the next thing you knew, the house would be full of soot.

Or if you jiggled that mantle just a little bit too much it broke and . . .

Oh, yes, and if you didn't replace it, why the flames spurting out of it would break the chimney.

Dorothy Personette, 77, Oregon

Finally they brought natural gas for lighting and cooking, but still we never had electricity.

Gas lights in a chandelier?

Yes, and they had those mantles that after they burned were just so delicate. I mean, if you just even looked at it sometimes, they would fall apart.

Cecila Lamb, 87, Michigan

Describe your typical daily routine as a homemaker.

(sighs) It was quite different to what it is now. You didn't have an electric button to push, and things come on. We had to get up and start a fire in the fireplace and make a fire in the stove, too, to cook your meals.

Bertha Andrews, 89, Alabama

I had a little wood cookstove, a little bitty thing. I bet it wasn't a yard square, hardly, and that was room for the wood and everything else. I couldn't even put a whole muffin pan in there. It was too big, and the [oven] door wouldn't close, so Roy had to cut it in two for me.

Virginia McIntyre, 63, Louisiana

I really enjoyed cooking on a wood stove. There's something cozy about a wood stove, and I never minded it at all. I had a modern range that baked beautifully. It was cozy in the kitchen. Even after we left there [rented farm] and bought this place, I moved my wood stove with me. I finally bought my first electric stove in 1951. I hated to part with my wood stove, but I didn't have room in the kitchen. If I had a big kitchen now, I would still want a wood stove.

Elizabeth McAdams, 69, Alabama

The first stove I had when I got married was a coal or kerosene [stove], and it was a cream and green [color]. It had four surface burners and an oven and broiler on the side.

I thought that was the most beautiful thing that I've ever owned. After supper, I'd get the dishes washed, and I would get some clean dishwater, and I would wash that stove and take another cloth and polish it.

My mother-in-law, she said, "Honey, if I were you, I wouldn't even cook on that stove."

Dorothy Tolley, 67, Arkansas

A Globe wood-burning kitchen range has lots of nickel to polish and a reservoir on the right side where water from the outside iron pump will be poured to become warm from the heat of the fire.
J. C. Allen Collection

My range was tan—I was very modern. It was a two-tone tan which I was later able to match, and painted the kitchen woodwork to match it.

I thought it was beautiful, but I never thought the stove and myself were compatible. If I wanted it hot, it just sort of simmered along and didn't get hot enough. If I wanted it just medium, it would just get red hot. I never really mastered the big old range. Many people loved them and used them a long time.

Marjorie Whitney, 69, Illinois

And what did you use for kindling then? This is a treeless prairie.

We could get ties, when the railroad put in new ties, lots of times you could get permission and go take those ties.

And in early years, lots of times we'd run out of coal and we didn't have kindling—they'd use cow chips. We kids would be sent out in the pasture to get cow chips. And sometimes they were a little bit under-done and soft, and you'd tip them over with a stick and let them lay and dry for one more day.

A combination wood-electric stove. The electric burners were used in the summer, but in the winter the wood/coal section would be used to generate heat in the kitchen.

One old lady that lived in the neighborhood, she'd take them home and set them on a slant up against the house, with the raw side toward the sun, and they'd bake through pretty quick.

If they were really good and dry through and through, they made a roaring fire.

But it's a lot easier to push a button on an electric stove.

Anna Sorensen, 83, North Dakota

This was a treeless prairie in the early homestead days. What did they use for fuel?

Coal. We used buffalo chips for quick-starting fire. That burns just like wood. So we'd go out and pick buffalo chips in little wagons and haul it to the house.

Minnie Ness, 81, North Dakota

We went out into the ranch pastures near the windmill water places for the stock and picked up dried cow chips. It got to be quite a sport to see how far you could throw a dried cow chip. There is a saying, "Out in the West, the wind draws the water, and the cows cut the wood."

Billie Jones, 72, Louisiana

We mentioned REA coming. How has that changed your homemaking?

Oh, that really changed it, because then we got electric stove, electric refrigerator, electric iron and electric lights. It was just wonderful.

What did you enjoy most?

The electric stove. Push that button and there you had heat. Didn't have to chop wood or carry coal to get some heat to cook on.

Anna Sorensen, 83, North Dakota

We, the Home Demonstration Agent and I, took around demonstrations to different clubs about electricity. We took a candle and gave them the measurements of how much light you'd get from a candle and then how much you'd get from an electric light bulb.

Mara Meyer, 84, Indiana

And one lesson from Extension was on the use of electricity. So many people thought we couldn't afford it, and the lesson was "We Can't Afford *Not* to Use Electricity."

Elsie Canary, 78, Indiana

Can you describe the impact of electricity?

To me, Heaven arrived the day we got it. I remember hearing Roosevelt on the radio making a speech, and he said, "We are going to have electricity on every farm in the United States." I could not imagine that man had any idea of what he was talking about.

Edith Gladden, 63, Missouri

What impact did electricity have on your homemaking?

It's made a *wonderful* impact. I wouldn't want to go back to the old days and the old ways for anything. Some folks sing about "Praise the old days." Well, the old days was alright as long as you didn't know something better, but since you've had these things you don't want to go back.

I think electricity is wonderful. It's like so many servants in the house. It amounts to that much; it saves that much time and labor. I think it's wonderful we have electricity.

Bertha Andrews, 89, Alabama

REFRIGERATION

My mother, I can remember, she kept milk and butter and stuff like that in what we called our parlor, 'cause we kept it shut off in the wintertime, and it was like an icebox in there.

The cooked foods she usually just made up enough that we could eat it up.

Hope Kessler, 86, Indiana

When we were first married, we had a spring for water, and there was a building over this spring which kept it fairly cool. You'd run cold water into a tub and set your milk in it.

Isabel Schoeff, 81, Indiana

How did you keep your cream and milk cool?

We kept it in the basement a lot, and sometimes we'd put it in tubs of cold water. There was a time we put up ice, too, and we'd take ice chunks and put in the tub of water and set our milk and cream in it.

Minnie Ness, 81, North Dakota

If it was a hot summer day, we had to run down in the basement, if we'd had dinner with butter, if there was extra butter left, we had to run down in the cellar with that every day, because it would melt on us.

Cora Lykken, 89, North Dakota

Where did you keep your milk?

We kept our milk in the well. It was a nice big well, and the water would be so cold. We had a big extra bucket, and we'd set the milk and the butter in this bucket and swing it down in the well.

Then we'd take turns—who had to go get the milk out of the well. It wasn't such a fun trip, because we had been taught that we was to draw this out of the well and not spill it. Not let it turn over and spill, because if we had that would have ruined the well. Back in those days several families used water out of the same well where the milk was hung. So we'd be very careful.

When we'd get that milk out of the well, it was so cold sometimes that the children had to wait just a little while to let their milk warm up. But that was due to us not being used to anything that was cold.

Opal Cypert, 68, Arkansas

Cooling with water in a springhouse. The partially submerged covered crocks probably contained milk, butter and leftover food.
J. C. Allen Collection

We even dug a hole out in the ground and put sawdust in it, with a block of ice, that was our refrigerator. When the club women got together and talked about these things, it helped everyone.

Jane Morgan, 63, Mississippi

We had what you call the iceless refrigerator at that time, too. I didn't help build one, but there were a lot of people in the community that had them. They'd put water in the top, and they had a drape thing down over them and this water would be seeping down on this drape, and I guess that's what kept it cool. It had shelves in there. I just really didn't know how they made those things. Where we lived, we had a spring and we put our milk and stuff in that.

Orrie Little, 78, Mississippi

Cooling with ice. This large oak icebox contains ice in the upper lefthand corner and food in the other sections. Note the pan beneath to catch water as the ice melts.

We had a windmill and we had a cooler, we called it—a box where the water ran through from the well. It ran on through this box to keep our milk and our things so we could use them.

Ruth James, 78, New Mexico

Father dammed up a spring and it made quite a pond. Then up on the south bank, they dug back in and made a cave. In the wintertime they would saw that ice when it was froze good and thick. Then they'd just pull it up the hill—we had one horse that was dependable—into that icehouse. They'd put in a layer of ice, and a layer of straw. Then they'd put in another layer, and filled it clear full. There was enough ice there [that] it would keep until the latter part of the summer. The neighbors used some of it. We made gallons of ice cream.

Sophie Bigge, 82, Kansas

We had an old icebox that was made. Wood, lined with tin. Bought ice by the block, wrapped it up in newspaper, and then wrapped it up in a burlap sack. Tow sack, we called it then. Weren't allowed to touch that ice, because my grandmother didn't allow you to chip off of it.

Julia White, 60, Tennessee

There were a few families that had what we called an icebox. And they'd put ice up in the top of the fridge in the kind of place where it kept from thawing out very fast. And then, what water come off from there, that'd drip into a pan down under the icebox. They had to empty it every so often, and if they forgot, it would run all over the floor. They were pretty nice, because in there you could keep your milk and cream—not as cold as we keep in the fridge nowadays, but it was kept pretty cool there.

Do you know where they got their ice?
They'd cut it in the wintertime out of the big slough with a kind of saw—an ice saw, they called it. They'd saw it into chunks and then they put it in—they had a building down there, near the slough where they put it in and added sawdust that was packed around it. And that kind of insulated it, so it didn't thaw out very fast. They'd keep it for quite a bit in the summer.

Anna Sorensen, 83, North Dakota

We had an ice refrigerator, with ice that the iceman left at our place. He had to come down with a pair of tongs and a cake of ice and put it in the refrigerator. Then we had to empty the pan from underneath it, you know, in order to keep it from running all over the place.

But it was a good way, and it helped our food stay fresh.

Cecelia Lamb, 87, Michigan

Our first refrigerator was a kerosene refrigerator. We were proud to have such a new thing in our home, because it was something.

We did our best to take care of it. Our Home Agent, she stressed taking good care of our refrigerators. Then when we got our electric refrigerator, it was hard to replace at that time. That was in 1943, so we were very conservative about our things.

Aileen Cole, 78, Tennessee

What would you hate to give up the most, comparing the things you have now with the things you started housekeeping with years ago?

If I had to do without, I believe my refrigerator. Because I could dab around to wash my clothes, and I could have candlelight or coal oil lights, and if necessary I could take a broom and sweep.

But I couldn't fix cold things, or keep things, and I would miss cool things.

Vernell Saltzman, 81, Indiana

A battery telephone connects the farm house with the outside world.
J. C. Allen Collection

TELEPHONE

I remember when we first got telephones up in that country. That was an exciting time. They organized a telephone company and started building a line out from Sutherland very early, before the first World War. But they kept running out of money. My dad had subscribed to

it, and we were supposed to get a telephone, too, because we had paid
in as much as the others. But they ran out of money before they got
the line built that far.

Then the first World War came on, and you couldn't do anything
like that during the war. Then they finally got more money and the line
finally came on over to our place.

And it was such a great help. Almost everybody up there had
phones. It was just wonderful to be able to talk to your neighbors. But
I remember my father—when he first talked to Mr. Harris, who lived
two and a half miles from us, he talked pretty loud to him. But when
he talked to Mr. Trigow, who lived six miles from us, he really yelled.
Dad never got over that. He always felt that he had to raise his voice
according to the distance away that people lived.

Those were the days when we were all on the same line. Each person
had a certain ring—two longs and a short, or three shorts, and you
answered your own ring. Of course, you listened in on all the rest [of
the rings], too (laughs).

**Was it like it was at home—five longs was an emergency—everybody
get on the line?**

I believe it was one long, long ring—was the emergency. When the
phone rang longer than an ordinary long, and kept on ringing, then
you all ran to the phone. That was our emergency call. Every line had
its own, and everybody rushed to the phone when that happened.

Nellie Yost, 76, Nebraska

Did you have telephones?

Yes, we did have telephones. There was just one main line. The men
of the neighborhood put the telephone line up, and they kept it in
repair. It was run by two batteries, and everybody was on the same
line. Of course, that wasn't too many people, because it was not settled
very thickly.

Everybody heard everybody's else's ring. When you'd get a ring, why
everybody would take the receiver down and they'd listen. They was
welcomed in on the conversation then, if they wanted to.

Well, I remember that telephone had batteries. My mother would be
talking to someone, and they'd sound like they was far away. She'd tell
us, she'd say, "Go get a cup of water and take out to the outside of the
house and pour down on the ground rod where it was grounded." And
my—they'd just begin coming in as plain.

Our ring was two longs and a short. You had to remember all those
rings to get anybody. We didn't have a telephone directory—we just
had to remember. Some was three shorts, and some was five longs, and
just different things like that. If you wanted to call somebody, and

you'd forgotten what theirs was, then you'd call somebody that you knew knew their ring, and they'd tell you. Then you'd just call them right then, before you forgot it.

Opal Cypert, 68, Arkansas

My father did the work. There were five men in the community that put the money together and built the telephone line and my father kept it up. I don't know what they paid to have what they called Exchange, where they connected uptown. Otherwise you rang yourself. Exchange didn't have a thing to do with it. But they paid so much a month to the central office in Vicksburg to be connected to them.

Everybody had a ring. One thing that shouldn't have happened was that everybody listened in when everybody else rang, because everybody's phone rang. If one rang, everybody else's rang, too. And you could hear receivers go up and everybody was listening to what you had to say.

You had to be careful what you said.

If you weren't, they'd call you down. I know I was called down one day. We were talking about a ballgame and how it had gone off, and someone said, "That wasn't the way it was."

They gave themselves away, didn't they? But at least you knew somebody was listening, so you were careful what you said.

Ruth Irwin, 83, Mississippi

My first telephone—let's see—it was in 1942, and it was a crank-type wall phone. Whenever your phone rang, well, your ten neighbors would pick up the phone, too.

It was really a party line. A lot of times when you were in a conversation, somebody would come on the line and say, "Is that you, Mabel? Do you know your cows are out?" Or, "Are you going to be home?" or something like that. Pretty soon you'd have three parties on the line and sometimes four.

Edna Dagnen, 67, Washington

Rural telephones came along. Now, honey, that was something. We had to get a $5 deposit to get the telephone lines in. You had to put up $5.

And I just told them what was what. I said, "You're here, and you're old, and you may need a doctor, and you got nobody." And I said, "The time's come that we actually need telephones."

Anyway, I had only one man refuse to put up his deposit, but when he saw everybody else was doing it, then he went in and did it.

Eunice Cameron, 80, Florida

When I moved to Eagle Nest back in 1948, there were no telephones. And then, when we finally received telephones—which was in the early '50s—it was a pay phone. You paid even if you called someone in Eagle Nest. It cost you 12¢. There were only seven phones to begin with in town; that was a privately owned line. But now Mountain Bell has telephones up there, and there's telephones all over the valley.

I'm curious about this paying for each call. Did the operator mark it down, and then send you a bill for 12¢ for each call?

It came in on our bill just like our long distance calls do now. I guess you couldn't call them direct yourself. You had to call the operator and have her call. And if it was someone on your line, you had to

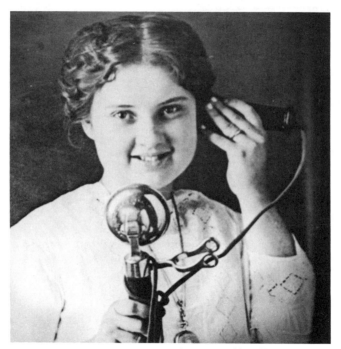

A young wife talks on a newer version of the battery telephone.

hang up while she rang the other person, and then you both picked up your receivers and you were talking.

Jalie Martin, New Mexico

I remember as a child in Kansas when we had a telephone put in, my father was running a store and when my father called home, my little brother James was put up to the phone. He didn't believe it was his father talking to him. That was very exciting.

Later we had a phone that sat on a desk, and that was quite a revelation.

When I came home from the ACWW meeting in Dublin, I stopped in Chicago to call my son and I picked up a new-fangled phone where you had to *punch* the numbers.

Eva Gill, 80, Nebraska

Did you have telephones on the Mesa when you lived up there?

Years ago they did have a system that was connected to the Bell system, but they lost it. And during my time there was no telephone. But we are getting a telephone in now, and it will be in before spring. It's coming up from Des Moines and across the country over there.

You think everybody on Johnson Mesa will have it?

You would be surprised. People that don't live there except maybe two weeks in the summer ask for it. It's a grand move for us. It will cost like $9 a month, it'll be a little over $100.

You can't make many trips to town for that. The telephone is one thing I always missed in moving back to the canyon in the summer. So I'm glad.

Nona Berry, 81, New Mexico

Does a telephone make a difference?

Oh, absolutely. I talk to my children every weekend or so, and it's nothing that you can't write, but you hear (their) voices and visit with them. It's cheap travel. My long distance bills are high, but it's still cheap travel.

Frankie Carruthers, 76, New Mexico

The telephone is great. It's a way to visit; it's a way to take care of business calls; it's a way for me to talk to my mother every week, and that I enjoy. It saves time; it saves money; it's a convenience. I guess (it's) a joy, too.

Jessie Halsell, 68, New Mexico

WATER

I think one of the most encouraging women I ever knew was my mother-in-law. She lived on this ranch before us, and she used to say, "You've got it so much better than I had it."

There I was, washing on the board, and pumping my own water, and wading around milking the cows.

But she told me that when they homesteaded there, they didn't have this 50-foot well. She and her daughters would go over to a spring and dip water out of the spring. They carried the water in a barrel on an old stoneboat, and they would bring the water back on that. She said, in the wintertime, the water that slopped on their skirts would freeze, and she said by the time they would get home, their skirts would just tinkle with the ice that was hanging on it.

Pumping water on a snowy 1930s morning.
J. C. Allen Collection

So, womanlike, there came a time when she had got enough of it. The well had been started when they bought this piece of land. And she said, "Next summer, the first thing we do is we finish that well." So they finished the well. And here I was complaining about having to pump water.

Yes, every generation has it a little better.

Dorothy Personette, 77, Oregon

I'm sure you didn't have running water.

No. I used to get aggravated, because they always called on me to draw a bucket of water. I was the youngest, and they thought every time they had to have water. We just had well water.

The water was heated right in the stove, on the big wood range. Reservoir, they called it.

Elba Johnston, 79, Oklahoma

In the dry years, we had a time with water, because the wells all went dry. We went from one neighbor to another to get water, because the water we had at home was so hard that you couldn't use it for anything but the cattle. It was an awful job to haul that water.

Minnie Ness, 81, North Dakota

[In the Dirty Thirties] the one thing that kind of plagued us was having water. That was a problem throughout the county. There were creeks, the river on the south and a large creek to the north. But the underground flow was not sheet water. It was in veins. So, to have a good well they had to hit a vein. They didn't always. They had places perforated with holes, and didn't get any water.

But anyway, almost every place had cisterns. They had eave troughs to catch the water. And we had windmills.

Sophie Bigge, 82, Kansas

We hauled our water from a slough, or else from a well. From the well, that was hard water. So when we'd bring that up in a barrel [to use for washing], then it was to put lye in—dissolve lye in hot water and put in there and let it stand until it "broke." Then there was always a white scum, or white settling, at the bottom. But the slough water we didn't do that with. We'd just bring that up and heat it.

Margaret Lien, 68, North Dakota

Our water was very hard. All west and south of Yukon [local town], the water was very "gyppy." We could break it to wash by putting lots of lye in. This hard water, if you didn't get all of that wash water out, it just plain curdled and you talk about tattle-tale gray! With hard water, you'd just have little teeny-tiny curds of that gray stuff that formed in your rinse water, if you didn't break your rinse water very well, and it was something you really hated, was water to look gray.

Sarah Ball, 74, Oklahoma

Water supply was a large problem in our part of the county. Almost everyone hauled water in barrels and tanks from the canal for domestic use.

Mrs. J. E. Kunkel, Idaho

Water and Plumbing

In the early years, homemaking meant carrying buckets of water from the pump out of doors. And, of course, there was the well-worn path in the backyard.

Lillian Eckert, 70, Alaska

A pitcher pump brings water inside the house in a newly-remodeled farm kitchen.

We carried water from a spring about a half a mile away. Carried it in a pail. We also used that, the spring, as our refrigerator. Kept butter and things like that.

You took your Saturday night bath in a tub. It was a good thing if you wasn't the fourth or fifth one down in the family, because you might have had to take the same water.

You weren't going to change water, when you had to carry it a half mile, were you?

Josephine Nixon, 90, Wisconsin

My mother was a very clean housekeeper—we could eat off of the floor of our dining and kitchen area. She'd say, now, if the kitchen and the bathroom areas were clean, everyone would say you were a good housekeeper.

In those old days we had hot bathtubs that were made out of wood and it was a chore to burn the fire underneath it. It was quite a chore to keep it hot. We had the old Japanese tub, which meant that you did not bathe in the tub with soap and water—you did the washing outside and then rinsed, and *then* you got into the tub and soaked.

Now that is an ongoing thing, with these sauna baths and Jacuzzis, and here in those days I used to think "Yuuk, I have to build the fire under the bathtub again." I wish I had one of those now.

Misaye Uno, 65, Colorado

The Fuller brush man came around, and he had a bucket with a hose attached and a brush on the end. I could [use this] and stand in the washtub and take a shower, which was really something special to me.

Vi Cottrell, 69, Washington

And I was going to tell you about—we didn't have indoor toilets like we have now, flush toilets. I'll tell you what we did have. We had a good old kind of a porcelain chamber they called it. We called it a pot. And we had it under the bed with a big heavy cover on it. And that was all the toilet—indoor or outdoor—there was.

Mother used to have to get outside with it several times and empty it way out behind someplace. And one time she got so embarrassed, she came out with this thing, and she met one of the neighbors right in the door. So from then on, she had an old piece of cloth she threw over it when she went out the door, because she didn't want to be embarrassed again.

And, in 1904, when my dad built the barn, he finally had enough pieces left over so that they could make an outhouse. And were we happy. We were so proud of that outhouse. One big hole and one little hole, and did we enjoy it!

What did you use for paper?

We were lucky if we had a good Sears, Roebuck catalog. And if we had a Sears and a Montgomery, we always took the Sears, 'cause the Montgomery was so stiff and scratchy.

Anna Sorensen, 83, North Dakota

We had to use the lantern [to go to] the outhouse, because we didn't have no flashlights. Then we used catalogs for toilet tissue, and we'd

save apple wrappings [paper used to wrap boughten apples] and whatever peach wrappings we had for our company to use.

Minnie Ness, 81, North Dakota

During that time in the early days, when nobody had running water
at all, and everybody had the path rather than the bath, the govern-

Taking a Saturday night bath in a
galvanized wash tub beside a cheery
baseburner heating stove.

ment came out with a program and made cement toilets. Most of all
the farm families did apply to get one. It was a much more sanitary
way of taking care of that type of thing than what most people had.

Sarah Ball, 74, Oklahoma

I guess when we got a bathroom and water in the house was the biggest convenience that we thought we had had in many years.

Margie Brookshire, 60, Kentucky

THE HOMEMAKER AND HER ORGANIZATION

"I think my whole life has been based on being an Extension Homemaker. There's not a day passes that I don't use something that I have learned through being an Extension Homemaker, and I don't think a day passes that I don't live better by being an Extension Homemaker. I have used my Homemaker skills in everything I've ever done."
Jane Morgan, Mississippi

The women who have
belonged to Extension Homemaker clubs over the years have
strong loyalties and long memories.

They remember when the Extension Service perceived the
need for education in the field of homemaking. They remember
how they welcomed the opportunity to belong to groups of
women who, like themselves, were seeking information which
would be useful to them in their daily life.

They remember with affection the dedicated Extension
Agents who brought them this information.

They remember how they enjoyed the friendly warmth of
the Extension Homemaker clubs they joined and how much
these clubs meant to their social life.

They remember, sometimes with laughter, some of the lessons and demonstrations of these early clubs.

But, most of all, they remember and appreciate the tremendous impact all these factors have had on their lives.

THE ORGANIZATION

Predecessors

I remember the Tomato Club. You planted a plot of tomatoes and there was a prize given for the girl that canned the most tomatoes out of their plot. That was when I was ten years old.

The agent came to our house; they had the canners. You canned the tomatoes in cans. Well, anyway, you waited till you had a lot of ripe ones—you had a washpot—and they put the tomatoes in a bag, and put them in this boiling water and scalded them. We helped peel them and we helped pack them in the cans. Then they [agent] sealed them, and you put them in the cooker and cooked them. Then you took them out and you put them in this other tub of water to see if they were sealed good.

The air spewed out if they weren't?

Yes, the air spewed out. You took that one out and soldered it over, and put it back.

Did you have 4-H later? I wonder if that Tomato Club wasn't sort of a forerunner of that? Sounds like they were trying to get the youth interested.

Eunice Cameron, 80, Florida

Tell us about your 4-H work.

We only was allowed to take one phase of work, and mine was a tomato crop. I was allowed to plant one acre of tomatoes, which we did.

A child planted one acre?

Well, my father helped. So when it came time to harvest them, why we bought a canner. It was different than today's because it was an outdoor canner, under a tree—a big tin box—and it had a firebox under it that heated your water. We bought tin cans and canned our tomatoes. Then you had to leave a little hole in the top of the can, and then you had a sealer that you used to seal them.

Then our Daddy bought labels with my name on them, and I sold them in the stores there in Rush Springs.

For this project, I won a trip to Washington, D.C., which I didn't get to take, because I had a ruptured appendix when I was supposed to go.

This is fantastic. I never heard of an outdoor canner. How did you process the tomatoes?

There was a big zinc or tin tub that set over this fire, and the fire was underneath. The water boiled, and they were processed by the boiling water.

Did you make a profit on your acre of tomatoes?

Oh, yes, that's one of the things that helped win the trip—was the amount of money that we were able to make off of this one acre of tomatoes.

I'm so sorry you did not get to go to Washington and meet President Wilson.

Zelma Wood, 77, Oklahoma

On June 1, 1912, the Kankakee County Farm Bureau was formed, and shortly afterward the Young Men's Country Club was organized. They were having difficulty getting the boys together for social occasions, because there were no girls.

Several women in the community were contacted to see if we could get a girls' group interested. We were all for it and soon had Young Women's Country Club started. We were all high school girls or older. Soon many city girls wanted to join, but they didn't want to be called Country Girls, so the University asked us to change our names to 4-H Clubs, which we reluctantly did.

As many of our girls were getting married, we were asked what we thought of getting women interested in a new organization. Working with an advisor from the University of Illinois, we soon had enough members to comply with the government requirements.

We had to pledge $1500 to have an advisor assigned to the county, and that seemed a lot of money, but Mr. George Schroeder of the Farm Bureau said, "I have learned that the best way to get things done is to wade in and then swim out."

So we did just that, and we formed the Home Improvement Association on June 4, 1915. Miss Bennafield was our first advisor, and she arrived on June 4, 1915. Miss Bennafield was our first advisor, and she held its first canning demonstration, with Mr. Ferrill of Washington, D.C., as the instructor. This was the first local demonstration of the cold pack method of canning. Everyone was sure it would not work— that it would not keep.

Our club had brought 21 books and a bookcase to start a library, which was located in the telephone service. So the canned products were put on display there, so when people came to pay their bills, they could check on the cold pack method of canning. They were there several years, before we decided they were old and didn't think they would be very good to eat now.

It was renamed Ladies Home Bureau in 1922, and in 1962 our name was changed again, this time to Extension Homemakers Association. We didn't mind what we called ourselves.

Alma Thompson, 85, Illinois

One thing we haven't mentioned was the Farmers' Institute. Back in the '30s and '40s, the Farmers' Institute was one of the big activities of Extension work. We would have two speakers from Purdue, a man and a woman. And they would present their subject matter in both morning and afternoon programs. There would be a pitch-in dinner and following that, there would be exhibits and shows. A corn and

Rural women had led isolated lives full of hard work. Extension clubs brought them together once or twice a month to learn about new methods in home economics which could be used in their daily lives.

small grain show and the ladies would bring in their cakes and other materials for competition. [A retired agriculture agent]
Wilbur Whitehead, 76, Indiana

And the ladies exhibited quilts, baked goods, jellies, jams, canned goods, a little art. They gave ribbons, blue, red and white, just like in 4-H. But the Institute has gone out with the times. A lot of Home Ec clubs started with ladies getting interested at Farmers' Institutes.
Mildred Weaver, 65, Indiana

I bet you've had trouble with all the name changes since you have been a member so long. First, the Tomato Club, then the Poultry Club, Home Demonstration Club, Extension Homemakers Club and now Extension Homemakers Association.

You're right. I often say Home Demonstration Club now, instead of Homemakers.

Well, you know it's all the same program, continuing adult education through our land-grant college. The name changes have just kept abreast of the program changes.

Theo Hammond, 82, North Carolina

Members of the early Extension clubs
often came in buggies, rode horseback, or
walked.

STARTING CLUBS

I believe our club at Glade Spring really grew out of interest in 4-H activities. You know the older clubs were called Poultry or Tomato Clubs.

Our first get-together was an organization meeting, and we ladies all carried a bit of sewing with us, and took along the youngest of the family.

Really, our first meeting was a stitch and chatter session. Everyone wore hats (chuckles) and no one complained when one child chose to taste the cherries on a guest's hat. We shared recipes and talked about preserving foods, and child raising and many other things.

Linnie Arnett, 65, Virginia

About 1920, or perhaps before that, I remember going to town on horseback for Extension demonstrations and for Extension club meetings. This was before there was any county agent or home agent in the county.

One of the reasons I joined the Extension club is that I was a young homemaker and had a growing family and I found new ways of canning and homemaking.

Our first meetings were held in our homes. Our club had about 20 members, and most of us came a long distance. We rode horseback, I and two of my friends rode. My first friend rode a Shetland pony, and the other friend rode a horse that was medium size, while I rode another horse that was so tall I could hardly reach the saddle on it.

Minnie Murphey, 90, South Dakota

Some of us were invited to the Ontario Club, and there was a specialist who came up to this club. They were making baskets—like Indian baskets. It was a real nice meeting.

Then we decided if that was what Homemakers was like, we'd like to have a club of our own. So there were about five or six of us met at one of the ladies' houses and got our club started. That was 61 years ago. I've been a Homemaker for 61 years.

Were they all-day meetings?

Yes. They'd come in the morning. We used to serve quite a lot of food at the meetings, especially new dishes. If we made something new in the morning, why we'd serve that for dinner.

Josephine Nixon, 90, Wisconsin

I was asked to help start a Homemakers club in a certain area. Now it was right out in the sticks, 28 miles from the nearest town, and the women in this area never got to go anyplace, never had any activities outside of the home.

In fact, many of the husbands considered that women should stay in the home—that is where they belonged and they weren't to go anywhere else.

So it was a great thing the day we started Homemakers, because we gathered together many of the women in that area, and they were so thrilled to be able to come and learn many things that they knew other people knew, but they didn't know. And they were so interested and happy to be able to have a few hours away from their own homes.

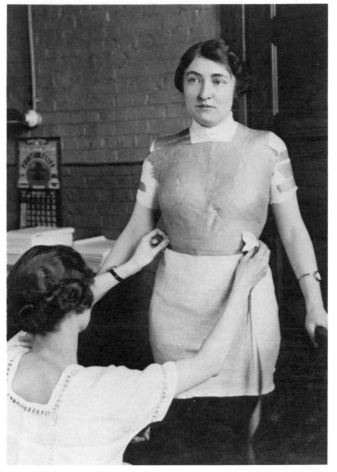

Making dress forms with gummed tape over a knit garment produced lots of laughter, as well as a useful product.

Do you recall some of the topics?

I can't recall the exact topics, but I do remember that the big thing that these women liked to do was learn about sewing and cooking. They knew sewing as taking a feed sack and cutting out a dress, but they didn't know anything about patterns or how to get material. They knew the basics of cooking that had been handed down from their mothers, but they liked to learn new recipes, and they were interested in learning.

Ethel Jury, 55, Kentucky

I've really been a Homemaker member all my life, because my mother organized one of the first clubs in Madison County, Alabama, and from a little girl on I've been going to Homemaker club meetings.

My mother was interested in learning how to can chicken, back around 1930. She went into the county agent's office and she came home. Didn't many people in the community have transportation at that time, so she got her neighbors together and she taught them how to can chicken. So this was the way the club was organized. She found out that the women were interested in learning other things as well, and she contacted the Home Demonstration agent, and she helped them organize a club, so I've been going to club meetings all my life.

Sue Moman, 55, Alabama

One day I went into town to a grocery store, and I saw two women in there who were on their way to the county annual meeting. They were so excited and happy that it made me wish that I was going along with them, and I began to wonder about having a club in our neighborhood.

I invited my friends and neighbors who were interested to meet in my home. In September of 1952 we organized the Fairview Homemakers Club. I have never missed a meeting in 29 years, and I have attended practically all the county meetings and several state meetings and several national meetings. My membership in the Homemakers club has been a major role in my life.

Mary Fouts, 72, Kentucky

My first meeting was in Barnstead Parade. They were trying to get a younger Homemakers group going in this particular area.

I think we started one of the first evening groups around. The idea was that our husbands and fathers of our children could take care of the children in an evening, and we'd have a night out to learn things that would help us become better homemakers. I've been in for almost nineteen years, and I've certainly learned a lot in Extension. I owe Extension a lot.

What were you interested in?

In everything. I found that it had something for every field. I believe there's always something you can learn in anything. Of course, being a new homemaker and a new mother there was a lot for me to learn. I figured if I could find a teacher—Fine! I was with people my own age who would have this common interest and problems, and a willingness to learn.

Carolyn Dame, 40, New Hampshire

We have clubs that meet at night, where most of the women work [outside the home] and they don't have time for all the programs that the women that have the day meetings do.

I helped organize a Homemakers club and there are only two women in that club who are not employed outside the home. They have been able to carry on and hold an office and take a lesson. This has worked out well. They have three generations of members in this club. They have the grandmother, the mother, and the granddaughter all in the same club. The granddaughter was elected as our county vice-president and I was very proud to say that I had helped in organizing this club.

Margie Brookshire, 60, Kentucky

Early Meetings

Can you tell me why you decided to join?

Because I was young when I married and knew very little about being a wife and mother, so I decided the Home Demonstration club was the thing for me to join.

Do you remember your first meeting?

It was on July 20, 1920, and we met at Jones Spring Church grounds, just in sight of my home. We decided to meet outdoors that afternoon at the spring.

What topic did you have that afternoon out at the spring?

We made organdy flowers. At that time organdy flowers were very popular. Some were wearing them in their hair, some trimmed their hats and some wore them for corsages.

Letha McCall, 91, North Carolina

Since your coming to Alaska was a Department of Agriculture project, you probably heard about Extension at an early time.

Yes, the first summer we were here, in 1935, the state home economist from Fairbanks visited the Valley and spent some time with the women in the community. We weren't acquainted with any of the brands that were available in the stores, so she gave us much information about the type of food that we could expect to get. She acquainted us with life in our new land, and gave us many tips on how to make the most of what was available for use in our homes. She instigated the organization of Homemaker clubs.

In 1936 an extension home economist was assigned to the Valley and continued to encourage clubs to organize. Our regular monthly clubs were not only happy social contacts for the exchange of ideas, but we learned many new skills from our programs. Newcomers are always made to feel welcome and encouraged to join.

Lillian Eckert, 70, Alaska

Children often outnumbered club members. Here are nineteen children, with eleven adults, making for a lively club meeting.

Do you remember when you joined the Home Demonstration club?

I do remember when I joined. We used to have our meetings at Macrons High School. The agent stayed at our home a lot; and my grandmother [with whom I lived] was a member. It's just been a part of my life.

Julia White, 60, Tennessee

I rode horesback down and took my two children. The lady that was giving the meeting, she had a big quilt all ready for the ladies to quilt.

They quilted and they had their lunch, and the little children—there was quite a few little children—played in under the quilt (laughs).

We had an all-day meeting that day, and the men enjoyed themselves playing cards.

Lillie Badgley, 85, Montana

When we started out, we had 33 members. And at some of those meetings there was as many kids as there was grown-ups, sometimes.

You took the whole family.

Well, they hadn't invented babysitters at that time. So if you were going to club, you took them with or you stayed home. Pa, he was out farming—he couldn't stay home with the kids.

Anna Sorensen, 83, North Dakota

Can you remember the first club meeting you ever went to?

I was invited as a guest, and I was really impressed with it. Of course, there were children running in and out. Once in a while we'd have to stop and blow somebody's nose or take one to the potty or something. One little fellow jumped off of a footstool and hurt himself and cried. I remember we had to stop the lesson for that.

You told me about a time at your house?

Well, I had a fairly small house with a little back room that overflowed with toys. I said, "I'll be just fine if it doesn't rain." Well, of course, it rained, and that day we had children and even *guest* children. Nineteen children and eighteen members.

It was really fun. We had a walk-in closet that went between the two bedrooms, and the kids liked to race back and forth through that. Right in the middle of the program one of the little fellows came in with one of my nightgowns hanging on his head. Oh, my! But we just took it all in stride.

Evelyn Rigsby, 58, Indiana

I was seventeen when I joined. They had a pilot program from Lansing, and my mother and her neighbors were very interested in it. They lacked one member—they had to have twenty.

They decided that Lansing would never know that I wasn't eighteen yet, so they put my name in, and I have been a member ever since.

I've been a member 61 years and I've always enjoyed it. I've never had a class that I didn't get something out of. They've been wonderful.

Rubie Gillion, 80, Michigan

I was five years old and I went with my mother and grandmother to the Decatur Home Economics Club. I was considered a member, for I remember paying my nickel as dues. I was in kindergarten then, and I skipped class to attend. After I got in the first grade, they wouldn't let me skip school anymore, so the next time I went to Homemakers was a month after we were married. I was invited to go to a club meeting then and I joined the first night, and I've been a member ever since.

Donna Marbach, 41, Indiana

Can you tell us a little bit about your early Homemaker club activities?

Well, we met in the community hall, just about two miles from where we live, all of the women around in our community. And we'd have a meeting, and we'd have a luncheon, and of course, we'd have a gab session, and then we'd go home.

Dorothy Carlson, 78, Idaho

Community Extension clubs are a social as well as educational experience, with members of all ages.

Our first club meetings were a very special day. The hostesses made it a point to have something very special. They used their good china, and tried to have a menu that would be just a little different from what their previous meeting might have been. When you missed club day, you just missed something that was very special.

We looked forward to the meetings—the information they gave there, and the sociability that was involved. It was really the social life of the community.

Marie Carlile, 67, Montana

I had much benefit from each meeting in many, many good ways. The fellowship meant so much to me. The potluck dinners meant so much to me, because I love to eat. We had different dishes, and I'd go home and copy the dishes. We exchanged receipts and had a good social time. We were very special to each other.

Clara Nichols, 82, Indiana

Our county agent told us one time to not try to outdo the other one when we served refreshments. She said, "Just something simple, and cut it down to just one or two things."

So one day she was going to be our guest, so we just got together that day and served crackers and bologna and a glass of water. And that tickled her nearly to death. She said, "That's getting it down right where I told you to get it." From then on, nobody tried to outdo the other with so much refreshments.

She put it in the paper, "Simple refreshments were served."

Edna Maddox, 70, Indiana

First Meeting

Can you remember back when the first meeting was?

I sure can. We were married in October and took possession of our ranch in November, and I was invited to the Christmas meeting of the ladies in the club in this community. It's a ranching community and all the people that live in this area that live on ranches—they belong to it. It's called Sweetwater Homemakers.

The Christmas meeting is always the big meeting. It was an all-day meeting. We went at eleven o'clock in the morning and we had a turkey dinner with all the trimmings. Then we'd have a real brief business meeting and then we'd have a gift exchange. No formal lesson, just a real nice social afternoon.

Mary Raymond, 60, Wyoming

Do you remember your first meeting?

I sure do. I was invited to go with an old member from the unit to take the lesson and I was to be an observer. I went to the meeting, and

the program was given, but the other member didn't show up. So I had
quite a time, giving a lesson when I was so new.

Catherine Wycoff, 90, Illinois

The Prospect PM Club was organized in 1948 and as a newcomer to
the area, one of the ladies came over and asked if I would like to
become a Home Demonstration club member, so I have been in
Extension Homemakers for 32 years, and I still belong to the Prospect
PM Club.

Can you recall the first meeting?

Well, I am a Japanese-American and I was invited, and it was just
during the World War II time and some of these people in the area had
very anti-Japanese feelings. I had a few moments wondering how I
would be received, but I was well received and I'm very glad that I did
join.

**It's nice to know that people, even in those days nearer World War
II, when there were so many bitter feelings—it's nice to know that you
were well received in your own community. I'm glad to hear that.**

Misaye Uno, 65, Colorado

When I married, I came to the Smith River community. The friends
and neighbors all belonged to the Smith River Club and they invited
me to join. I attended a meeting, and after the first meeting I became a
member.

I was a new bride at that time, and that was the way they welcomed
me to the community. I think they gave us a chivaree. They also gave
me a shower shortly after coming to the neighborhood.

So the Extension Homemaker club was really a home-oriented group?

Yes, they were the Welcome Wagon; they were your friends and
neighbors. They let you know that this was going to be a home that
you would really enjoy living in, in the community.

Marie Carlile, 67, Montana

I have mentioned my inexperience as a farm woman. It was rather
interesting that a few months after we had been making our home and
doing things [in the house] and my husband was getting active in farming, he said to me one day, "You know, there's a young woman down
at the County Extension Service that I think you might like to talk to."
Which made me think that he felt that I needed some help and guid-
ance (chuckles). So that was my first contact with the home economists in the county, which was a very rewarding one.

I became interested and learned that there were neighborhood
groups called Home Demonstration Units. So the first meeting of the

Home Demonstration Unit for me was in my own home, where we organized the unit for the neighborhood. This was in the 1930s.

Evelyn Alden, 74, Kansas

As a young bride, my mother-in-law took me by the hand the first Thursday of September—I was married in August—and said, "Come with me and we'll go to our Extension group. It's just over the hill."

Alice Wand, 65, Oregon

Why Joined

What prompted you to join a Homemakers group?

I had this friend in Little Rock who kept inviting me to go with her. To be honest, I finally went with her just to please her, because she had asked me so many times. And that's how I got started.

I say this very honestly—I really can't imagine what my life would be like if I had not gotten involved in Extension club work 20 or 21 years ago. I have told my friend many times since that I tried to avoid her at times when I'd see her coming, because she was always wanting me to go to club. She would say, "I know you would like it. I know you would enjoy it and learn lots from it."

Well, she was so right, and I'm so glad that she stayed after me until I did go.

Ann Webb, 48, Arkansas

I first joined when my eldest son was just a year old, which makes me a member of Homemakers for 26 years. I joined because I wanted something to do, and a friend of mine told me, "Oh, I belong to a fantastic group." We met with these ladies, and they *were* absolutely fantastic. They were from all walks of life. A lot of them were farmer's wives, we had a banker's wife among them. And I learned so much from these ladies and they were so warm, hospitable and outgoing.

Dorothy Tyrawski, 58, Delaware

What prompted you to join?

Well, I had recently moved with my husband and four children into a town where I had once lived as a small child. I was looking for both education and homemaking, and companionship with my new neighbors. I was pleased to accept the invitation of my grandmother and aunt to join them in attending my first meeting.

Young mothers could take their pre-school children to the meetings, just as my mother had taken me with her earlier. Our meetings were from 10 a.m. to 3 p.m. with potluck luncheons.

Priscilla Lloyd, 56, New Hampshire

I joined shortly after we were married—partly because my husband said that, "Ma always has gone, and you have to, too, with all the other farm wives." Everybody just belonged to Extension. It was completely new to me, but he said, "You definitely have to go," so I went. Here I am, still a member 25 years later, and enjoying it very much.

Marge Kleinjan, 45, South Dakota

When I first joined, as a new homemaker, there were a lot of things I needed to know. I had been out of the housekeeping business for some years. I'd gone through school, and taught school for a year, and spent two years in an office.

Then I got married and all at once I needed to be efficient in housework again—in laundry and cooking and baking and just everything that goes to make up the work of a homemaker. So I really needed it as a kind of refresher course.

As a girl, when I was home and doing those things, I had my mother to supervise me and tell me how. Then, when you're married and on your own, you don't have a supervisor. So you have to learn for yourself. This was very helpful to me in teaching me the methods of homemaking.

Nellie Yost, 76, Nebraska

My littlest boy, he always went [to club]; he wouldn't stay with Grandma. The older boy would stay with Grandma and Grandpa. He didn't want "to go to any hen parties," he would say. My dad put that in his head.

But the little one wasn't about to stay there. He was going along.

My father wondered about that. He said, "Dean, why won't you stay? Why do you want to go to that for, anyhow?" So Dean came up close to his granddad and said, "Grandpa, they eat there." He wanted to be there for lunch (laughs).

Sophie Bigge, 82, Kansas

The Story of a Club

I got in touch with the home agent, and she told me to ask quite a number of ladies in Meire Grove who wanted to join. Thirteen or fourteen were going to join, and we started the club. We've kept it up now for 45 years.

We decided we were going to serve the same meal every time. It consists of a sandwich, pickles, coffee and cake. We kept that up.

Elizabeth Meyer, 84, Minnesota

[Same club] All having little children made it harder for us to get away from home, and our husbands were kind enough to stay with the children so that we could get out occasionally. At first we had meetings in the afternoon, but later we changed to the evenings. Then some of the men began to attend with us. They'd play cards.

Different ladies joined our club from time to time, but they'd soon drop out. The old faithful ones always stayed on and on. We shared many experiences, both happy and sad. Several ladies lost their husbands. Several of the ladies later left the farm and moved to different towns, but they stayed on with our Homemakers group. One couple moved to St. Cloud, but they still came back 40 miles for our meetings.

But in 1976 our best seamstress died. Since then, two more ladies have died. One is too sick to attend meetings and one is in a wheelchair at a nursing home. The remaining six of us, plus the two remaining husbands, still stick together through thick and thin.

We had thought of having a more appropriate name than just the Meire Grove Homemakers. Last fall we decided that the name Persistent Pals was right for us.

We don't work as hard at the lessons anymore, as many don't pertain to our lives anymore. We are old in years, but we're young in spirit. It has been a great experience. We worked hard and we have happy memories.

Marcella Meyer, Minnesota

State Meetings

I want you to tell me something about this short course that you attended for a week in the early years.

Well, that was schooling through the Home Demonstration work in Raleigh. It was called Farm and Home Week.

That was usually held in the summer months, wasn't it?

Yes, in August. You see, we were through with laying the crops by and we hadn't started gathering [harvesting] and by that time you had your vegetables and fruit [canned] and your jellies and jams and pickles all made, so you had more leisure time.

We had specialists and each one had classes in their own particular training. And it was just like going to school. We stayed on campus in the dormitories.

Did you sign up for special classes?

We signed up after we went down there. We couldn't take all they had to give us, but I took everything I could squeeze in.

I know that was a real experience—getting away from the home grind, and I bet you went back a better mother and a better wife.

Oh, yes, I did! I went back all just so full of ideas. They didn't know each day what I was going to suggest doing that day, because I was so bubbling over with everything.

Letha McCall, 91, North Carolina

Many counties had Extension Homemaker camps, where homemakers came to spend two or three days. There would be educational programming, but there would also be games and laughter.

One of the highlights of each year was going to the Conference at the University of Illinois. We had excellent speakers, and they made us realize how fortunate we were, to be members of this organization. One of the speakers mentioned that this was equivalent to a college education in Home Economics.

Marjorie Whitney, 71, Illinois

It was in the '20s and '30s, and each year the women would go to Columbia for what they called Farmers' Week. I always thought it was really a good thing, because it included the women and the men. The men would go to their meetings, and the women would get together and they would talk about their food, their clothing, their homes, and their children.

It was at one of these meetings that I was elected president. It was so different then from what it is now. It was my second trip to Farmers' Week. The meeting was held in the old Jesse Hall. The nominations were made from the floor, and I think about how hard it would be to do that at this time. Everybody had a vote. We even had mothers there with their children.

Lillie Stuery, 79, Missouri

I think I have gone 39 years in succession this year. The first time I went, it cost us $4.50 to stay all week. We went on Sunday and came home on a Saturday. We took our own bath towels, sheets and pillow-cases, and food out of the garden. We took string beans and potatoes and lettuce, that sort of thing. We brought it to the kitchen, and the ladies that worked in the kitchen took the food and cooked it. We picked up our meals on trays and then brought the trays back to the counter. We kept our own rooms in order, until we come home. We thought that was beautiful; we enjoyed it so much.

Rubie Gillion, 80, Michigan

My mother-in-law used to tell me about when she would go to State meeting. It was held at Camp Robinson, which is out from North Little Rock. The main thing I can remember is she said that they used to sleep in tents. When we go to State meeting now for two or three days, I can't imagine us sleeping in tents, but back in that day and time, the ladies did.

Ann Webb, 48, Arkansas

I became president of my [local] club, and that was when I attended the first short course, or University Days, at Fairbanks. The women from the outlying districts would meet in Anchorage and stay with some of the Anchorage ladies. Then we would all ride the train to Fairbanks, which was a twelve-hour ride. We had one railroad car full of ourselves, so we had a grand time going.

We were met in Fairbanks by the women of the Tanana Valley and the Fairbanks ladies, and taken to the University.

How far is it from Anchor Point to Fairbanks?

It's about 430 miles.

How long did you stay?

We arrived on Sunday afternoon, and caught the train home on Saturday.

What were some of the things you did during that week?

We had different classes, we had get-acquainted parties, and we were shown some of the countryside around Fairbanks. We had educational classes on many different things.

Did the educational classes have an effect on your homemaking and on your life?

Yes, it had a great effect.

Gussie Mumey, 67, Alaska

I always enjoyed going to Clifftop. We always had an influential speaker and different visitors when we had our annual meetings there.

How many members did you have?

Frankly, I do not remember, but we did have a large number, because of the ten counties, all of the black homemakers went to Cliff-top at that time. The real name was Washington Carver 4-H Camp, at Clifftop, West Virginia. That is where we held our county and area council and all of our state meetings.

Margaret Hill, 65, West Virginia

I might mention Mini-College. It's jokingly referred to as The Camp for Runaway Mothers. It's five days, toward the end of June, put on by the Oregon Extension Homemakers Council, in cooperation with the Extension Service and the Oregon State University.

There are some very wonderful classes. You can have your pick of many, many classes. They are taught by volunteers and by some of the staff of Oregon State University.

It's just wonderful! They treat you like a queen or a king. You stay in a very nice dorm. You have wonderful food prepared for you, and the classes are top classes. What more can you want?

Alice Wand, 65, Oregon

It first was Farm Woman's Week. Then the women from the city liked to come and felt they were being slighted, so it was College Week for Women. Now it is Homemakers' Week, because the men think they would like to come. We have had men in the last few years. I said that after the men got equal rights, they got to come (laughter).

Rubie Gillion, 80, Michigan

I thought all the state meetings in Jackson's Mill were really, really outstanding. They were so helpful in every way. If you were just a member, they were helpful in that you learned to lead a lesson and you were helped if you were on a committee. And if you were an officer they were all helpful. It was such a treat, it was such a privilege for a member to go as a delegate from their club to the programs at the Mill.

They say there was a fellow that said that he had heard his wife talk so much about Jackson's Mill that he didn't know—when he died—if he'd be able to get to heaven or not, but that he certainly hoped that he'd be able to get as far as Jackson's Mill.

Pearl Faulkner, 78, West Virginia

National Meetings

Why did you go to Washington in 1934? What was your purpose?

They were planning on starting a national organization, and [the advisors at] Purdue thought I should go and represent Indiana. A lot of people, state officers, were there and we met at the Department of Agriculture auditorium. Henry Wallace was Secretary of Agriculture then, and he came to our meeting, and his wife was always there. She was very nice.

Each state had something special they got up and talked about. My subject was music because we had a chorus in Indiana, which no one else had. We had a wonderful state [music] leader, Al Stewart, and we had this great big chorus, so I was to tell about Indiana being the singing state.

I remember I was so frightened when I got up. I didn't think I would be, but I was, because they put a microphone on me and I'd never had one on before. There were journalists and recorders from different publications, and that was published in different articles.

I don't think they really organized for a couple of years after that, until in 1936 when there was another meeting in Washington when the [Associated] Country Women of the World met.

Lora Herrick, 89, Indiana

[Ed. note: Mrs. Herrick was Indiana State President in 1934-35. She is telling about a Rural Homemakers Conference where representatives of state home economics extension groups were invited to participate, and where action for forming a national organization really began.]

They were planning to get an organization of the state councils made into a national organization. So at the time the Roosevelts were in office in Washington, Mrs. Roosevelt invited women to come in, and that was when the National Extension Council started.

[Ed. note: Mrs. Alden was National President 1958-60. She is speaking of the formation of the National Extension Homemakers Council in 1936 in Washington, D.C.]

Then the first annual conference [after that] was held in Kansas, at Manhattan. We had a state leader, Georgia Emma Smirthwaite, and she had been working [on this]. Through her efforts and invitation, the conference came here [Kansas].

They had the meeting in Benzil Hall, because that was about the only and the first women's dormitory.

Eleanor Roosevelt, wife of President Franklin Roosevelt, greets a Homemaker member. Mrs. Roosevelt was very supportive of the Extension Homemaker organization.

This would have been in the '30s?

Yes. [Ed. note: The conference in Manhattan was in 1937].

Evelyn Alden, 74, Kansas

We [Tennessee] have recently gone into the National Extension Homemakers Council. Do you think this will help?

People all over the United States join up and find out what the others are doing.

A women's group of five hundred thousand members can do a lot of things.

Yes, they can. Join hands.

That's a plus for our state.

Julia White, 60, Tennessee

In looking through some old handbooks from the National Extension Homemakers Council, I had one from 1957 and one from 1980, and in reading the objectives in the bylaws, [I found] there is just very little change—just a change in wording, just a word or two.

I am sure this is because their aims have remained so constant through the years.

Nellie Depew, 68, Indiana

The trips we take to National every year are an institution in themselves.

Bess Jones, Georgia

How many meetings of Extension Homemakers have you been to that were out of the state?

Thirty-two. And I declare, it's wonderful to go to them. It's something new. You see new and different country; you see different things; and the more you become acquainted with other people, the broader one's viewpoint does become.

Elba Johnston, 79, Oklahoma

I've only missed one national meeting since 1941.

Mary Moore, 73, New Mexico

I've been to national meetings all over the United States, and sometimes we had to fly. Being able to do this, it makes the world so small.

Frances Caldwell, 57, West Virginia

Yes, I have attended national conferences. I think I have been to five.

Do you think that was one reason you wanted to [join] Extension Homemakers, that you had attended many national meetings and got caught up in the enthusiasm of them?

Yes, I think that is it. It was very educational. They always had tours arranged for men, and I have always liked to travel. So it was educational, there was quite a bit of traveling and it was something worthwhile.

Ansel Peterson, 76, West Virginia

[Ed. note: Mr. Peterson is one of the newer male members of NEHC.]

I find the association and the general tenor of the meetings so rewarding. That's the reason I like to go.

I believe you enjoy making new friends, too.

I do, and you keep seeing old friends from all over the United States.

Henrietta Phillips, 69, North Carolina

Tell us about your trips to National, and what you do to foster friendships.

Well, I went to my first meeting in Florida and I just took a lot of things I'd made, to show them that there was no point in them getting old. That they could do things with their fingers and their hands. I say, "Now reading is wonderful, but don't just let that be your only hobby, because your eyes will give way and you can't read, but if you can use your fingers, you can crochet and not hardly look. You can do lots of things."

Then I'd just give them out to people, to swap them for their wares. They all brought something. I didn't know they did that till I went to Florida and saw they brought so much.

I took some china-painted plates and gave them to the ladies from Hawaii. They always bring me such nice things. And I always take something for each of the women who come from Puerto Rico. And I try to give out something to each state. Something original, that I've done.

Mary Skelley, 76, Oklahoma

One time I went to National meeting, in Columbus, Ohio. There I had the opportunity to meet all those real deep south [women] from Georgia, Mississippi (chuckle) and towns down there. And we visited and learned so much from each other.

But the thing that stayed in my mind was that one of the Georgia girls said, "You know, I get the biggest lot of fun of the way she talks." (laughter) And I said, "Well, I expect to you girls it sounds like sticks breaking, with our voices sharp and the words so short." And she said, "Ah love ta heah you tahlk." (laughter).

Elsa Skiles, Washington

Oh, that's a fun, neat experience. It makes you realize that Extension isn't for your own immediate community. It's state-wide. It's national. It gives you a feeling of, "Hey, you're a part of something!" It gives you a good feeling when you come away from it. You've learned something. You're somebody.

Saundra Zook, 39, Oregon

International Meetings

Mrs. Lefman was privileged to attend the meeting of the Associated Country Women of the World in Washington, D.C.

This was the third such meeting. The first meeting was in Vienna in 1930, the second was in Stockholm in 1933 and now the third one in the United States in 1936.

Through their membership in the Associated Country Women of the World, Extension Homemakers reach out to women all over the world. Shown is Olive Farquharson, England, past world president of ACWW, with a group of American Indian Extension Homemakers.

[Our county picked me as one of their two representatives] and I didn't see how I could go. Back in 1936, nobody was very rich. Maybe you'd like to know how much money it really took. The tickets from St. Louis to Washington, D.C. were $33.50. That took care of the railroad fare to and from Washington, hotel accommodations for two in a room with a bath, and breakfast and evening meals en route and while in Washington. We were told we would probably need about $15.00 extra for transportation to and from St. Louis, for some noon meals and for the banquet, making a total of $48.00. That sounded like a lot of money.

Our county had sales to get a little money. My own local club said, "Forget about the money. You are going to Washington." They had a bake sale, gave me the money, said, "Now, you're going to Washington." Then another one came along and said, "Here, I've got a hat that would look pretty good in Washington. Take it and wear it." So, first thing I knew, I was packing and getting ready to go.

We took a bus to St. Louis, and I was so sick I didn't know whether I was going to live or die. He stopped; I got off the bus; set foot on the ground; and was perfectly all right. I got back on the bus and said, "I'll just stay sick, and I'll just ride."

We got on the train, and the same story. I had never been on a diner and I wanted to go to the diner, but I was so sick I couldn't even eat. But there were [women from] three states close by on that train, seems like 400 people. And I believe there were two husbands and one son. They took inventory on the train and the oldest one was 76, and one woman had left a 14-month-old child. That was the youngest one. So they were traveling all ages and all people and all having a good, good time.

We were very anxious to get there, because we had slated on the program, the first thing a garden party at the White House lawn, which we all wanted to go to. We had directions on how we should dress. You were supposed to wear one of your best dresses and white gloves, because Mrs. Roosevelt wanted to shake hands with all of us. She didn't want to shake hands with bare hands. I had a 25¢ pair of little thin white gloves and I carried them in my purse.

Our train ran a little late, [and we didn't have time to get to the hotel to change]. So we just changed clothes right there on the train—right there in the car seats—to get ready to go to the party. We were ready to go when we got off the train.

When we got on the [White House] lawn there were 8,000. I think they had expected about five or six hundred. They had little cups and little tables scattered around with the punch; everybody was to have their cup. Well, you can imagine 8,000 people trying to grab for a cold drink. We were ready for it; it was hot. So it didn't make any difference if somebody had used the cup we used.

Mrs. Roosevelt and President Roosevelt were there. President Roosevelt came out and had his few words; then he was followed by Mrs. Roosevelt. Mrs. Roosevelt wanted to meet us all, so she just came down in the crowd. She was literally encircled with personnel guarding her, and just walking like she was in a little circle. So we were reaching . . . and we could shake hands with Mrs. Roosevelt. We didn't get the white gloves on, but it didn't bother her. She wasn't the President's wife. She was just one of us and talked to us in the same manner all the time that we were there.

I was amazed at the places we visited in Washington, D.C.; the people we met; the meetings we attended and the wonderful messages and lessons we learned; plus meeting so many, many lovely people from all over the world and making notes and comparing our life and their life.

Some of the topics that were specially emphasized included motherhood and safety [in childbirth]. We weren't so familiar with hospitalization and it was up to the home to take care of things then. That was one thing that was discussed and discussed from all those different countries.

Educational lessons were brought to the club meetings by Extension agents or by members of the club who had attended a training session.

Food and eating habits was one of the things that was emphasized, and it's being emphasized today, too. Another subject was rural women and their economic problems. And they emphasized the cultural interests of women. We had entertainment that showed what they had, and that, coupled with the craft exhibits from many of the countries, showed us that they were interested in more than just making a living, and I think that is true of Extension clubs, too.

We had a lot of good music. Some of these foreign countries are great with their music, especially with their folk dances. They usually did all those in native costumes, which made them quite pretty. So we enjoyed that a lot.

Farm women came for a purpose: "friendship and understanding will lead to peace among all people of all nations." We hoped to dispel racial hatred. The will to peace was the underlying theme.

One great enjoyment of the convention was to meet and talk with women from other states and nations. After all, they were just country women of the world, happy to be together and interested in the same topics of homemaking. It was quite a thrill.

Verna Lefman, 84, Missouri

I was state president in 1936, and our Indiana Homemakers Chorus was invited to sing at the opening session of the ACWW meeting in Washington, D.C. There were over 7,000 women there with 44 states represented and 28 foreign countries, and we sang for that *great, great* organization.

We were privileged to sing in Constitution Hall where the opening meeting was. As we were going down off that huge stage, I heard Mrs. Roosevelt [Eleanor] ask if our chorus, joined by any other choruses who were in Washington for the meeting, would come to the White House and sing for the President at the lawn party that afternoon.

Of course, we were so thrilled about that. We decided to sing "Home on the Range," because it was such a favorite of his. We had to go eat lunch and get back to the White House in just a short time.

We had white dresses on, and while we were getting together to practice just a little before we went to lunch, Al Stewart, who was our very popular director, said, "For goodness sake, don't get any gravy on your dresses." The funny thing was, he had on a Palm Beach suit, and he got some gravy on that suit. We laughed about that so many times.

You know where the balcony is, and there is a driveway? Well, right across the driveway is a big enclosed place, and we had lots of room there. And we did sing for the President and enjoyed it.

The White House lawn was beautiful. It was covered with women. It had kiosks all over where cold drinks were being served. Mrs. Roosevelt was such a gracious lady. She went all over that big lawn and she shook hands for a long, long time with anybody that wanted to shake hands with her. That was a gracious thing for her to do, because I know that hand must have been awfully tired. But the women were so thrilled.

We had the week in Washington together, and everything had been so exciting. The farewell meeting was held right back of the Lincoln Memorial, facing Arlington Cemetery. It was a beautiful summer evening. The Navy band was playing. Everyone was so sad, because they had met people, and the meetings had been so wonderful, and then this was the last one.

A lady from Germany was the speaker, and it was the most beautiful talk on "Peace." And we were so full of that, because for a week we had talked about peace.

And I've thought so many times since. That was in 1936. And by 1939, we were at each other's throats. And many, many times after the war started, I thought of that dear lady giving that farewell address in that beautiful setting where everything was so peaceful.

When we left to go home, everyone was filled with high hopes that there never would be war again. That was the last meeting of a perfectly wonderful week.

Mildred McCay, 85, Indiana

Through their membership in the Associated Country Women of the World, Extension Homemakers are represented in the United Nations organization. They maintain a representative who works with the NGO's (non-governmental organizations).

What impresses you most about these [ACWW] conferences?

The impression or feeling that I got is the cooperation that goes on between the women of the world. After you've gone to a conference like this, you feel that—well, your community is your home—and with the women of the world, you bring all these communities together, and you feel like a much larger person. The women help each other and you are surprised at how far some of these small suggestions, given from friend to friend, how far they go all the way around the world.

Gussie Mumey, 67, Alaska

I think that's one of the best organizations that we have, as far as getting information around the world. We would do much better than your heads of states.

Dorris Graves, 70, Oregon

Can you tell me what Associated Country Women of the World means?

It means that we are women who keep our own identity in our own country [in our clubs]. Now in Northern Ireland they are called Women's Institutes, and in Maryland we're called Maryland Extension Homemakers. Each one has its own name, and then they are under this umbrella of the Associated Country Women of the World, meaning we are together, and yet each one is autonomous. They have to have some sort of program to bring women together [to be eligible to belong]. They have to have the same aims to educate women and to be interested in world peace. And families—we're very concerned with families.

That is why we're at the United Nations—because we're interested in preserving peace; to draw countries together; to help women to help themselves. And these are some of the greatest aims of the United Nations.

Would you like to mention other subjects?

I wanted to talk a little bit about my UNICEF work. I was the ACWW non-governmental representative to the United Nations, and to all these committees we work with at the United Nations.

And people kept saying that, if organizations such as the ACWW, the Red Cross, the Zonta International, the Quakers, the Baha'is, the United Methodist Women, the Baptist World Alliance, the Catholic women, the many Jewish women's organizations that work with them—if all of these people would work on one project together, rather than each one separate, we'd get somewhere.

Since I was the representative to UNICEF, they asked me if there wasn't a project that would help mothers so that they could help their children. UNICEF had been strictly for children, but they rethought, and said, "How can the child be helped if the mother is ignorant?" So we pinpointed Kenya as the place we would work for this first project.

And in Kenya, at that time, women had to walk eight to ten miles to get three gallons of water in big metal containers that they carry on their backs, with a leather thong that goes up over their foreheads. And they would have deep indentations in their forehead from carrying this water. This leaves their hands free so they can carry their babies.

And if they could have spigots in their town, then they could stay home with their children. So we raised money—little bits from different clubs that would send money to the project. And we sent it through UNICEF and they would distribute it to buy pipe. The women dug their own ditches to lay the pipe.

When the project was three years old, our ACWW conference was in Nairobi, Kenya, in 1977. So I went there and met with the women in Kenya who were working with the same committee I was working with.

One day I was invited to go out to a harambe, which means little town. We had helped them replace their mud roofs with corrugated iron, and, water being scarce, they would pitch these roofs so that the water ran into a big barrel, and they'd catch ever single drop of water.

And we saw these women coming to this harambe with pieces of the corrugated iron roof that they'd tied with a string, and these were their drums for the entertainment. They'd drum on their drums, and their headwoman would chant something and then the rest of her club would answer. It was a very tribal thing, and beautifully done.

Then they had all these officials in a line to do a little dance as they contributed in the pot of money toward this [project]. They would give them a baton that would show they were leading the group. And the president motioned to me, and I said, "Oh, no, not me." "Yes, you." So here I am with the baton in my hand leading the dance, with several hundred blacks dancing with me.

It was wonderful. These things are memories you'll never forget. People say, "Well, how did you get the job that you've had at the United Nations all these years?" I said, "I was a Homemaker [member] in Maryland on a farm, and this is it." (laughter) That was the beginning and now, all the people I've known and helped!

Eileen Moon, 62, Maryland

LESSONS AND DEMONSTRATIONS

How Lessons Were Given

I went out to peoples' houses to show them about canning. I went to a house one day, and we canned tomatoes all day. We had a hot water canner in the yard. From that outdoor canner we went up the back steps (which were kind of rickety) to where we were packing the jars. I was a young woman, but I was so tired when I got home.

Pearl Laffitte [retired agent], 80, Florida

As a Home agent I went to every club in the county four or five times a year, demonstrating a lesson. That became quite a chore. When I came, there were five clubs, but at the end of three and a half years, there were 28. So visiting every club became quite a chore.

Alice Gentry, 68, Indiana

In the beginning, the County Agent usually gave the lesson [to each club] each time they met. Then, quite a few years later, the Agent would come maybe two or three times a year and give the lesson. The

Canning together in a local school teaches correct methods and makes the task more enjoyable.

other times, members of the club were appointed to give lessons. One or two persons would go to town to a training meeting and would learn how to present the lessons.

Luella Hardie, 75, Montana

I started as an Extension Home Economist in Branch County. Our specialists from the university came out to the county with usually four or five lessons a year. She'd spend all day on the topic.

People either brought their sack lunch, or they went out to eat. And then they'd come back in the afternoon. We had complete outlines of the lessons, and sometimes we had more than one lesson on a subject. But it was all-day training by the specialist.

Luella Hamilton, 71, Michigan

Do project leaders play an important role in your club?

They surely do, since project leaders now bring the demonstrations, they play a *very* important role. We try to select the project leader that we think best fits the job. One lady is good in crafts, while the other may be good in cooking.

Hautie Nelson, 69, Tennessee

I have learned so much by participation in the lessons that we have received from our Extension Service throughout the years. I was always one of the first to volunteer to take a lesson for my club, because you learn so much more when you actually take it and give it back to the club.

Hazel Leininger, 59, Colorado

Lessons and Programs

The club programs have changed. Some of it is better, and some I liked better with the old ways. We paid more attention in the old club to their lessons than we do now.

I think that they used to have an all-day lesson, but now it seems like there's so much reading.

Minnie Ness, 81, North Dakota

What has caused you to continue your club activities?

Well, I don't want to miss one meeting. We are taking up so many topics, and I'm interested in them all.

Lora Torsey, 84, New Hampshire

Through the years, Mrs. McCall, have club programs been helpful to you?

Every program that I attended was very helpful, because I knew very little about homework, sewing, cooking, canning, all those things. I felt like I needed some of all—I can't single out one single project. I'll just say I always carried home something very valuable, every meeting I attended, and always learned something new.

Letha McCall, 91, North Carolina

In 1932, when I first joined, there were many lessons that were very helpful. They were all helpful to me. I found that the literature was helpful, and I filed them away. I've been asked to help people and I went and looked in my file.

Eva Gill, 80, North Carolina

The lesson material in my mother's day was next to the Bible. She followed the Bible and she followed her club lessons and all the instructions and information that was given to her.

Pearl Faulkner, 78, West Virginia

At the beginning I think they probably learned more basic things— how to make cottage cheese or how to take care of chickens, compared to lessons we have had recently.

We have expanded a lot of our programs to make them fit the needs and the times. The Extension program has really come along. They have kept up with the times.

Evelyn Alden, 74, Kansas

There's been a lot of changes in the programs, but that is necessary to keep up with the changes in everyday life and everything else that's changed. Our program is still education, and still covers the basic needs of today.

Hazel Johnson, 57, South Carolina

Lessons Remembered

The first thing we did was make a little handkerchief holder. We used a ten-pound sugar bag and just little scraps of print and had a little pocket for handkerchiefs and a little handle put on top, so you could hang it up. It's right cute. This is one I never finished—I found it crammed down in a trunk this morning. You see we put buttons on for eyes and worked a little nose and mouth. Then we hung it up on the closet door, and you put your handkerchiefs in here.

And I think the second thing we did was make little hat racks out of sturdy cardboard, and covered it with wallpaper and then used bias binding to go around the edge. Well, hats have gone out of style, but I believe they're coming back, so this thing might come back in style.

Then I think about the next thing we did was to take burlap bags, washed them and then made a little buffet set, or a [dresser] scarf, or just what you wanted to make. We drew threads [to make them straight] and did a little embroidery on them.

Now that looks pretty kiddy [childish], but when I think about it now—we were just as proud of that then, as we are of the beautiful things we do today. So what we do today is a sign of progress, I think.

Mrs. Ray Cassell, 69, Virginia

The first lesson I remember Purdue giving was in the World War I era. My mother went seven miles to attend a meeting. A leader from Purdue gave a lesson on how to make hats. She got straw braid a half to an inch wide and sewed it round and round, shaped it over a bowl or a crock, put a ribbon band around it and a little bunch of flowers on it. You know then, you weren't dressed until you put on your hat.

Lois Waggoner, 76, Indiana

Here is kind of a list of some lessons I have remembered. Now when it came to straw hats—we bought this straw that was probably ¾ of an inch wide—kind of braided straw—but that didn't stay with me too good. My hat looked like it was going to seed. So I didn't do much in hats.

Then there were those aluminum trays that we etched. We bought this sheet of aluminum and then we took the pliers and bent it up around the edge, drew our pattern on the tray and painted it all but the pattern with flat black paint. Then we poured muriatic acid on and that etched your design. My trays are just as pretty as they were forty years ago when we made them.

Other things we did were refinish wooden bowls, and make leather jackets. Then we made wood fiber flowers, and silk hose flowers. And then the glove deal, that was fun. I don't know how many pair of deerskin gloves I've made.

Nellie Frost, 80, Missouri

There are a lot of things that we have done in the club over the years. We have caned chairs, refinished furniture, made baskets, aluminum trays, the fiber flowers. And I've made slipcovers with a pattern, and the cut lampshades, and splint stools. I didn't make a candlewick bedspread, but some of them did. And they made gloves and I made a down quilt for my daughter's little doll baby bed, for a demonstration.

Yes, you love this whole area of lessons, don't you?

Florence E. Reed, 64, Delaware

Does your club do a lot of crafts?

Yes, we do a lot of macrame. We enjoy that. Ruby Brown makes dolls; one [club member] makes big bonnets. We have each lady make one craft, and by the time we do that, we have a table full.

You all won first place on Achievement Day, didn't you?

We appreciated that.

Geneva Slaton, 82, Georgia

Through craft programs with lessons and workshops both local and statewide, I was able to develop my natural-born creative ability. The committee which West Virginia called "Let's Preserve West Virginia Beauty" caused me to fully realize just how important it is for us to protect our God-given natural beauties and resources. I have always loved nature, and it was such a boon for my husband and I to use so much natural materials in our craft work.

Beatrice McCann, 82, West Virginia

A well-remembered crafts lesson was given on metalcraft, with many women making aluminum trays.

I think that I've learned so much, and my life has been enriched by all kinds of lovely things that I would never have known. Some of these things are lost arts, and if we don't get women to share these things with us in our club work, they are going to be gone. And I think all of us have something. Myself, with the Ukranian Easter Eggs, that's an art and I brought it and shared it with Homemakers.

Dorothy Tyrawski, 56, Delaware

You joined in the late twenties. We had hard times then. How did the club help you cope with hard times?

At that time you didn't have too many places to go. We were just thrilled to be able to go to the Home Demonstration club, and if we could just learn a little, we were happy. How to strip honeysuckle and make baskets, or how to select our seed [that we saved each year] from the garden—those were some of the highlights of the club. Each month we'd take a nickel. That was a big offering, to take a nickel.

Aileen Cole, 78, Tennessee

I learned how to make soap, which during the Depression we really appreciated. We even made our own toothpaste—or tooth powder, I guess you would call it—which I used for a long, long time.

Mary Jonas, 81, Ohio

I remember a meeting, this was in the Depression years. An Extension worker came from another county to meet with a small group of ladies in my husband's mother's home.

She had brought a skirt with her that was made from a gunny sack and she told us that we might go out in the woods and dig roots and boil this for dye and dye a gunny sack and then make a dress or skirt or blouse, or whatever. She tells us how many sacks we would need, and then we would need at least five packages of bias tape to use for seam binding.

Well, for poor farm women who had very little to work with, I think we kind of sat there and stared at each other. And we were thinking, "Well, we got the gunny sacks to work with and we surely can get the roots to make the dye." But that five packages of bias tape—even though it was only ten cents a package—was just too much for us to think about. And you could buy calico for ten cents a yard, and it didn't take five yards to make a dress. So we were a little skeptical of her demonstration.

Jessie Halsell, 68, New Mexico

I think one of the most appreciated workshops they had was that in upholstery, where they refinished old furniture, replaced springs and did a complete job of upholstering. Another workshop was making of draperies.

And then an agent came up and set up a workshop and made patterns for us individuals in making dresses, swimming suits, girdles and undergarments.

Marie Carlile, 67, Montana

Lessons have really changed. Used to be the home decorating was more of making do with what you had. For example, one lady lived in a log house and she was so tired of looking at her log walls. So we had a meeting one day about what we could do with log walls.

You could have your husband help you finish it so you could paper, etc. Well, she came up with the idea that it would be cheaper to just buy gingham material and then use that to cover the walls. Now you read in the magazines where they are using sheets [on the walls]. But it was very primitive back then and it was trying to beautify what we had, with not too much to work with.

Mary Raymond, 60, Wyoming

One of the lessons that I remember that meant a great deal was in making drapes, and the length of drapes. Another lesson that I remember was on hanging pictures. So, when I visited in other homes and saw pictures that were not hung as prescribed in the lessons, or drapes that were half-way between the window sill and the floor, I said to myself, "Oh, yes, nobody here belongs to the Farm Women's Club."

Pearl Faulkner, 78, West Virginia

I had a fairly good dining room set, but I needed something to demonstrate how to refinish a piece of furniture. So I took a leaf from the dining room table and I refinished this to show how to refinish furniture. When this turned out so beautifully, my husband and I—well, he didn't know it was going to be a joint effort—we did over the entire dining room set, including a buffet, a china closet, six chairs, and the rest of the table. This took a couple of years. And I found that he could take finish off when the Baltimore Orioles were losing (laughs). He worked twice as hard when there was a real exciting time in the game.

Eileen Moon, 62, Maryland

We were taught how to set the table and how to entertain and to greet your guests as they came in and how to make them feel comfortable.

Now, we are trying to make each other feel comfortable in a psychological way. We didn't know then that it had anything to do with psychology. We were just taught to make your guests and your family comfortable in your house, so that all people in your house and members of your family felt comfortable at all times.

Are you saying they taught the skills more than the theory behind it?

Yes, I think we paid little attention to the theory. How it turned out was more important than the method.

And I think that a well-rounded houseperson should have charm. They should be more charming as individuals, so that they're a pleasure to meet and a pleasure to have in your company and a pleasure to have as a friend.

What has caused you to keep going all these years?

I guess that's because I have an inquiring mind. I've never had a class that I didn't get something out of it.

Rubie Gillion, 80, Michigan

[Memory of a retired agent] Another project during this period was the cotton mattress project. The project was for low-income farm families. We had to charge a small amount to each family that came to make a mattress. I think it was 25¢ that they paid. We had mattress centers all over the county, in abandoned schoolhouses mostly. The government furnished the ticking and there were several farm women who were glad of the opportunity to make the ticking—make the mattresses to be stuffed. They were paid 25¢ for each mattress ticking that they made, and many of them were *glad* to get that 25¢, and the ones that were doing this, they owned farms.

But money was just tight in those days.

Yes, you just were glad to get anything to do to make a little cash money.

What did they use to stuff the mattress with?

Cotton. The government sent a bale of surplus cotton that they wanted to get rid of. They sent you bales of cotton, to your county.

So you had all the materials furnished to work with. You just needed the labor to make them.

Yes. About 5,340 mattresses were made in Dillon County

That's a lot of mattresses.

And it took up a lot of the Home Agent's time to supervise that project.

Etta Sellers, 90, South Carolina

Some of the mattresses you see out on the street for trash are better than some of the mattresses a lot of our people had back in the earlier days. The government bought up tons and tons of cotton, and you could get the ticking through the Extension office, and then you sewed your mattress.

It was at a town house or a church, and you had sawhorses and planks and boards and things. You stuck that cotton in the mattress, and after you got it so full and even all the way around, then you put it on the boards. Then you had those long needles about two feet long. You had to tie down and up.

My mother, until she passed away, back in the early '70s, was still using those mattresses, and a lot of people maybe still are using them today.

Luella Hamilton, 71, Michigan

I remember we had a lesson where each of us made our own dress form. We helped each other. We each brought a roll or two of glued heavy paper tape, and each of us had to undress down to some kind of an undergarment that came down to the knees. Then we followed the instructions in the manual and wrapped that sticky paper around us— layer after layer after layer, covering over the shoulders and around the armholes and round and round the chest and waist and thighs—clear midway down the thighs.

Many homemakers of the 1930s took advantage of the opportunity to make their own mattresses by stuffing ticking with cotton and sewing it all together with long needles. This project was supervised by the Extension offices.

It was quite a long process and rather wearying. We had to stand around a while, while the paper dried a little, enough from the heat of the outer air and our body heat that it would hold its shape.

Then, very carefully, someone would split it all the way down from the neck to the bottom and we wiggled out of it like a locust wiggles out of its skin. Then they taped the two cut edges together again.

Then we carefully took those forms home and had our husbands saw out a thin board that was exactly the shape of the bottom opening of the dress form, and the form was tacked to that board. That held it securely at the bottom, so it couldn't cave in or mash in. Then we could fit our dresses over our own bodies, in a way.

They were fairly successful, because a ready-made dress form—a metal dress form—was expensive and not very many of us could afford them. However, if you got thinner or fatter after you made your form, (laughs) then you had to take that into consideration when you made your dresses.

I had never expected to have a dress form, so it was fun. When a group of women get together and have to strip down to fundamentals and work on each other, why it was a lot of fun. I enjoyed it—I think we all did.

Nellie Yost, 76, Nebraska

My dress form was a little less than perfect, but she was so good that once—I told them—it scared a burglar away (laughs). That really didn't happen, but this did. A friend of mine came and the dress form was standing in the corner and he went over and threw his arms around her and said, "Hello, Dorothy."

Dorothy Klock, 66, Oregon

We made these dress forms that you made on a person. You put layer after layer of that tape on, and they couldn't move, or they couldn't sit, or lay, or anything.

Well, this lady, we got a good start on her and she started to faint on us, and we didn't know what to do. We couldn't lay her down, we couldn't sit her down, and we didn't know whether to cut her out of it and ruin it—we didn't know really what to do.

So we tried holding her. A group got around her and we was holding her in our arms, and another group was there fanning her and washing her face and trying to bring her to.

We worked with her until we did get her out of it [the faint] and we asked her if she wanted to continue with the dress form, and she said yes. So we stood her back up and continued with her dress form.

But the clinch was that evening when we all went home. We didn't use cars much, we were all there in the neighborhood. And to see them all walking down the street with these dress forms in their arms!

Marie Unfried, 71, Indiana

Our nearest neighbors were Polish people. They made home brew over there. The father would sometimes get too much home brew and when he came over, he was kind of uncontrollable.

My mother had just had club there a couple of weeks before, and they'd made those dress forms that we made over cotton T-shirts. Well, one night this Polish man came over and we had the phonograph going. He grabbed Mom's dress form and was dancing a Polish dance around in the living room.

Evie Foster, 70, Alaska

My mother-in-law, she never attended a class that I remember of. But the class wouldn't be over, and the agent gone, until she'd be in my house, wanting to know. So the information that we gave to each other and to others—it spread like wildfire on Little Prater, and I guess everywhere in the county.

Corria Ratliff, 82, Virginia

All the topics broadened the homemaker's view. When I was married, all we had was a radio, if you were lucky. We didn't have the televisions. We had the type of telephone that might be out on account of a storm.

So it [Extension Homemakers] kept us in touch with the world. It gave us an unbiased viewpoint on many topics.

Alice Wand, 65, Oregon

When we first started Extension work, I can remember that women thought they had had a profitable Extension club day when they would go to club and could carry something home that they had made with their hands. Something out of paper, something out of anything that was available. Something that they could set or hang up in their homes. And I thought to myself, will we ever get beyond just something to carry home in our hands? I'm happy to say that today we're able to go to a club meeting and carry something home in our minds as well as our hands.

Verna Lefman, 84, Missouri

I think I get just as much benefit from [the programs] as the ladies do; they are all educational.

That is good to hear, because that means that a man can enjoy Extension Homemakers just as much as a woman can.

Ansel Peterson, 76, West Virginia

Have the programs varied throughout the years?

I think they really have. I think this is an organization that has definitely tried to keep up and has done a good job keeping up with the pertinent issues and questions that homemakers have.

I think we have to applaud the leaders and the Extension agents for this. And it reaches the Extension Homemaker members and then we in turn disseminate a lot of this information to people in our community. And, to me, that's really what it is all about.

Janet Cassell, 34, Virginia

EXTENSION AGENTS

Early Conditions

[Ed. note: In the list of suggested questions for the interviews from which this book is drawn, there was the question "In the early years of club work, were there individuals who impressed you?" Of course, there were many varied answers, but many, many narrators spoke with

Lella Gaddis, early Indiana agent, steps into her car, carrying a suitcase with demonstration materials. The license year is 1918. The crank was the method of starting the engine.

heartfelt admiration and respect of the Extension agents with whom they had worked. Since all names which were mentioned could not be included, it seemed fairer to include none. However, all people working with Extension work can be assured that Homemaker members admire and appreciate them—the interviews prove this.]

My mother was an assistant agent. She helped the lady who was the Home Economist at that time. She would put us kids in the back of her little Model T Ford. I can remember that little rumble seat. We always got to eat the dust on those dirt roads.

We'd go out in the country. Of course, we lived in the country, but there was some farther back in the woods than us. Babysitters weren't heard of then; she had to carry us with her.

These people were, well, they were ignorant in ways of fixing up their homes. They just didn't know how to even fix simple things to make their homes better, so Mama would show them.

I remember one time she showed them how to make beds. They'd just take a blanket and throw it in the corner of the room, and sleep on the floor. Anyway, Mom was to show them how to fix up beds, so they'd sleep up off the floor.

She had a way of talking to men. Sometimes we'd go to these places, and the men of the house—big boys and all—would be sitting around on the front porch, I guess just talking. She'd conjure them up, and make them go out and cut them a stick. She'd tell them to cut down a small tree, a little slim oak, and trim them off and make a post about four feet high

Mama had a good way of talking. These men and big boys, you know then, back out in the country, they thought it was women's work and men's work, and they didn't want to mix it. But Mama, she could talk those men into doing things they didn't know they was talked into doing, till you'd see them (chuckles) doing it.

Then she'd take hog wire [woven wire fencing], and it was about three inches square. It was right big wire and it must have been strong, because it would keep the hogs in the pasture. Of course, these farmers, they would have hog wire around. So Mom would take and make them cut a piece, and they would put nails into that corner post. I remember one time Mama said, "If you haven't got any rope, we can use old plow line"—anything that was strong enough to hold that wire [fencing] around that tree limb.

So the wire actually made the springs of the bed.

Yes, I don't know if you know anything about cotton picking, but back then we had cotton sheets of material and they'd lay their sheets out in the edge of the field and when you picked cotton you just stuffed your crocus bag of cotton on these sheets.

Well, Mama finagled so that she got these women to get a few of these cotton sheets. They were a little bit bigger than a bed, but it give Mama room enough to cut them out—and then she'd get them to sew two of these together and make a bag. If they happened to have cotton, she'd always encourage them to use the cotton, but if they didn't have it, she made them use pine straw [needles] to stuff the bag. That made a mattress, and that way they learned to make a bed. I remember she used to make them sit those posts in a little cup or a jar lid and she'd pour kerosene in that. I think that kept bedbugs and whatever was in the pine straw from living—I don't know, but I remember she'd make them put it in that little cup of kerosene. Ooh, that kerosene would stink!

Dora D. (Mother) Walker was first appointed to Extension work in 1911. She was appointed as State of Carolina Home Demonstration Agent on December 1, 1914. Here she demonstrates how to cut up and cure pork.

That seems impossible in this day and time, but those people did not know how to conjure them up a bed.

I guess Extension hasn't changed all that much, because we're still trying to help people to learn to live better.

Pat Gates, 55, South Carolina

I did all the surveys with the doctors. They would set up areas for the doctors to go out to the various schools and I'd help haul them. I remember Dr. Morris when he was a young chap and he came back to practice with his father here in Jacksonville.

I was assigned to take him to Cross Swamp which is really out across a swamp. That really was the lowest, flattest country I ever drove a car in, I can tell you. I soon discovered that he was nervous, but I'd gone over it so much that it didn't bother me any. I knew I could go through that creek all right and come out on the other side. But he was really concerned.

Pearl Laffitte [retired agent], 80, Florida

Miss Gertrude Humphreys organized a great number of women's clubs in Mercer County. I know that, with there not being good roads at that time, she had a difficult time getting to the different communities. Sometimes she would borry a horse and ride it; sometimes she'd have to hire a horse and buggy because it was too far and too muddy to walk. In our area we had the Tri-City Traction street car, and the agents would take advantage of riding some distance on the street cars. And sometimes they were able to hitch a ride with the mail carrier, or with people going or coming to town.

So my memory of Miss Humphreys is trying to get from place to place. It was a difficult job.

Pearl Faulkner, 78, West Virginia

In my term as president of the South Dakota Extension Clubs, we took the same program to different places. I can remember going across South Dakota with Dr. Russell from Kansas and Miss Hott, our state leader at that time. We were riding along and I remember Dr. Russell saying, "Where are we now, Miss Hott?" and she would say, "We're in Meade County." Then a few hours later, he would say, "Where are we now?" and she would say, "We're in Meade County." And he said, "Meade County must be a second Texas; every time I ask it's still Meade County."

But when we got there, we had the biggest crowd at the church for the potluck dinner. He was so amazed that the people came from so far, and I said, "Well, they are coming to hear you, Dr. Russell. They are so interested in learning about things to make life a little better." So we had a grand crowd and a grand meeting.

Cleo Tyler, South Dakota

We often drove a team fifteen miles and more over very poor roads to get our information, and then we passed on this information to our neighbors who couldn't attend the meetings.

And because the roads were bad and the distances great, the lecturers who came to give the programs had to stay all night in the homes. This was an advantage in many ways, and much information was given both ways. The settlers got more information, and the lecturers got a better insight into the problems of the people.

Mrs. J.E. Kunkel, Idaho

[Memories of an early agent] We were expected to be at work shortly after eight and work till five. Then, if there were any night meetings, those were in addition.

How were you dressed when you went to work?

I always had a dress on, and most places I went, I had a hat on. People were expected to wear hats.

You had your office in the basement of the courthouse, I know. What kind of facilities did you have down there?

Just a desk. The County Agent had a separate room, but I was in the same room with the office girl.

We had rats in the courthouse. We'd go out and see them walking across the pipes in the hall. The day I declared war was when they had eaten the candy right out of my drawer. So I declared war!

Every time we would see one, the office girl would get on top of that big table in the office and I would get the rod that raised the window. I always shut the door so he couldn't get out. I would corner that rat behind the files and beat him to death. I think I must have killed eight or ten that way. But she would get on top of the table and just scream at the top of her lungs, and I would kill the rat.

Alice Gentry, 68, Indiana

Getting an Agent

Did you have a Home Economist in the county when you first organized? I think there were [male] County Agents in most of the counties.

Yes, but we didn't have a Home Economist for years—a long time after that. And of course I was the one that had to go to the [county] commissioners and ask for a little help in getting a Home Economist. So we got the agent, and things went along fine then.

Sophie Bigge, 82, Kansas

In 1936 I was made chairman of the committee to get us a Home Demonstration agent. You can imagine what trying to run the county meant when you had no help except the general help the [male] county agents could give you. We worked very hard on that. Among other things, we had to raise a sum of money.

And we had to go before the County Council to get the appropriation. That happened to be the summer that I had to have all my teeth out, but that didn't stop me. I went on ahead anyway, and went to the meeting of the County Council and made an impassioned plea for [money for] the Home Demonstration agent, telling them we would fall to pieces if we didn't have her, and all that.

One of the gentlemen that was on the Council said, "If that woman can talk like that with her teeth out, I would sure like to hear her when she gets them in."

I take it they let you have your county agent?

Got the county agent and she was very good, and we did better after we had her. We could see the results in several ways.

Camille Hey, 89, Indiana

Most of our Extension programs are having penny-pinching with their budgets. Last year there was some question as to whether we would be able to retain our women county agents, which we felt was really imperative if we were going to keep our Extension Homemaker programs as active and ongoing as they are.

So we really put on a real campaign to go out and have a letter write-in campaign to our senators and county commissioners and newspapers—anywhere we thought we could have a little clout.

We must have hit them hard, because the county commissioners and other legislative people did go ahead and appropriate funds so that we were able to retain our County Agent.

How did you go about this campaign?

It was basically through letter writing and telephoning. Those of us who weren't able to go out and actually see people face to face because of transportation costs and time, we could always take the time to telephone. And by telephoning our members, we got them to sit down and write letters. I guess it was just a blitz.

Elsie Rieger, 59, Montana

Extension Home Economists as People

We had some agents that I was very thrilled with—they were very good. At that time they were able to devote much more time to working with the clubs themselves than they do now. So we became very close to our agents. They were almost like one of the family.

They had a job to do and they did it well. They were easy to get along with. They made things very pleasant. [And they taught us] to make housekeeping and homemaking an easy job.

Zilphia Edwards, 63, Louisiana

What about the leaders in Extension?

The professional leaders? I think the ones that I've been involved with have impressed me because they're so well-rounded. They can do a lot of things and be interested in a lot of things and therefore they are interesting people. I like to listen to what they say, and I like their willingness—if they don't have the knowledge—to research it and bring us the information.

Carolyn Dame, 40, New Hampshire

We had this "green" agent, she's just starting her job, and I'm serving my third year as county president.

And I told her one time that I didn't know who was learning the most with us working together. I said that I had really benefited from working with her as our agent, and she commented that she sure wouldn't have wanted to go through that first year without me.

But anything in Extension is a two-way street. You learn from others. When you're helping them, you learn—you can't help but learn.

Our agents, they're more than agents. We spend so much time together doing different things that I think they're almost family. Best friends situation.

Deanna Cook, 31, West Virginia

They [agents] were all so interested in their job. You never had the feeling that they were just doing it for the money. They were really working toward an ideal. They were unusual. I think that in order to be an Extension agent, you have to be an all-around person who is interested in humanity.

Cleo Tyler, South Dakota

I was very much taken with the agents, the county Home Demonstration agents. I thought they were something very special to me. And I tried to do and follow the things that they taught. I felt it was good for us; that we were getting so many things that were really *good* for us, to make us better homemakers.

Beatrice McCann, 82, West Virginia

All the Extension club leaders who were sent out from Lincoln were *very* good. I admired those young women very much. They were not very long out of college, and they were enthusiastic and very able.

They could make wonderful demonstrations for us of the many things that we needed to know.

They were all good. We didn't have a Home Extension agent that wasn't a good one. They were very different, but they were efficient. They were nice to work with, and I liked them all.

Nellie Yost, 76, Nebraska

Times have changed; conditions have changed. But the Home Demonstration and farm programs, they're still marching forward. I think there surely always will be a need for these wonderful programs.

And, Miss Sellers, there'll always be a need for dedicated women like yourself, who have devoted so much of your life to developing these programs.

Etta Sellers [retired agent], 90, South Carolina

BENEFITS FROM HOMEMAKER CLUBS

General Benefits

I think the Extension Homemaker club is a good all-around organization where you learn; you gain information; you gain insight into problems. [It is not] just cooking and sewing, which a lot of people have the idea that we are.

We learn how to deal with our emotions. We learn how to deal with family problems. It gives us a chance for leadership. It gives us an opportunity to go out beyond ourselves—to expand—to enrich our lives. I think that is one of the greatest things that has happened to me and to a lot of other people I know. It has really enriched our lives.

Sue Moman, 55, Alabama

If a young housewife, or even an old one, came to you and asked about Extension Homemakers, what would be the first thing you'd say to them?

I'd say, "If you can't have that, you're losing something in your life that you need."

Corria Ratliff, 82, Virginia

Well, I was a young housewife when I started and I had not had the responsibility of running a household. So first I had to learn to cook, and then to sew, and then my first child was born about ten months after we were married, so I immediately had to learn how to start raising a family. So you have to learn in a hurry.

When I used to attend Home Demonstration clubs in those days, I would learn little things that would help me out the next day when I would start to do something. I can truthfully say I learned more in Home Demonstration work those first few years than I had ever learned anywhere else.

Zilphia Edwards, 63, Louisiana

All-day club meetings were often broken up with some sort of group exercise.

It has taught me how to save and economize; it has taught me how to sew; how to can and preserve food. Without the Home Demonstration club, I don't think I could have made it. There isn't too much of anything that I can't do for myself.

Julia White, 60, Tennessee

Do you think the Homemaker club member herself has changed through the years?

I sure do. Her looks, for one thing. The Homemaker club woman—where we used to have homemade [looking] dresses, they're handmade now. The looks of the woman and of her home have improved. I think a lot of that has to do with Homemaker clubs.

Betty Newman, 50, Mississippi

If another man asked you what the benefit of Extension Homemakers was, what would you say?
I would tell him that I felt everything was most worthwhile.
Ansel Peterson, 76, West Virginia

I always felt like the club did more for me than I ever did for the club. It taught me a lot of things. I went into the club following a real serious nervous breakdown and by going to club meetings, I got myself able to get back to stand people and to be in a group of women.
Lots of times I couldn't stay all the time. But finally I got to where it was all right. That was the biggest thing it ever did for me. I don't know what would have happened without my club.
Nona Berry, 81, New Mexico

I was active in my Homemakers unit and I served on the county board. I think it was working with all the people in the county that probably led us to make the decision that we might succeed in business. I guess what I want to say is it made me self-confident.
Charlene Diel, 43, Illinois

At one of the two-county meetings the other day, this lady was speaking about that she thought Extension Homemakers had saved her life. They came here from another state; she didn't know anybody; her kids were all small; they didn't have money enough for babysitters; they were in a small town on the north end of the county; and there was nowhere she could go. Then someone said, "Come on, go with me to Extension."
She said that was something that she simply held on to. She has grown with it and now she's a committee chairman. I think it's one of those things that you can give to, and it can give to you. It helps a person to grow and develop her full potential.
Dorris Graves, 70, Oregon

I feel that the sociability of your own group in your own locality is another binding point. You have such a good time, you make so many new friends. In time of need, they're there. This builds up from your working and learning together. It's a fun experience. It really is.
Women need women.
Priscilla Lloyd, 56, New Hampshire

I was president of this local club [in Baltimore]. Within a year we had 150 members in that club. I'll never forget how wonderful they were to me. At Christmas we usually exchanged presents. You brought one present and exchanged with someone else in the club.

Well, I had just had a back fusion, and I was in bed at Christmas. After the club members came back from their Christmas program, they brought me a *big* basket full of presents. Instead of exchanging presents, everyone had brought one for me. I was going to be in bed for several months, and I opened up one of those presents every day, and it was a wonderful thing—the love and concern of these people.

That is the way with Homemakers. It isn't just the subjects we learn, but the friends that we make.

Eileen Moon, 62, Maryland

I've enjoyed being a Homemaker ever since I joined in 1964. I've enjoyed the fellowship of these fine ladies and they have taught me an example of what living right and living a clean life can mean. It's just been great.

I'm just so lucky to have stumbled on to a member of the club and asked to visit the club one day and then finally joined.

Elizabeth, I won't offend you, I think, if I asked you—you are Indian, aren't you?

I'm part Indian and I'm proud of my heritage, very proud.

My maiden name is Big Walker, and my Indian [given] name means Flying Eagle. That was given to me by my grandmother, as a baby.

I think back to the years that I've been in the club and how nice everybody's been. It's been an opportunity to reach out. I also pass this information on to members of my tribe. They're glad that all of us can live anywhere in the United States, and hold our heads high and be proud of our country.

Elizabeth Big Walker, Georgia

I think that the gift that I received from being an Extension Homemaker has been the many friendships that I have made in these past several years. My husband has been able to go with me and he has found great value through the Extension Homemakers contact of making friends.

The contacts that we have had with the Extension Service has given us an opportunity to learn many things and be in touch with areas that I'm sure we would not have been able to do, if we were just a plain farmer and his wife.

And I think that the very fact that we have been able to rub elbows and make contacts with other people—we feel that we have enriched their lives.

Misaye Uno, 65, Colorado

Being able to get out once a month and talk with other people is the best thing for me right now. Not working, and being home with three kids all the time, it's nice to get away and talk to other people, other adults, once in a while.

Sarah Adkins, 27, Ohio

Bob would keep the children, and that was my night out. I would go pick up my mom and then we would go on wherever the meeting was. This was just about the only thing I did just for me. The other things that I did were things the family did together. But Homemakers was always my special thing.

Mary Jo Depew, 41, Kentucky

One of the things that impressed me was the fact that the Homemakers club was such a rounded program. That there was information and material and helps, not only for the homemaker, but for the husband, or the father, and for all the children. So it was a program that was of benefit to every member of the family.

Pearl Faulkner, 78, West Virginia

The knowledge I have gained through the district, state and national workshops and educational sessions has improved my family's way of life. In fact, I think my entire community has benefited by my being a member.

Lou Ellen Peek, Georgia

To step out to lead and to teach, and to see the need. This is the part of Extension work that is really great—to look beyond ourselves and see the need of the community.

Sarah Ball, 74, Oklahoma

Extension has been a big part of my life. I think it's helped make me the person that I am, one way or another—the lessons, the contacts I've made with my own study groups, with the Extension agents and the state personnel. It's been very meaningful in my life.

Saundra Zook, 39, Oregon

It has helped me to change with the changing times. I think I understand better about the changes and am willing to accept the changes better from the education that I've had as a homemaker.

Vi Cottrell, 69, Washington

I've lived a happy life. The farm has played a great part in my life, and the Home Demonstration has played a great part in my adult life. I don't know what kind of a person I would be if I hadn't been a Home Demonstration club member.

What a beautiful tribute!

Hautie Nelson, 69, Tennessee

LEADERSHIP

When I was first asked to be the Hillsboro County Chairman, I just kind of looked at our Home Economist as much as to say she was crazy to ask me to do it. But she encouraged and supported me and helped me, so that I got over that.

It sounds like the Extension agents have done a good job of getting women out of their shy, backward feelings and inhibitions.

I think that they've helped do that for me, and I think they've helped many Homemakers. I think there is any number of them that you could mention across the country, that the reason they can do the things they do today is because of a county Home Economist.

I don't know of any other organization that I could have gotten involved in that gave me the self-confidence that I've gotten out of Extension Homemakers.

You are looking at a woman who would not—and still—has a hard time to stand up in her own community at a public hearing and say anything. I have to become very emotionally involved before I do. I was never one to get up and speak in front of a group of people. It just was too frightening for me.

Certainly there are many things that I haven't done in this world, like everyone else. But I think that I have grown as an individual because of my involvement, and because of that county Home Economist many years ago—"Get going, Eleanor!"

Eleanor Whittemore, 55, New Hampshire

[Editor's note: Eleanor did indeed get going. Sometime after this interview she became president of the National Extension Homemakers Council, which position she currently holds.]

When I first joined club—I'm sure people wouldn't think about it now, but I used to be very bashful and I couldn't any more have gotten up in front of people. When I had to give a book report in school, I would get so nervous I could hardly talk.

I really was anxious to learn more about homemaking and family living, so I joined. The first thing they wanted me to do was go get a lesson, and I said, "Oh, Lord, how will I ever do that?" But they were so good, so I said yes and went to get the lesson. There were supposed to be two of us, and the other lady couldn't come, and here I am, all bashful, and I thought, "What am I going to do?"

But Eve Goebel, who was later our state leader, was the specialist teaching the lesson, and she did such a beautiful job. And she even showed us the best way to teach [the lesson] so actually it was an ideal lesson for me to start on.

So I went back and taught it, and from then on, I got better at it. And it was a form of education in developing leadership, because I would never have dreamed I could stand up in front of a group and talk. If anyone had ever told me I would be state president, let alone

Members of the Extension clubs learn how to teach lessons to their fellow club members, after having been trained themselves by Extension specialists. This leader training multiplies the specialists' efforts and gives training in leadership to the Extension club member.

be a national president, I never would have believed them. [Mrs. Agness was national president in 1976-79.]

Donna Agness, 61, Indiana

How do you think that people get started in the training to be a leader?

Well, you take on a job and you do that one and then you just seem to kind of move from one thing to the other. Then all of a sudden you realize, "Well, I'm a leader," (laughter) not fully realizing that that's what you're doing.

Do you mean doing the program, is that the way you started?

You start off by being a chairman—maybe you're health chairman in your local club. Then you go to leader training in the county and it's your responsibility to bring it back to your club. Of course, you feel like you can't get up and do that program, but you manage to do it.

The next time you do one it doesn't bother you as much. The next time, a little less. Of course, you always feel a little nervous. I think that just goes along with it.

But when I went in the club I would hardly say anything, and I ended up as state president.

Thelma Barnes, 61, Florida

I remember the first time I got up to give a lesson. I was so nervous, being my first part, that after I gave it, I just picked up my baby and walked out the back door and went home.

Edith Gladden, 63, Missouri

I have learned a lot, because the first time they asked me to take the lesson I was panic-stricken. But after I worked on the lesson and gave it a lot of time and thought and was able to present it . . . seems like after that first lesson, I was on my way.

Dorothy Tolley, 67, Arkansas

One of our objectives in Home Demonstration club work is to develop leadership. Of course, basically, we are dealing with education. When we go to a club meeting, we hope to learn something in the area of home economics. But leadership is an objective, too. Have you seen people develop their leadership potential?

I surely have. It's helped a lot of women.

The shy young homemaker . . .

And some of them are not that young. But you see them overcome it when they are in club a short while. We always tell them we won't ask them to do anything that they can't do. But you'll find that it won't be long till they'll be doing everything that everyone else is. Reaching out and growing.

Hautie Nelson, 69, Tennessee

How many jobs or offices have you held on the state board of the West Virginia Extension Homemakers Council?

I have been a member of the advisory committee to the executive board and I have been state secretary.

Did you come up through the ranks, holding offices in the Farm Homemakers Council?

Yes, I did. I was secretary at one time, and then from secretary I was elected the vice president, and then I became state president of the Farm Homemakers Council from the year 1963 to the year 1965.

Were there any other presidents following you?

No. I was the last president up to integration. I was the last president at Washington Carver State Camp.

Margaret Hill, 65, West Virginia

I wanted at one time to be president of the PTA and I always felt like I wasn't capable. I didn't think I could get up in front of people. Then I started Extension work, and by the time I felt like I was capable, my daughter was out of school, and I never did get to be PTA president.

But now I have been every officer in our club. I've had three state offices and from there I was on the national board as treasurer. And from there I was treasurer of the Country Women's Council.

That is quite an impressive list of offices. So the leadership training that you have had in Extension Homemakers has been as valuable as the homemaking skills?

I know that it has helped me to get up in front of people and I have learned a lot and have helped our family. It has been many things to me.

Mary Moore, 73, New Mexico

Mother Mack [mother-in-law] was elected to the state council. She was a member of our parish council and was the president of the parish council at several different times.

She was a very good leader; so sincere and such a good Christian that she did what she thought was best in everything she had to make decisions about.

At the time she was state president she was able to go to the national council meeting in one of the northern states and just the next week after that meeting they were having the Associated Country Women of the World—the ACWW—International meeting in Canada, and she was fortunate enough to go to this international council meeting.

Now that was just the biggest thrill to her, because she had stayed home in the country and reared her family, because back in those days you didn't get to do too much going. Then after they were all gone from home, all of this started happening. We were all so happy for her, because she really did enjoy it.

Virginia McIntyre, 63, Louisiana

I have said that to get people to do a job, you've got to help them to know what it is they are supposed to do. I think this is where Extension Homemakers has benefited me *so* much, because there was not one job I was ever asked to take that I didn't have somebody back of me, helping me. You know [in the county] your Home agent, your past president; and on the state level you had your State Leader and your past presidents you could go to; and on the national level you had your leader from Washington and the past national presidents, who had all been leaders, and they were all willing to help to develop the person.

And I wrote this material and it is still being used—about leadership.

That has been passed everywhere. As I remember it, the main thing you said was that it takes a lot of help, and no one does it all by themselves.

No way can you do it all by yourself. Any organization that has a successful [function] and the leader says, "I did it," I am sorry for that leader.

Sorry for the leader and sorry for the organization, both.

That's right. They all have to work to make it a success.

I have often said, in a way it isn't leadership at all—it's coordination. You coordinate other people's efforts, because no way, as you were saying, can you do it yourself. You need to be able to coordinate other people's helpful efforts together.

Nellie Depew, 68, Indiana

I am in a lot of leadership things, and I don't back off of leadership. I would rather be a leader than do the work. I can always find people that are ready to work (laughter).

You're a delegator (laughter).

I've always enjoyed working with people, and I'm always amazed at how much they will do. They really do come up with a lot of things. If it wasn't for them I wouldn't get anything done. I really should have no credit for anything, because every time I start a project, someone else really carries it.

I need that talent.

Oh, I don't know whether it's a talent, or just plain laziness (laughter).

Rubie Gillion, 80, Michigan

The skills are important and I know that's what they teach primarily—the cooking, and so on. I think they *are* important, but I think the other things you learn are even more so. By having all of these leadership opportunities, being an officer and on lots of committees, I've learned to be a leader. I've used that in other places, like in the church or in other organizations and things I've belonged to. It helped always, because I knew how to organize and how to do things. I know I learned it mostly through Extension, because you don't learn it in college or school or anyplace else.

Betty Wenig, 51, Ohio

It's a matter of growing through learning and learning by doing.

Elsie Rieger, 59, Montana

Family Support and Involvement

My mother was county president and I thought that, at the time, that was a great honor. I was real proud that she was able to do that.

So, in like manner, I felt honored when I was elected county president.

Pearl Faulkner, 78, West Virginia

I would like to say that the reason I am a Homemaker club member is the fact that my mom was a Homemaker club member and the club that I belong to was established in her home. She is a charter member and she has been very active on the county and area level.

She has been a good example for me to follow, and if it had not been for her, I might not have been a Homemaker club member at all.

Mary Jo Depew, 41, Kentucky

I have a daughter that has gone on, and she's in state Extension work. I'm sure that some of the seeds of that, she picked up while we were at Extension club meetings. She was in the way, no doubt, and getting told to keep out of the way, like kids do. You just took your children right along with you.

And your daughter is president-elect of the Missouri Extension Homemakers State Association at this time.

Nellie Frost, 80, Missouri

I've always had such a big mouth that it was easy for people to say, "Let's send Corry." When the time came to go to town or have one of these meetings, I had a dandy mother-in-law that would say, "I'll keep the baby. And the boys'll stay here, too."

I've had a lot of backing-up in my life. I think if there's anything due me—any greatness or anything that I feel thankful for in my life—it comes from Little Prater people. They've always backed me.

Corria Ratliff, 82, Virginia

[Interviewer's note: Mrs. Ratliff is a very modest person and failed to mention that she was Virginia State Mother of the Year in 1975. Several EHC members accompanied her to Richmond to receive the award from the Governor. On the morning of the award, much to her surprise, her seven sons and other kin arrived by charter bus to be present at the ceremony in the state capitol building.]

It is all well and good that our husbands like the organization and the work. And my husband certainly did.

He supported you in all your activities in Extension?

He supported me, and he loved to go to the workshops and any of the meetings that I went to. He loved to be there. And he made so many friends, and he thought so much of the women that belonged.

He knew that they all had the same goals, that of being better homemakers and wives.

Beatrice McCann, 82, West Virginia

I was privileged to become the President of the National Extension Homemakers Council, the national president.

How did your husband feel about this?

I'd like to say that one of the main helps that a person who's involved outside the home can have is an understanding husband. He is dead now, but the memories I have of coming home and how good he was, and the interest he showed in hearing about what had happened are with me. I always felt that he had pride in what I could do.

Did he keep the home fires going then?

Yes, he did, and he even watered the violets. He would stick his finger in to see if they were wet.

Evelyn Alden, 74, Kansas

You obviously have had the support of your husband in all of your activities.

Oh, yes. Couldn't have done it without the support of Horace. I owe a lot to Horace for his willingness for me to go and do whenever [I was] called upon.

Tell us what he requested of you when you were State President.

That I should never leave town without seeing that my gas tank was full, and that all four doors of the car were locked.

He wanted to preserve a good wife.

Zelma Wood, 77, Oklahoma

THE HOMEMAKER
AND HERSELF

*"I can't think of anything in the
world that's greater than being
a homemaker. It's a joy."*
Jessie Halsell, New Mexico

With the coming of labor-saving equipment in the home, the amount of labor and the number of hours required to do the basic work of housekeeping has been reduced.

Homemakers can now make decisions on how to spend some hours of their day, when previously there simply were no extra hours.

Many homemakers are now employed full or part-time outside the home and combine their traditional role with this newer role. Women who have elected to be full-time homemakers now spend more hours in community and volunteer work.

This change in work load has not changed the values of homemakers. Themselves trained to be honest, truthful, devout, kind and hard-working, they train their children in the same virtues.

They view the care and training of their children as one of the most important tasks in the world, and devote much thought, energy and love to the process.

Homemakers recognize that changes have occurred in family life, as women participate more fully in the decision process and in the task of breadwinning.

One thing never changes, however, and that is homemakers' devotion to their family and their home. They believe that homemaking is important and fulfilling, and they glory in the happiness and content it brings to them.

STUDIES IN COURAGE

Mary Skelley, 76, Oklahoma

I was born the day the town of Snyder blew away. I was two hours old. I think they told me eighty people were killed, and they have a monument.

Yah, I was like Mark Twain. I came in with a storm and I'm going to go out with one. I've been blowed away six times, so I may be blowed away and killed. I don't know.

Tell us more about when you were in tornados, or were blown away.

Well, there was the time in 1911. We had just come in the house, and it hit just like that—the biggest hail and everything. There were four of us children then. Mother put us under an old big Home Comfort stove, and that protected us. We were just crying; my mother was crying; we were all crying, and she was holding the door shut.

That house moved, and it moved again. Just like it was yesterday, I can remember it. It raised up just like we were flying and it fell down just like that and squashed everything. If it hadn't been for that stove, we'd have been killed by the ceiling.

Was there another storm?

Yes, when we lived at Piedmont. My sister was four days old. My father saw it coming and he told us to go to the cellar and he'd take our mother. He told her to stay in bed and he'd come back and get her. It hit and she got up and it blew her off the porch. We don't know just what happened, but she never did walk after that. She lived six months and died.

I raised the baby then. I fed her the first bottle. I was just thirteen years old. My grandmother came to live with us, and she was crippled. Couldn't get around at all, but she kind of bossed us kids around some.

Then I decided I wanted to go to school. I had missed so much. My father had kept me out of school three years to take care of this little sister. So I missed that much school. Then she [sister] was big enough to go with him, and my grandmother was there, and he could leave her with her.

We didn't have buses—we had to walk. We walked four miles to school every morning and every night back.

So I started in the eighth grade there, older than all the other kids were, but I got through that and started to high school. If a teacher was absent or something, [they] always called on me to go down and teach for them, and I was tickled to death, because I had decided way back yonder I wanted to be a teacher.

Then I went to high school three years. I finished in three years, because I was determined I was going to get through. I was behind, and I wanted to catch up as much as I could.

I had one dress. My grandmother had an old velveteen skirt, and she made it into a skirt for me. Every fall I'd get a new middy blouse, and I wore that velveteen skirt three years to school, just changing the blouse. I'd wear the blouse and I'd wash it out on Wednesday night and on the weekend.

We went with holes in our clothes, and I know we were dirty. I don't know how people stood it—you know, a bunch of kids. Our grand-mother died; we just didn't do like we do [now].

But I was always the type of person—I wanted to learn—I wanted to do like somebody else or better. I'd learn from seeing other people do something. Watch them. I did that all the time.

So when I finished high school I wanted to go to college. I wrote to all the colleges around to get a place to work for my room and board. That's the only way I could go. But I couldn't find a thing. Three days before it was supposed to start, Mr. Sugg [superintendent of schools] came down. We was out in the field picking cotton and he said, "Mary, Walter McCallum [former superintendent] said if you could go to col-lege, he wanted you to go, and he'd let you work for them for your room and board at Stillwater." So I was tickled to death.

Now they weren't able, but he wanted to help me through. That was his mission in life—to help somebody. He helped me. So I just got busy right quick, and Aunt Mary made me a dress out of shirting material, and one out of cretonne [curtain material]. That's all I had to go to school in. I wore the same old high top shoes, and the same old coat that I had worn all through grade school and high school. I had two pair of black cotton stockings.

What year was this?

September, 1925. I went to the bank and borrowed $35 from Dr. Richardson, and he said, "Pay it back with your first check." The school board had already told me if I could get this certificate they'd give me a job. I felt like I was privileged, for all of them to be looking out for me like this.

You had a lot of friends.

So anyhow, that's what I went to school on. So it took the $35 to buy my books and my tuition, and the McCallums gave me my board and room for working for them. And I worked hard. I wanted to go to school. I had always wanted to go to school.

Now which school was this?

Oklahoma State University, Oklahoma A & M. Then I finished. I got that two-year certificate to come back. One of the school board members had a daughter and he wanted them to give her a school. Well, he decided he wouldn't sign that contract for me unless they gave her a school. I was broken-hearted. I didn't know what to do.

So we talked with Dr. Richardson, and he said, "I'll go down and talk to him." He went down and took him a little drink of liquor and they called me that night and told me that I could have it [the school].

And then you signed a contract that you didn't go any place through the week. You couldn't date through the week; you dated on the weekend, if you wanted to. But you had to be in by nine o'clock. You had to go to church three weeks out of the month in that town, no matter if you belonged or not, even had to teach Sunday School class.

Times have changed, haven't they?

I went back to school that next summer and stayed with the McCallums again and worked. So I went back every summer and worked for my room and board. Taught in the winter and went back in the summers. Got through with my first degree, and a life certificate in 1934.

Now during this time I was teaching. Had four years over at Lone Rock, during the Depression. I took that job because I got $110 a month in a two-room school, and that was a *big* price. Well, the Depression come along and we got a cut in our wages, so one year I taught for nothing for four months and I got $50 a month for the other four months.

But I paid my room and board to these people—Carl and Lavina Wilson—when I got my first check. I paid $13 a month room and board out there in the country—a little three-room house we were living in. I slept in what they called their living room, and we all ate in the same room and just was part of the family. That's the way we lived—had to.

We didn't have any water. Sometimes his well would break down and we'd all wash in the same pan of water. We'd all take a bath in the same tub, but they always let me take my bath first; then they'd take theirs in the same tub of water. Can you imagine? We wouldn't do that now. We don't even drink out of the same dipper now, and then we drank out of the same dipper all the time.

Then they come down and asked me if I'd go up to East Walnut and teach in the high school and be principal. So I went up there and stayed two years. Then I went to work with the Farm Security and was a Home Supervisor and was, ever since then, a Home Economist.

You were the Home Economist in what developed into the Extension Service?

Yes.

Phyllis Sullivan, 49, West Virginia

Ifirst joined, well it was Home Demonstration back then, because my husband is a Methodist minister and our first church was a country church. I soon found out if you didn't belong to Home Demonstration, you weren't "with it" there. And I've never regretted joining.

At my first meeting there was a new agent (she's now specialist in women's programs at WVU). She taught a workshop on flower arranging, and I found I really had a talent for it. I taught flower-arranging workshops and finally was employed in a flower shop.

And from this I also started making pictures for the walls, using natural dried materials. And my family and I really enjoyed going out into the woods to gather those things. I taught people to do these pictures, and even today I still meet people that say they have a picture they made from those workshops.

And I've always said since I've had multiple sclerosis that that is the one area I never did get quite enough of, was working with flowers and natural materials. I said that when I get to heaven, what I'm going to do the first half of the first day I get there is going to be arranging flowers, and the second half I'm going to spend listening to Johnny Cash sing.

You get a lot of satisfaction from your creativity, don't you?

Yes, I can't do it anymore, and I guess one of the greatest satisfactions is that I can look around on my wall, since my hands are so stiff and I can barely write, let alone do creative crafts, and I can see the pictures I have painted or the arrangements I have made and all these crafts I was exposed to in Extension Homemakers and it is such a great satisfaction to see them on my wall.

Another area I enjoyed was leadership and there is a story behind how I got to be area representative. I had only been a member of Homemakers Club about a year when I went to my first spring county meeting. And they were having nominations for a candidate for their area representative. Someone nominated me, and I didn't decline, because I didn't know what to decline from. I remember saying, "You need to tell me what I'm being nominated for." And our agent said that I really didn't have to worry because there would be eight people running (one from each county) and my chances of winning were almost zero.

So I accepted, then went to the area meeting. I was song leader there, and anyone knows that I am real enthusiastic and I love to sing and I guess I made a big ham of myself that day, enough of a ham that it got me elected. I *know* that is what did it, because I sure didn't have any background in it. Our state president said when she heard that a greenhorn, with only one year's experience in club work, was going to be voting on a state level, she almost died. But she has told me since that it was the best thing ever happened to get a younger woman on the board. It had been basically an older woman's organization. Not that there's anything wrong with older ladies—they taught me what I know now—but there certainly was room for younger Homemakers.

And one of the specialists asked me to make a list of young Homemakers that I saw that had potential talent and might work for the future of our Extension Homemakers work. So I did, and out of that list of names I gave her, I would say about three-fourths of them have served on a state committee, or as a state officer, and two of them went on to serve on the national board. So that was a way we really got our young Homemakers involved, and it has been a blessing to our organization.

I served three years as area representative and then I served as Better Living Projects Committee chairman for three years, then I served as state secretary for one year, then I was on the ballot to be state vice president, but a week before the election came the diagnosis of multiple sclerosis, so I had to make a quick decision as to whether I should go ahead and run for vice president, or be the coordinator of the upcoming national conference. I knew I couldn't do both, my physical health wouldn't permit me, so I decided for the short term, which was coordinating the national conference, and I have never regretted it. I loved being coordinator.

Can you still participate in Extension Homemakers?
Well, that's one good feeling I had, because after I coordinated the conference, it took us about a year to wrap it up, and then I sure did let down on Extension work for two or three years. Then all at once I

got myself back together again, and began to do things again. For instance, I did the state handbook for two years, because that was something I could do at home and work with the publisher on the phone.

You're still working on the Young Homemakers program, aren't you?

Yes, as much as I can, since I am basically a bed patient and in a wheelchair now. I write a column for our state newsletter. It began as a season-type column, but then I got into hints for the handicapped and physically disabled. The title of my column is "Thoughts from the Wheelchair" and I try to tell family, friends and organizations how they can help disabled persons, and also how the disabled person can help themselves.

And another thing I can do, even though I am so limited in my travel, is something which I'm kinda proud of. I do ads for the newspaper for the florist shop I used to work for. I pick out little cartoon type things and I staple them on a paper and I think up the thoughts that go along with the cartoons and match the ads to the time of year or occasion. And, thank goodness, the newspaper puts up with my awkward handling of the ad, because I take a rough piece of yellow paper, staple the picture on it, roughly outline what I want them to say and give them directions. When it's finished, you can barely read it, but when it comes out, it's just a beautiful attractive ad. I'm proud of them, I keep a collection of them, and I think anything I do with my talents stems back to my work in Extension Homemakers.

There's another thing I want to elaborate on and that is leadership development. It has been the big thing in my life with Extension Homemakers and as I've mentioned in this interview, my first home demonstration agent has been such an influence on my life. I always kidded her and told her, "Here I am, I am your product. You made me what I am today. If you don't like it, then that's just tough luck, because I am one of your products."

I can never overemphasize the importance I feel toward leadership development in the Extension Homemakers program, and I hope and pray that emphasis will continue.

And I also do meditations, because I've had a lot of experience in church work and doing meditations for a group comes easy for me. I have even taught classes at conference and I try to teach the women to do unusual devotions and I suggest ways and give handouts. I still get mail from people telling me how one of my devotionals triggered something in their life that was good and they write to tell me how much they appreciate what they learned. So I feel that that's how my Extension Homemakers work has reached out and helped other people.

Your meditations are one of the highlights of the fall and spring conferences. I remember three or four years ago when you announced that this would be your last time to attend.

Yes, I stayed active in club work two years after the '76 conference, and I can remember doing the last meditation up there that night and I remember thanking the people for what they had meant, because I actually thought that was going to be the last devotional I would ever get to do for them. That's how fast I was going downhill. I remember telling them how much Extension Homemakers means to me, has meant to me through the years.

And this is the way I still feel about it today. If you ask me what Extension Homemakers means to me, I would have to say God comes first in my life, and then it's kind of a toss-up between my family and Extension Homemakers, because without one I couldn't do the good job on the other one. And that's just kinda the way it is.

Phyllis, thank you so much for giving us this interview this afternoon.

Thank you for letting me still be a part of the Extension Homemakers program, even though I am what they call physically disabled. I am disabled in my legs, but, thank goodness, I'm not so disabled in the head (both laugh).

Celia Lausted, 48, Wisconsin   I was born, the fourth child, in the middle of the Depression, in 1933. My family was struggling then, but I have to take you back a little further than that for you to understand.

I'll give you a brief picture of my mother. Her problems started before she was born. Her mother—my grandmother—was the youngest in a family of eight. Her mother died, and at the turn of the century, without any of the social services available today, it was necessary for each neighbor to take one child to help that man raise his children.

A maiden aunt and an unmarried uncle raised my grandmother, or at least she called them aunt and uncle. Then she met and married my grandfather. But when my mother was born, my grandmother became very, very ill. She went back to her aunt and uncle and they took her in and cared for her until she died. That left my mother, at the age of fifteen months, with no family.

These people were older. They kept her as long as they could, but at the age of ten, she was put into a children's school. From there she lived in foster homes until she was old enough to work out as a hired girl. There she met my father and fell in love at a very young age—seventeen. Okay, that's a history of my mother.

She met this man who was older than she was. He had been raised as an only child in [a home] where there was no love and sharing. It was a very bitter atmosphere. So even though [his parents] were well-to-do people and had considerable farm property, he was not about to go back to their home, after serving in World War I and coming home not too well.

I was the fourth child born into that family [that was] already in a hardship situation, with a mother who had very little education and very little experience in the world, and a father who was not well.

Then his father died and my father inherited a considerable amount of property. He began to spend it freely and began to run around and drink. This led to a divorce between my father and mother. During the divorce proceedings all the property was sold, and it was put into trust to help raise the children, and then to be divided after my father's death. You see women had no rights within marriage. Since the divorce took place, my mother got absolutely nothing.

But nothing was ever done with this estate. At the time of the divorce, there were six children, but my mother received no help to raise these children. A guardian was appointed to that estate, and that estate was not settled until I had been married and I went back to settle that estate.

That's the key factor in my interest in these things. My mother was left destitute with six children to support—where there was money available to be used for them.

She had no alternative but to remarry. We were itinerant farmers. He would work at one place for a year and then move to another farm for a year, and then move on. You can see the impact on the children as they move from place to place, without the roots they need and should have.

This marriage lasted through one more child and ended. My mother was left with one more child to support. The older children were beginning to leave home, because by the time you reached eighth grade you had to support yourself. There isn't money to take care of you, feed you, clothe you, so you get out and get a job.

By this time, Mother remarried the second time. I was old enough to begin to realize that I was different; that I didn't have the clothes; that I didn't have the opportunities that other children were having; and that there was a problem in our family. I might also say that both step-fathers were alcoholics, and the alcoholic situation with my second stepfather was just very, very ugly and disagreeable.

So by the time I was ready, at the age of thirteen, to leave home, I was ready, willing and able to go. I didn't want to deal with that any longer.

But I realized that to make any changes in my life, there had to be some education, so I had the gumption to not quit school. By living with a family and working for my room and board, I was able to stay in school. At least I was surviving and it was a much better environment to be growing up in.

My home economics teacher in high school was very understanding. She didn't know a lot of the details of my problems, but she was very understanding and encouraging. The principal of my high school, during my senior year, came to me and said, "Celia, I think we can help you with a scholarship."

[College] was very difficult for me financially. I borrowed money to go to school on and I worked. I remember one of the hardest days in my life was my college graduation day, because there I had accomplished a long-term goal—a goal that I had really fought for and really worked for—and there was not *one* person there from my family. It was a very hurting experience (speaks sadly).

Now at college graduation I had already signed a contract to teach home economics, and I went into teaching. But you see during college I also met a very wonderful man (laughs). He was a very loving and gentle person, and very understanding of my situation. I was *determined* to repay that loan before I got married. He said, "I'll wait for you."

With the kind of determination I had, it took me one year to pay back that money. I took one-third of my salary each month to pay back the money that I had borrowed to go to school on. So after I had earned enough money and paid back what I had borrowed, we did get married and came out to the farm.

I had felt that I was not in a position to do anything for my brothers and sisters. I had to educate myself first, but when I did get that education and my husband and I married, my youngest half-brother lived with us for two and a half years. My oldest daughter was born during the time he was there. It opened a whole new doorway for us, because ever since then we have had foster children at our home—sometimes two at a time. I've given a lot of myself to them.

I got involved in Extension Homemakers and began to learn about inheritance tax and the estate tax problem. My childhood had led me directly up to a problem that I had to deal with later.

[I was involved in settling two estates and saw the problems of ownership] and then my own father passed away and I had to settle his estate and I found out what had happened when I was only five years old. During all the years that I was growing up, there was money sitting in that bank that should have been used for the support of us children, and never was. The guardian of the estate helped himself, instead of helping us, and the attorney involved did nothing to correct the situation. The estate had been bled down to four thousand dollars, to be divided among six children who were all adults and self-supporting. At the time when we needed it, it wasn't there.

So whenever the Extension offered a class on estate planning, on probating an estate, or property ownership, Celia was there listening and asking questions. Then I began to realize that it's not necessarily the inheritance and the estate tax that was the basic problem. The basic problem was the attitude toward wives—that we are not a partner with our husband. It goes back to that old English common law that says a wife is the *property* of her husband. So when two people go to see an attorney to buy a piece of property, the attorney is addressing the husband as if the wife isn't there. She thinks she's there and her husband thinks she's there, but the attorney is addressing her husband.

[Celia Lausted became active in the movement for marital partnership property reform. She was appointed to the Commission on the Status of Women, and began an active speaking campaign.]

In 1978 I spoke 57 times through the state of Wisconsin. During the next three years I spoke 186 times.

What kind of audiences are you talking to?

Of course I started out with Extension Homemakers, and they have been staunch supporters of what I'm doing. I would say that the Home Economists have been delightful, also. But it's expanded beyond that. It's expanded into the Farm Bureaus and the Farmers Unions, and the NFOs and many of the producer organizations [all farm-related organizations].

Now it has expanded even byond that. I'm going into the League of Women Voters and the American Association of University Women, and the Business and Professional Women, because it has another scope, beyond farm women. If you're a professional woman, with your own salary, you no longer have proof or claim to your private income. You're actually giving a gift of your salary to your husband. Women don't know that.

[Mrs. Lausted attended a luncheon with Mrs. Walter Mondale and the Senate wives, where she talked of her concerns.]

The whole movement that President Reagan has picked up on—eliminating the estate tax between husband and wife, and the tax on interspousal transfer, and increasing the family exemption and increasing the gifting—is right along the whole thing of what I've been promoting and pushing.

Four years ago it wasn't happening, and here it is! It's happening on the federal level. I may have had just a tiny spot in helping promote that kind of reform. It's just really exciting.

[An award from the University of Wisconsin, an honorary recognition and the university's highest award, bears this citation: Celia Lausted of Colfax—zealous homemaker and devoted mother to her own children and foster mother to many others in need, full partner to her husband in a farming enterprise, inspirational crusader for justice in inheritance tax equity, and successful activist for statutory change.]

Is there an advantage to belonging to an Extension Homemaker Club in today's society?

Oh, absolutely! I wouldn't consider dropping Extension Homemakers. I'm still willing and ready to grow.

Lura Hess, 90, Ohio

I was born in a log house by a fireplace on an old-fashioned lounge. The land where we lived was very, very rough. One hill was (I think) a thousand feet above sea level and it had landslides in it. The ground on them high places would slide down and big rocks would turn up. My father one time cleared it off to farm it—that steep thing! We farmed with horses, and the horse could hardly stand up on it. He had to plant the corn with a jabber, and I had to take my hand and pat the dirt down. He let it go to grass after that.

My mother boarded the schoolteacher so as to have somebody to go to school with me, because the road was two and half miles around to the schoolhouse. Sometimes we went across a farm where they had great big cattle so we had to look out for that.

We wore high-topped shoes with woolen stockings to our knees and what you call bloomers made out of shirting cloth. It was heavy material, and my mother made them. And a wool dress on and a hood. She made nearly all my clothes.

When I got older, I never picked up with boys very good, because my mother was always telling me to watch it. She was always scaring me of the boys. But I met Ora Hess and we were married on March 15, 1911. Now we was two simple kids. He didn't have any money. Just had his farm equipment and he had $78.00 in his pocket when we went to housekeeping. That's all we had.

[The Hesses were tenant farmers. They moved often with their increasing family and had bad luck with crop failure and loss of livestock.]

What was it like, taking care of fourteen children?

Well, I look back over that and wonder. I never thought it was too bad. I was always awful busy, and I never went any place at all.

My children tell me that I was talked about when I was young and raising my family—that the neighbors didn't think very much of me. They said I was called trash.

And I said, "Now, listen, I never was trash!" I said, "I had all of you children, but you never went hungry, and you never went naked. I was always respectable and I always remembered I had a Savior, and I was not trash."

Well, they said I was talked about, but it didn't worry me any. I never thought about it. You don't have time to think about it. I remember one time when we lived back of Slabtown that I was never out to the road for two solid months. I think that was the year I was carrying Betty.

You don't have time to think about pitying yourself. By the time you draw water out of the cistern, hand over hand and carry it around to the kitchen door and come up three steps with it and put it on a coal stove and put that water in there and boil it, and then wash and carry enough water to rinse the clothes—you don't have time to think what anybody's saying about you (laughs).

I always raised a garden. I always calculated to have new potatoes and fried chicken on the Fourth. And I didn't fail very many times. I didn't have no brooder house to raise my chickens in. I raised them in a hog house with a lantern [for heat].

And this place [didn't have a privy] and you couldn't go any place to hide, because they'd see you from the road. So we had quite a time going out. So there happened to be a square box out in an old shed and there happened to be a toilet seat out there. So the boys they fixed a toilet out in the corner of the barn. You backed in—that was the only way you got to go in.

I sewed their clothing, out of anything I could get to sew out of. I even made overalls for the little ones. I used up my wedding dress to make Carol or Betty a crawling suit. I done sewing and mending. I never let them go raggedy. I washed about every day. I had to with that bunch, because I didn't have so much clothing.

I baked all the bread we ate. When there was four of them going to school, I would bake bread and when they'd come home I'd have a big baking of bread just out of the oven, and I'd have one loaf of bread less when they got done with it. Then they went and done their chores. I've baked enough bread to make a road from here to New York.

Now you say you've had fourteen children, and lost six of them?

Yes, I've always blamed myself for losing my baby. I got up one Monday morning and there was frost all over the trees and snow on the ground, and the sky was beautiful sunny. I sent two children to school and I had three to home—two up a-goin' and a baby, ten months old. I was washing and the baby was asleep. I had to go out to wash about fifty feet to a place to wash with my washing machine with a gasoline engine.

I went in to see how the children were getting along, and the baby waked up. I brought him out and put him in the high chair and I told Master, the oldest one, to get him something to play with. I never could remember where I had had this bottle of acid, but Master give it to the baby, and the baby pulled the cork out and spilled it on him. We didn't save him.

I thought that morning when everything was so beautiful and the kids was all so well, and I was going to get my washing done—I had it all done but the overalls—I thought it was going to be the most wonderful Christmas we ever had, but it was the saddest one.

How old was the baby?

Ten months old. He'd taken two or three steps—lovely little thing. I never got clear entirely over it, but I pass it away, because I cannot do nothing about it. But that was the first one I lost.

Then three years after that, I lost Master—he was the one that had handed the baby the acid.

It was wheat harvest time and Dad was out in the field and a thunderstorm was coming up. It was just about noon. He was bringing the horses in, so I sent Master—Ora McMaster was his name—I sent Master with a coat for him to take down to his father for him to come to the house in.

Well, this storm came up before any of them come back and we had the awfullest splitting clap of thunder. Then the sun came out.

We waited quite a little bit for them to come to the house, so I said to Eathel, "Go down to the barn and see what is keeping them." I can hear that kid coming up yet. He was about nine years old and he said, "Oh, Momma, they're all dead."

My, oh my, I didn't know how I'd ever go to that barn, but I started to the barn. And I got down a ways, and it didn't seem like I was going to be able to make it. I said, "Dear Lord, let me go on!" And with that I took up courage and went on.

Master was sitting on a rock in the doorway. I put my hand on him, and I said, "I can't do nothing here." I looked and Ora was laying with his head and shoulder right under where a horse's hind feet should be. She was a kicker, but she was huddled over against the stall as tight as she could be.

I went in and hollered at him, but he made no move at all. I said, "Oh, can I get him out of here?" I picked him up by the shoulders and pulled him clear out to the side of the barn. How I did it, I'll never know.

Eathel was with me down there and I said, "Eathel, go to the house and call the doctor." He said, "Mommy, I can't." Well, we had hogs all around the barn and I said, "Well, you will *have* to stay with them, then [to keep the hogs off of them] till I go."

By the time I got back from calling the doctor, the yard was full of people come to help. The doctor came and took Master to the house and laid him down on the porch. He said, "He is gone. I can't do nothing for him."

Ora was in bed about ten days. Wherever there was metal on him, he was burnt brown. He had had overalls on with two buttons at the side waist and just the shape of them was on him. I didn't know whether he was going to make it or not.

We had the funeral in the church, because we couldn't have it at the house [because of Ora]. My brother-in-law took me to the funeral. When I came home from that funeral, I went upstairs to change my clothes. When I got changed and was all ready to go downstairs, I never will forget the feeling that I had. I thought, "I never can go on." I just fell over on the bed and laid there a little bit.

But then I thought, "This won't do. I've got to go downstairs and see how Ora is." So I got up, and from then on I was able to make it. But I never had such a feeling, and I've never had it again. Just seemed like I was all in.

[Mrs. Hess' last child, a girl, was born dead, and a fourteen-year-old son died with appendicitis. In later years a son in the Army died with kidney disease, and recently a son was killed in an automobile accident.]

I've had some serious commotions in my life. I often wonder why in the world I didn't get discouraged—I don't remember getting discouraged with all of that.

You'd be surprised the things that a person can live with. I've said if it hadn't been for the Lord with me, I never could have made it. I sure depend on him.

It's been nice talking with you, Lura.

I thank you for bothering with me.

SUMMING UP

What values were implanted in you as a youngster?

The necessity of being clean, decent, virtuous, truthful, loving, willingness to work, and, oh, above all things, honesty. Belief in God, belief in love for one another and respect for parents, moral behavior and manners.

Floy Chapman, 80, Illinois

A happy mother and children.

What gave you confidence to deal with your life?

I guess Mother gets the credit for that. She always told us we could do anything in the world we wanted to do. All we had to do was to set our goals and go in that direction.

Elizabeth McAdams, 69, Alabama

We learned to be honest. People then, even if they couldn't write, their word was worth a lot. If you said you were going to do something, well they knew that that was the way it was going to be.

Mary Moore, 73, New Mexico

My family made me feel that I had the responsibility to do my best; to do what I could do. It was a philosophy of life that gave you a lot of individual resource. You weren't dependent on the other person. You were complete and had the ability to cope with things yourself.

There was also the maxim, "If at first you don't succeed, try, try again." Our goodbye when we would leave for school was "Do your best today," and it wasn't just like goodbye, it was kind of a thought-provoking thing.

Marjorie Pontius, 65, South Dakota

My parents had good elementary school educations and did not consider themselves inferior to others because they did not have more education or money. In fact, they believed that anyone who was willing to work, who would live right, and manage well could attain anything he really wanted. This is America, isn't it? It is the land of opportunity, isn't it? Hold yourself up and work. It can be done.

Floy Chapman, 80, Illinois

My mother was very adamant about a good education. She felt that was pretty necessary for her children. So we were influenced and encouraged to get all we could.

Evelyn Alden, 74, Kansas

What difference do you see in the role of young girls than when you were growing up?
The young girls can get an education and make a living. They don't have to marry like we did. It's a lot easier for the women today than when I was growing up.
Roles have opened up for women, where before they could be a school teacher or a nurse and those were the only occupations open for women.
Now they can be anything.

Edna Wood, 77, Nebraska

Men don't want women now, if they can't do more than just one thing. They want smart women. They want women who know how to save what they bring in, and most women have to get out and help their husbands to make a living now.

Julia White, 60, Tennessee

I think women are perfectly capable of doing most anything that a man can do, especially if it is a matter using brains.

Mildred McCay, 85, Indiana

I like being a woman. I wouldn't change that. But I also want to have the right, if I want to do a job and I have the ability to do it, I want the chance to do it.

Have you seen firsthand cases where women are discriminated against?

Sure. All the time. They will promote a man right up, and they will leave the woman sitting there.

Libby McKinney, 53, Indiana

Homemakers of the period. Strong, self-reliant and devoted to family life.

Well, I've had my equal rights all of my life, and I don't think much of it. I said if a woman wants to get out and work like a man, that's all right, but I had to do it whether I wanted to or not. I worked in the fields. I plowed. I cultivated. I disked. I done everything a man does, and I wasn't enjoying it one bit.

Ozetta Sullivan, 73, Indiana

I feel like with what I am doing right now, I am the most liberated person in the world. I feel like if I had a job, I would have to be there at 9:00, but now when my husband comes in and says, "Would you like to go with me?" I'm free to go. I feel like I'm just about as liberated as I can be.

Jane Gillooly, 34, Indiana

I think there have been social changes in that women are regarded now as being equal. I think that is good, however—I still like to have my chair pulled out and I like to have car doors opened for me. I think women who do the same work as men are certainly entitled to the same wage, but I still don't want to lose my femininity. I want to keep the fact that I am a woman present.

Jalie Martin, New Mexico

I'm glad I'm a woman.

That's a fantastic statement to make.

But I still like for men to be gentlemen.

Juanita Harden, 49, Indiana

You know, men need liberation, too.

How would you liberate the men?

Give them an opportunity to cry along with their kids and to help take care of them. Give them a bath once in a while and do some of these things that they would like to do.

You know, back when women didn't work outside of the home, having to be completely responsible for the financial part of raising a family must have been quite a responsibility.

It must have been terrible for the men to feel "I really must support you at all odds."

That was in the days of eight, nine and ten children, too.

Nellie Depew, 68, Indiana

We never worked, and the man was the keeper of everything. I remember one time when I saw a woman ask her husband for a dime and he wouldn't give it to her. And so I told my husband, "Listen, I want some money. I'm not going to run to you every time I want a dime." So whenever we went anywhere, he gave me a little money. He didn't have much to give, but he gave what he could.

Hazel Dolkey, 79, Indiana

When it came to deciding and managing, did you feel you were an equal with your husband?

No. My husband went in the other room and shut the door and done the bookwork. When I was left a widow, I knew nothing about managing money. And my dad always took care of the money. It was just the way it was.

Edna Winter, 76, Indiana

What about changes in the family decision making?

That has greatly changed. In earlier days, it was what the father said. He made the rules. But in the past few years, this has changed. They work together more. They have more of a democracy going in the family. Children are asked for their opinions and the families talk things out among themselves and make wise decisions. Everybody is pleased, rather than just one person being pleased.

Betty Alvey, 60, Indiana

I think now the homemakers probably makes lots of the decisions and helps make lots of others. I think a lot of this is because she's working, too, and wants to have a say in how her share of the income is being spent.

Floy Jacobus, 54, Indiana

The women I know, I think they have always helped make the major decisions. I think that is the way it should be in a family. The husband and wife make the major decisions. I wouldn't want to be asked about every little decision that is made, because I make some decisions that I don't ask; but when it comes to major decisions, they should be made together. I think a good marriage has always been that way.

Sarah Ziegler, 53, Indiana

There isn't anything more honorable, or that takes more ability than being a homemaker. It takes patience, it takes knowledge, and it takes endurance for a woman to really be a homemaker.

There is a difference between a homemaker and a housekeeper. A housekeeper keeps a house clean, keeps it picked up, cooks meals. But a homemaker does it with love. Love for her family, love for her mate. There is a lot of difference, and I am proud to be a homemaker.

Jalie Martin, New Mexico

I think homemaking is the greatest vocation—the greatest job there is. If a woman keeps her home properly and makes a comfortable home and the family feels comfortable in it, with a husband and children and a mother who is interested in her children and their welfare—that's wonderful.

It's a big job, it's a tremendous job, and it's a very important job. I don't see how anyone can look down on it, because she is training future citizens of our country. She is making a happy, comfortable home for her husband. She's got the biggest job in the world.

Nellie Yost, 76, Nebraska

We lived different places, but you know, you have to make a home where you are. Home is not just a house—it is a place where you make

The standards of honest and hard-working parents were handed down to the next generation.

it a home by living in it. I think they [family] all appreciate life at home more than anything else.

Elba Johnston, 79, Oklahoma

I think right there in the home is where our country starts. If a woman could be a good wife and mother and homemaker, it's something that they should really put a shrine around, instead of speaking it down.

Nona Berry, 81, New Mexico

I think to raise a child and have him or her become a person of value to his community is probably the most rewarding and fulfilling thing a person could do. I look on homemaking as a very honorable profession.

Vi Cottrell, 69, Washington

What is your biggest satisfaction as a homemaker?
I think my biggest satisfaction is in knowing that I stayed at home and was a homemaker and raised my kids. To me, that has been a real satisfaction. I feel like that my time that I spent doing it was worthwhile.

Thelma Barnes, 61, Florida

Do you think motherhood was a satisfying role?
I thought it was very satisfying, and I enjoyed it very much. It is something you work at and give your very best to. It's something that is a deep and very real responsibility.

And yet there is so little done in preparation. It is just up to the individual to do the very best they can. That was one of the areas where Extension club was very helpful.

Marjorie Pontius, 65, South Dakota

I think it is so important that there is a central figure in the house. I mean, the father is there and the children are there, but it's always been the mother's role to be the central figure in the home.

Carol Kobat, 56, Indiana

What advice would you give to a young homemaker today?
Consider the joys that are associated with homemaking. Your home life depends on you. Let's face it, it depends on the mother. The more she puts into it, the happier your whole family is going to be.

Edith Gladden, 63, Missouri

Do you feel that a commitment to homemaking deprived you of opportunities for self-fulfillment?
No, I never thought that anything I did deprived me of any opportunity to do something else. I liked what I did, so I was satisfied.

Mabel Thompson, Louisiana

You're living in a time when homemaking is disdained by many American women. How do you feel about that?
I still think it's the basis of home life. I think it's very possible to have a career and yet have an enjoyable home life. I don't have any griefs of having to work most of forty years outside the home. Yet I

managed to have a home life, and I don't think it was any detriment to me.

I think the attitude that homemaking is degrading somehow is ridiculous.

Edith Gladden, 63, Missouri

I think homemaking's a noble profession, and my hat's off to the women who can manage a home and work. I wanted my girls to work, and they all did—all three of them. We spent quite a little, and they gave up some things to get their education, so why not use it? I'm all for women working.

Catherine Wycoff, 90, Illinois

Have you been a full-time homemaker the entire 48 years [since you've been married]?

Yes, I have. Now, I've worked out of the home; I did factory work for eight years, but I was a homemaker all the time.

You just had two jobs.

I had two jobs and I enjoyed it. And then I worked for another company for six and a half years. But I was still a homemaker. I always put my home first, and the job second.

Hautie Nelson, 69, Tennessee

When I was a small child, I made up my mind that when I grew up I was going to marry a good man and raise a family.

Do you think you would have got that satisfaction from being a career woman?

I wanted to teach school and I wanted to be a good teacher, and I believe that I was. But after I met my husband, I wanted to marry him and I did.

I hear people say their family kept them from doing this or that. My family never kept me from doing anything, because we did what we wanted to do.

Nona Berry, 81, New Mexico

I think homemakers are a tremendous force in society. I think sometimes we don't take ourselves seriously enough because a lot of us don't work outside the home. My husband gets upset when I say I don't work. He says, "You work. You work hard. You are a non-salaried person." I think he's right. If we are not careful, we put ourselves down, simply because we don't make a salary.

I think, as women, we have a tremendous contribution in our society when you think that we are raising the future generation. Today our sons and daughters have more choices than we had, and hopefully it won't be too confusing, with us there to guide them and help them through the difficult years. Our homes are important as bases where our children grow up and go out into the future.

We should realize that we are important, too, and we can develop our personalities, our own being, as well as help our children.

Sue Cole, 43, Indiana

Homemaking, to me, should mean [being] a part in community life, not just shut up within the home.

Frankie Carruthers, 76, New Mexico

To me, it's very important for the homemaker to have an input in the schools, in the home and the church.

Emma Baker, 79, Indiana

The volunteer work that I do for Extension Homemaker clubs, the church and charitable organizations gives me great satisfaction. My mother, in raising a big famly with less time to give to outside activities, was happy with her neighborly deeds of caring and sharing. But as a clubwoman, Extension Homemaker and volunteer for many things, I am able to keep busy.

Linnie Arnett, 61, Virginia

I think my college education and my teaching have prepared me for my life as a housewife and mother and community volunteer. It's given me a perspective on things that are important and worthwhile doing.

Karen Retzlaff, 34, North Dakota

We live in a time when homemaking seems to be a nothing thing.
Women seem to want to take on different roles outside the home.

That upsets me a little bit when people say a "nothing." I spoke to my husband rather harshly the other day on that subject. He says, "What are you going to do today?" I said, "I have plenty to do today— not nothing." Running a household, certainly that's not nothing. That's big business. You've got to be on top of it, and you've got to keep up with the interest rates, along with the penalties if you don't pay. I think there's a lot to it.

Carolyn Dame, 40, New Hampshire

I've preferred the term home executive instead of housewife. A woman who takes care of the family and does the chauffeuring and does the meal getting, cleans clothes, having everything run smoothly— she is an executive, really. She's a home executive. That was one of the things that Extension clubs emphasized—the dignity of the responsibility the mother carries—that it is partnership, not just a housewife.

Marjorie Pontius, 65, South Dakota

Right now, some women are feeling like homemaking is not a way of life that they want to go by, but I cannot conceive of any woman that does not have a desire to have a home, or a nest of some sort. That is a built-in impulse.

A loving husband and wife with three
fine children.

I do not feel that being a homemaker and mother deprived me of any opportunities. In [my] soul-searching, I find I have more fulfill- ment and love and accomplishments than I ever dreamed that I could attain.

Billie Jones, 72, Louisiana

What is your biggest satisfaction as a homemaker?

It's so great and so wonderful to be a homemaker. I think it's one of the greatest things in the world. It's a joy to me to have a home and to have a family—to have someone to love, to have someone to respond to that love, and to return that love. I can't think of anything in the world that's greater than being a homemaker. It's a joy.

Jessie Halsell, 68, New Mexico

What is your biggest satisfaction as a homemaker?

I think the fact that my husband and I get along so very well, and we have many happy moments together of sharing.

Misaye Uno, 65, Colorado

As far as my husband is concerned, he isn't just a husband because he married me and had to get along with me, but after 62 years, we're still friends. And I think if you can keep a friend for that long, your homemaking has been a success.

Elsa Skiles, Washington

You mentioned your husband—he died how many years ago?

He died December 19, 1971, so we were married sixty-four happy years.

What would you say to a new couple being married today?

Never let the sun go down on your wrath. If you have any differences, anything you've argued about, settle it before you go to sleep. And keep up your courtship after you're married.

And you always kept yours up?

I did, I did. And, well, I won't tell you that now.

No, go ahead.

I can't [do it] without crying. [I got] this Mother of the Year award, because my husband always worked in the background. I'd go to conventions, be gone a week, he was always at home, he didn't want to go. Kept the children—mothered them just the same as I did. I knew when I left the children with him that they'd be cared for just like I cared for them.

And I think now of all the honors and attention that I've had, and that he stayed in the background, keeping buckle and tongue together.

Letha McCall, 91, North Carolina

Do you remember what you received your award for—the Distinguished Service Award?

It was given for the service rendered not only in the Extension Clubs, but the community and church.

Now we have your name on this award, but not your husband's. Would you tell us your husband's name?

Peder L. Phillips, my sweetheart.

Florence Phillips, 88, South Dakota

My husband was a very fine man and we enjoyed each other. We kept right on enjoying each other all our lives.

Why?

We never went to bed angry with each other. We disagreed; I don't say we didn't (chuckles), but on the big things we managed to see eye-to-eye on anything.

Do you think you did anything different to make it so you enjoyed each other all the way through?

I have always said that women [are] in a relationship as far as men [are] and it's up to them [both] to see that it works. I think that loving

Many happy years together reflect
in these faces.

and showing that you love is the main thing in marriage. I think that I am quite loving, but I could never outlove my husband. He would tell me how nice I looked and how well I did. He would tell me, "When I can see you, my world is all right. It's when you're away from me that I don't feel the same. I've got to have you where I can see you." Now if that isn't a reason to get along with somebody, I don't know.

Rubie, your body gestures when you start talking about him—you just start swinging on your chair. You look just like a fifteen-year-old girl that just fell in love.

Rubie Gillion, 80, Michigan.

I think the most important thing in a home is love. I think that people ought to tell each other in the family, "I love you."

But we think we don't have time.

It saves a lot of time and anxiety if you'll just do that. I used to have a little saying for my husband. I said to him, "You belong to me." And he would say, "Yes, and you belong to me." We did not want to do things that were not approved by the other, because we belonged to each other. Sometimes I think that's the reason we have so much divorce. People have forgotten that they belong to each other, and they've forgotten to say "I love you." When things go wrong they've forgotten to say "I'm sorry," and they've forgotten to say "thank you." Those are the things that count in my home.

The last words my husband said to me when he died in the hospital was "Love you." Then he just closed his eyes. I think that love is everlasting.

Ruth Irwin, 83, Mississippi

ACKNOWLEDGMENTS

With a nationwide project, almost completely done through volunteer work, no list of acknowledgments could possibly include the name of everyone who has contributed. Much of the membership of the National Extension Homemakers Council has contributed, if not by active participation, at least by enthusiasm and support.

The volunteer interviewers conducted the interviews which are the basis for the whole project. Many of them, in addition, transcribed the interviews they had done, spending many additional hours in this process. Their contribution was invaluable.

Equally to be thanked are the narrators—the people who talked to the interviewers and shared their experiences, memories and judgments. They have offered us their finest compliment—their trust—as they shared their lives with us.

Because of space limitations, this book can contain only a very small portion of the fine material contained in the interviews. Each interview, however, has been read and studied many times. Each one was extremely useful for background and research, both in this project and for historians who will be using the material in the future.

The conclusion of this section contains a list of the narrators' names and of the interviewers' names. They are arranged alphabetically, according to their state. Without the people in this list, there would have been no project.

Many thanks go also to the people who shared photographs, other visual materials and written histories with the project. These things added another vital dimension.

Although this was a lay project, we have endeavoured, from the beginning, to consult experts in the fields which the project touched. Our consultants were a major factor in the success of the project.

F. Gerald Handfield, Assistant Director of Field Services, Indiana Historical Society, has been with the project since its inception, serving as chief consultant to the Indiana pilot project and continuing with the national project. Both studies owe a great deal of their depth and scope to his knowledge, enthusiasm and expertise.

Cullom Davis has been evaluator and consultant to the project. Dr. Davis is Director of the Oral History Office at Sangamon State University at Springfield, Illinois, and is the author of a popular text-

book on oral history. The project has benefited greatly from his ex-
oral history. The project has benefited greatly from his expertise in oral
history and from his experienced counsel on practicalities of the work.

D'Ann Campbell, Dean of Women's Affairs at Indiana University,
Bloomington, Indiana, has been the other chief consultant since the
beginning of the project. She served as coordinator of the 1983 seminar
and her strong belief in the need for this kind of documentation of
homemakers has been a constant inspiration.

Paul Wilson, photographer and producer, recorded the visual materials and produced the slide/tape show *Voices of American Homemakers*
which was another dissemination of the project. His professional expertise, his good humor and his complete dependability were unfailing.

Charles Morrissey, adjunct professor, University of Vermont,
helped in planning the project and was chief instructor in the workshop
for training interviewers. He was also a participant in the seminar held
midway through the project, in 1983.

The seminar was coordinated by D'Ann Campbell, and other partic-
ipants were Susan Armitage, Women's Studies Program, Washington
State University; Dama Burkhart, Dean Emerita, Purdue School of
Home Economics; Joan Jensen, Department of History, New Mexico
State University; and Alice Shrock, Department of History, Earlham
College. The very fine research done by these participants was an out-
standing feature of the project.

An especial acknowledgment goes to Margaret Boilanger, past
NEHC treasurer, who has been the fiscal agent for the project. She has
kept perfect records throughout.

The Oral History Committee of the NEHC has given good advice
and hard work to the project. The present committee is Della Geffe,
Idaho; Mabel Givans, Delaware; and Katherine Van Holten, Florida.
Barbara Corey, Florida, also served in the early part of the project.

The board of directors of the National Extension Homemakers
Council has been encouraging and supportive through the years of work,
as have been the USDA advisors Ava Rodgers and Jeanne Priester.

The financial support of the National Endowment for the Humanities made the project possible, and the helpfulness of their staff, particularly Program Officer Sally Yerkovich, made it pleasant.

The Indiana Historical Society has made its personnel, facilities and
files available, and Purdue University and Indiana University have served
as cooperating institutions.

Much gratitude must go to my long-suffering family, who have given
help freely in many phases of the project and have always been full of
enthusiasm and encouragement. Two grandchildren, my first, have been

born during the course of the project, and this has shown me in a very personal way the constant evolution of woman's role.

And my deepest gratitude must go to my husband who has always been fully supportive, understanding and appreciative of my deep commitment to this project.

LIST OF SOURCES

INTERVIEWEE, *INTERVIEWER*

ALASKA
Lillian Eckert, *Nancy Rowland*
Evie Foster, *L. Burgoyne*
Gussie Mumey, *Rieta Walker*

ALABAMA
Bertha Andrews, *Nina Langley*
Sallie Bell, *Mildred Ennis*
Ouida Harwell, *Opal Price*
Elizabeth McAdams, *Miriam Watkins*
Sue Moman, *Jean Moon*
Jean Moon, *Sue Moman*
Opal Price, *Madge Becton*

ARKANSAS
Opal Cypert, *Katherine Skelton*
Vivian Jefferson, *Katherine Skelton*
Essie Simmons, *Minerva Houser*
Dorothy Tolley, *Minerva Houser*
Ann Webb, *Minerva Houser*

COLORADO
Lois Kevan, *Hazel Leininger*
Hazel Leininger, *Misaye Uno*
Nadine Marchun, *Hazel Leininger*
Pearl Mehl, *Hazel Leininger*
Jeanette Salbert, *Misaye Uno*
Misaye Uno, *Hazel Leininger*

DELAWARE
Florence Reed, *Jean Skibinski*
Dorothy Tyrawski, *Jean Skibinski*

FLORIDA
Thelma Barnes, *Louise Lindberg*
Eunice Cameron, *Louise Lindberg*
Elsie Gould, *Adelaide Moores*
Mabel Hughes, *Adelaide Moores*
Emily Harper, *Louise Lindberg*
Pearl Laffitte, *Louise Lindberg*
Katherine Taylor, *Adelaide Moores*

GEORGIA
Geneva Parsons, *Geneva Parsons*
Geneva Slaton, *Mary Hartley*
Glenwood Homemakers, *Mary Hartley*
Past Presidents, *Mary Hartley*

HAWAII
Kazuko Kurose, *Charlotte Nakamura*
Betty Sakate, *Gladys Brown*
Mary Soon, *Charlotte Nakamura*
Julia Souza, *Bert Kikuchi*

IDAHO
Ruth Bright, *not known*
Dorothy Carlson, *Ruth Bright*
Mrs. Hepworth, *not known*

INTERVIEWEE, *INTERVIEWER*

ILLINOIS
Floy Chapman, *Eleanor Ross*
Charlene Diel, *Eleanor Ross*
Alma Thompson, *Eunice Pagel*
Marjorie Whitney, *Eunice Pagel*
Catherine Wycoff, *Eleanor Ross*

INDIANA
Iva Crouse, *Carol Schroeder*
Beulah Grinstead, *Wanetta Edgerly*
Pearl McCall, *Ruth Colbert*
Masa Scheerer, *Mona Harley*
Neva Schlatter, *Julia Binkley*

KANSAS
Evelyn Alden, *Athol Reusser*
Sophia Bigge, *Athol Reusser*
Brenda Van Meter, *Athol Reusser*

KENTUCKY
Margie Brookshire, *Mabel Bertram*
Mary Depew, *Mabel Bertram*
Anna Evans, *Mabel Bertram*
Mary Fouts, *Mabel Bertram*
Ethel Jury, *Mabel Bertram*

LOUISIANA
Irene Clause, *Irene Clause*
Zilphia Edwards, *Rebecca Fortenberry*
Billie Jones, *Doris Ashley*
Virginia McIntyre, *Doris Ashley*
Mabel Thompson, *Elaine Vidrine*

MARYLAND
Eileen Moon, *Jeanette Green*

MICHIGAN
Wilma Bre, *Bethel Schmidt*
Edna Christian, *not known*
Gladys Fox, *Frances Michalek*
Rubie Gillion, *not known*
Luella Hamilton, *Petra Swanson*
Edith Huffman, *not known*
Emma Jones, *Joan Luerr*
Agnes Klein, *not known*
Jo Kraii, *not known*
Cecilia Lamb, *Rhea Thayer*
Estella Myers, *Joan Luerr*
Blanche Ockerman, *not known*
Arvilla Parshall, *not known*
Myra Spike, *Eleanor Stewart*
Ethel Watkins, *not known*

MINNESOTA
Persistent Pals, *Mary Meyer*

INTERVIEWEE, *INTERVIEWER*

MISSISSIPPI
Ruth Irwin, *Mrs. E.R. McKnight*
Orrie Little, *Marian Carmichael*
Jane Morgan, *Marian Carmichael*
Betty Newman, *Mrs. E.R. McKnight*
Mrs. B.N. Simrall, *Mrs. E.R. McKnight*

MISSOURI
Edith Fennel, *Donna Howard*
Nellie Frost, *Betty Reynolds*
Edith Gladden, *Janet Vaughn*
Verna Lefman, *Betty Reynolds*
Lillie Stuery, *Betty Reynolds*

MONTANA
Marie Carlile, *Arlene Stoner*
Lillie Badgeley, *Arlene Stoner*
Myra Daniel, *Arlene Stoner*
Lora Foster, *Arlene Stoner*
Luella Hardie, *Arlene Stoner*
Pearl Herndon, *Gayle Muggli*
Elsie Rieger, *Arlene Stoner*
Daisy Taylor, *Arlene Stoner*

NEBRASKA
Anna Coburn, *Selma Stevens*
Eva Gill, *Norma Schneemeyer*
Edna Wood, *Tootie Johannsen*
Nellie Yost, *Sandra Hansen*

NEW HAMPSHIRE
Carolyn Dame, *Goldie Roscoe*
Priscilla Lloyd, *Goldie Roscoe*
Helen Merrill, *Goldie Roscoe*
Lora Torsey, *Goldie Roscoe*
Eleanor Whittemore, *Goldie Roscoe*

NEW MEXICO
Frankie Carruthers, *Beatrice Stagl*
Marie Cauhape, *Beatrice Stagl*
Nona Berry, *Mary Popejoy*
Ima Fairly, *Beatrice Stagl*
Jessie Halsell, *Beatrice Stagl*
Ruth James, *Mary Popejoy*
Florence McDonald, *Beatrice Stagl*
Jalie Martin, *Mary Popejoy*
Frances Matthews, *Mary Popejoy*
Mary Moore, *Mary Popejoy*

NORTH CAROLINA
Theo Hammond, *Virginia Harris*
Nancy Madre, *Virginia Harris*
Letha McCall, *Virginia Harris*
Henrietta Phillips, *Virginia Harris*
Lucy Wilson, *Virginia Harris*

NORTH DAKOTA
Margaret Lien, *Arlene Sagness*
Cora Lykken, *Maryadele Knudsen*
Mary Mootz, *Maryadele Knudsen*
Minnie Ness, *Arlene Sagness*
Karen Retzlaff, *Maryadele Knudsen*
Anna Sorensen, *Arlene Sagness*

INTERVIEWEE, *INTERVIEWER*

OHIO
Sarah Adkins, *Eva Barger*
Lura Hess, *Eva Barger*
Mary Jonas, *Eva Barger*
Mary Shultz, *Eva Barger*
Jeanette Stratton, *Eva Barger*
Nellie Stratton, *Eva Barger*
Winifred Thrush, *Eva Barger*
Betty Wenig, *Eva Barger*

OKLAHOMA
Sara Ball, *Hester Sickles*
Elba Johnston, *Hester Sickles*
Mary Skelley, *Hester Sickles*
Zelma Wood, *Hester Sickles*

OREGON
Marie Brown, *Dorothy Klock*
Dorris Graves, *Dorothy Klock*
Dorothy Personnette, *Dorothy Klock*
Alice Wand, *Dorothy Klock*
Saundra Zook, *Dorothy Klock*

SOUTH CAROLINA
Ellen Chadfelter, *Eleanor Cottrell*
Hazel Chamblee, *Margaret Vernon*
Bee Cochran, *Pat Gates*
Mildred Davis, *Patricia Clarkin*
Alice Edwards, *Patricia Clarkin*
Ethel Farlow, *Carol Lawrence*
Pat Gates, *Bee Cochran*
Ethel Gordon, *Eleanor Cottrell*
Ruth Hockett, *Carol Lawrence*
Nona Jennings, *Bee Cochran*
Novie Jerrell, *Carol Lawrence*
Ethel Jobe, *Betty Varner*
Hazel Johnson, *Bee Cochran*
Flossie Lewis, *Lottie Watkins*
Lucille Monroe, *Margaret Vernon*
Etta Sellers, *Bee Cochran*
Mattie Shepard, *Lottie Watkins*
Mrs. L. R. Tesh, *Eleanor Cottrell*
Margaret Vernon, *Lucille Monroe*
Eunice Wagoner, *Dewey Baldwin*
Gerry Williams, *Patricia Clarkin*

SOUTH DAKOTA
Marge and Carla Kleinjan, *Linda Svec*
Christine Gaffin, *Arlene Erickson*
Byrdie Johnson, *Evelyn Beug*
Minnie Murphey, *Laura Grubl*
Florence Phillips, *Arlene Erickson*
Marjorie Pontius, *Linda Svec*
Iriska Stroschein, *Linda Svec*
Ina Tate, *Linda Svec*
Cleo Tyler, *not known*

TENNESSEE
Aileen Cole, *Marian Mariner*
Oma Lewis, *Marian Mariner*
Hautie Nelson, *Alpha Worrell*
Tressa Waters, *Marian Mariner*
Julia White, *Marian Mariner*